Forest Insects in Europe

II

Forest Insects in Europe

Diversity, Functions and Importance

Beat Wermelinger

CRC Press
Taylor & Francis Group
Boca Raton London New York

CRC Press is an imprint of the
Taylor & Francis Group, an **informa** business

First edition published 2021
by CRC Press
6000 Broken Sound Parkway NW, Suite 300, Boca Raton, FL 33487-2742

and by CRC Press
2 Park Square, Milton Park, Abingdon, Oxon, OX14 4RN

© 2021 Taylor & Francis Group, LLC

CRC Press is an imprint of Taylor & Francis Group, LLC

Reasonable efforts have been made to publish reliable data and information, but the author and publisher cannot assume responsibility for the validity of all materials or the consequences of their use. The authors and publishers have attempted to trace the copyright holders of all material reproduced in this publication and apologize to copyright holders if permission to publish in this form has not been obtained. If any copyright material has not been acknowledged please write and let us know so we may rectify in any future reprint.

Except as permitted under U.S. Copyright Law, no part of this book may be reprinted, reproduced, transmitted, or utilized in any form by any electronic, mechanical, or other means, now known or hereafter invented, including photocopying, microfilming, and recording, or in any information storage or retrieval system, without written permission from the publishers.

For permission to photocopy or use material electronically from this work, access www.copyright.com or contact the Copyright Clearance Center, Inc. (CCC), 222 Rosewood Drive, Danvers, MA 01923, 978-750-8400. For works that are not available on CCC please contact mpkbookspermissions@tandf.co.uk

Trademark notice: Product or corporate names may be trademarks or registered trademarks and are used only for identification and explanation without intent to infringe.

Library of Congress Cataloging-in-Publication Data

ISBN: 978-1-032-03031-9 (hbk)
ISBN: 978-0-367-45700-6 (pbk)
ISBN: 978-1-003-18646-5 (ebk)

DOI: 10.1201/9781003186465

Publisher's note: This book has been prepared from camera-ready copy provided by the authors.

Contents

Preface	IX
Author	XI
Acknowledgments	XIII

1 Diversity and functions of insects 1

1.1	Diversity of species and lifestyles	2
1.2	The forest habitat	2
1.3	The most important insect groups in the forest	8
1.4	Ecological functions and economic significance	12

Ecological functions

2 Insects and plant reproduction 17

2.1	Pollination of flowers	18
2.2	Dissemination of seeds	27
2.3	Influence on plant competition	28
2.4	Feeding on flowers and fruits	29

3 Turnover of green plant biomass 37

3.1	Caterpillar feeding	38
3.2	Other plant feeders	44
3.3	Plant-sap-sucking insects	48

4 Decomposition of wood 51

4.1	Colonizers of living trees	53
4.2	Pioneers on dead trees	55
4.3	Insects of the decomposition phase	61
4.4	Secondary dwellers in feeding galleries	76
4.5	Colonizers of tree fungi	78
4.6	Natural enemies of deadwood insects	82

5	Exploitation of animal waste	89
5.1	Colonization of carrion	90
5.2	Processing faeces	94
5.3	Other animal waste products	100

6	Maintaining soil fertility	105
6.1	Improving the soil structure	106
6.2	Decomposing organic matter	108

7	Food for other organisms	115
7.1	Food for birds	116
7.2	Food for other vertebrates	120
7.3	Hosts for microorganisms, fungi and parasitic worms	125
7.4	Insect products	127

8	Natural enemies	133
8.1	Predatory insects	134
8.2	Predatory spiders and mites	158
8.3	Parasitoids	163
8.4	True parasites	174

9	Antagonists of bark beetles	181
9.1	Prey and host location	182
9.2	Predators	183
9.3	Parasitoid wasps	190
9.4	Woodpeckers	195
9.5	Pathogens	196
9.6	Impact of antagonists	198

10 Ecological significance of red wood ants — 201

10.1 Life forms and natural enemies — 202
10.2 The ant nest — 211
10.3 Establishing a colony — 214
10.4 Ecological functions — 217

11 Transport of organisms — 223

11.1 Vectors of invertebrates — 224
11.2 Vectors of fungi — 226

12 Maintaining stand vitality — 231

13 Shaping of ecosystems — 235

13.1 From microhabitats to landscapes — 236
13.2 The larch budmoth in Switzerland's Engadine — 238
13.3 Bark beetles create new habitats — 251

Economic significance

14 Economic damage — 255

14.1 Leaf- and needle-feeding insects — 257
14.2 Sucking insects — 263
14.3 Bark beetles and other bark colonizers — 264
14.4 Transmission of plant diseases — 277

15 Insects and human health — 281

15.1 Disease-transmitting ticks — 282
15.2 Caterpillars with urticating hairs — 284
15.3 Stinging insects — 289
15.4 Medically useful insects — 289

16 Usable insect products — 293

16.1 Edible products — 293
16.2 Commodities — 297
16.3 Insects as food for human consumption — 302

17 Introduced species — 305

17.1 Invasive species in forests — 306
17.2 Other alien species on woody plants — 310

18 Endangered forest insects — 313

18.1 Endangered forest butterflies — 315
18.2 Endangered deadwood dwellers — 317

Bibliography — 327
Photo credits — 337
Glossary — 339
Species and subject index — 343

Preface

Until recently, insects have been predominantly perceived in Western civilization negatively as pests or a nuisance. Terms such as 'detrimental' and 'beneficial', however, reflect purely human interests and say little about insects' ecological functions. The diverse roles played by insects and other invertebrates in almost every ecosystem, including our forests, are often poorly understood or ignored. In recent years the general public has become more aware of the ongoing decline of insects and their importance in virtually every ecosystem is more widely recognised.

This book describes the manifold ecological functions in forests of insects and some other forest arthropods, and illustrates them with a wealth of photos. Insects, perform most of these functions not just in forests, but also in other terrestrial ecosystems. At the same time, some forest insects may have a direct impact on human well-being. For example, they may impair important ecosystem services or adversely affect human welfare. Conversely, some insects provide usable products. Separate chapters and sections are devoted to red wood ants, the larch budmoth and the natural enemies of bark beetles because these insects are particularly important ecologically.

The basis and motivation for this book have been the around 14 000 insect photos I have obtained during the 25 years forest insects have occupied me professionally. I began to take photos of insects while completing my diploma thesis on the alder leaf beetle, and I soon became hooked. Insect photography quickly turned into an intense and pleasurable passion. Instead of collecting and pinning insects, I found it more rewarding to capture the huge variety of shapes, colours and behaviours of insects with photos 'in the wild'. This led, over time, to the production of an extensive, well-searchable database of photos. By far the majority of the photos in this book are therefore 'homemade'. Although they were shot almost exclusively in Switzerland, the selection is representative for a large part of Europe.

In the course of my research and teaching activities, I have accumulated a great deal of information about the ecological roles insects play. This has provided the basis for selecting and structuring the content and photos of this book. Over the past three decades, my work as a research forest entomologist at the Swiss Federal Institute WSL and as a lecturer at the Swiss Federal Institute of Technology ETH have perfectly complemented my passion for insect photography and have been mutually inspiring.

The success of the German version of this book ('Insekten im Wald – Vielfalt, Funktionen und Bedeutung'; 2017) prompted me to translate this book and adapt it slightly to fit a more general European context. As in the German version, the text has been written with both specialists and interested laypeople in mind. I have tried to avoid using too many technical terms and to explain any I felt necessary in both the main text and a separate Glossary.

The nomenclature is based on the online database Fauna Europaea (www.fauna-eu.org) as of May 2016. Where available, common names of insects are given in addition to the scientific Latin names. This book cannot, of course, claim to be a comprehensive compilation of forest insects or an identification key. The species presented here are intended to illustrate the functions discussed in each chapter. Some may also have been selected because the available photos of them have a particular aesthetic quality. Thus, the book is intended to not just inform, but also to increase our appreciation of the aesthetics and subtleties of this seemingly odd group of animals, many of which are unfamiliar. If this book succeeds not only in communicating the importance of insects, but also in catching the reader by surprise, then it has achieved its goal.

Beat Wermelinger
Adliswil, January 2021

Author

Beat Wermelinger, Dr. sc. nat. ETH, is a biologist in Adliswil, Switzerland. He is Senior Scientist at the Swiss Federal Institute for Forest, Snow and Landscape Research WSL, Birmensdorf. His research topics include bark beetles and natural enemies, forest insect biodiversity, disturbance effects, climate change and neozoa. He is also a lecturer at the Swiss Federal Institute for Technology ETH, Zurich, and the Swiss Arboricultural Association.

Acknowledgments

First of all, I would like to thank my wife, Ursi, for her (almost) endless patience during our hiking/photography tours, for her understanding and moral support in writing and translating this book on countless evenings and weekends, and for sharing my passion for the fascinating world of insects.

For the identification of many insects or spiders, I have been lucky enough to count on help from a large number of specialists over the past decades. Among the many species shown in this book, several were identified by Matthias Albrecht, Roman Asshoff, Ruth Bärfuss, Hannes Baur, David Bogyo, Dieter Bretz, Yannick Chittaro, Peter Duelli, Christophe Dufour, Beat Forster, Anne Freitag, Christoph Germann, Jean-Paul Haenni, Ralf Heckmann, Xaver Heer, Doris Hölling, Klaus Horstmann, Marc Kenis, Seraina Klopfstein, Iain MacGowan, Bernhard Merz, Andreas Müller, Rainer Neumeyer, Giuseppina Pellizzari, Bruno Peter, Sigitas Podenas, Matthias Riedel, Ulrich Schmid, Ute Schönfeld, Daniel Steiner, Alex Szallies, Hans-Peter Tschorsnig, Kees van Achterberg, Jakob Walter, and Denise Wyniger. Any mistakes in this book are, however, my responsibility. Should you spot one, I would be glad to receive feedback about it (e-mail: b.wer@hispeed.ch).

Sincere thanks go to my work colleague, Doris Schneider Mathis, for all her identification work and other entomological assistance over the past decades, and to my late work colleague Beat Fecker, for identifications and photos. Many colleagues provided me with valuable information and live insects to take photos. Peter Duelli, Doris Hölling, Beat Forster, Daniel Cherix, Thibault Lachat, Martin Obrist, and Tom Wohlgemuth checked smaller or larger parts of the German text for comprehensibility and scientific correctness.

Special thanks go to Silvia Dingwall for thoroughly revising my English manuscript, and to Sandra Gurzeler, Jacqueline Annen, and Clarissa Bräg, who typeset the text and nicely incorporated the many photos.

Lastly, I would like to thank CRC Press for publishing this book and, in particular, Alice Oven who guided me in a very friendly and cooperative way through the publishing process. Matthias Haupt, from Haupt Verlag, kindly returned the English copyright to me to make the English version possible.

Diversity and functions of insects

1

Insects are among the oldest land creatures on Earth. The first terrestrial insect species developed around 400 million years ago, even before vascular plants and long before the dinosaurs. The origin of insects is estimated to be 480 million years before our time (Misof et al. 2014). At first, they fed on spores, fruit and seeds, but they were soon able to obtain nourishment from the green parts of trees and even from lignin-containing or woody parts. Petrified fossils and insects preserved in amber indicate that the basic construction plan for insects has functioned efficiently for hundreds of millions of years. Thus, all have an outer skeleton, three pairs of legs, two pairs of wings, an open circulatory system and a simple tracheal system for oxygen transport. Insect species were the first living creatures to conquer airspace. Some were enormous, such as giant dragonflies with wingspans of more than 70 centimetres. They were able to reach such huge sizes because the oxygen content of the air then was higher than it is today. Large species could supply their organs with

The mountain ash sawfly *(Pristiphora geniculata)* belongs to the Hymenoptera, one of the most species-rich insect orders. Like many sawflies, their larvae take on a characteristic defensive position when disturbed to deter potential enemies.

sufficient oxygen even though they had to rely on simple tracheal breathing (Polet 2011).

1.1 Diversity of species and lifestyles

Insects are the dominant group of organisms today, not only because of the number of species, but also because of the diversity of their ecological functions. So far, approximately one million insect species have been described worldwide (Stork 2018). This corresponds to about half of all known organisms and more than two-thirds of all animal species. As the British biologist Robert M. May put it (with some exaggeration), "Essentially, all organisms are insects" (May 1988). This may not be as far-fetched as it seems considering the number of insect species that probably exist today. Estimates vary widely; barcoding-based analyses suggest approximately 10 million species (Hebert et al. 2016). Most have probably yet to be discovered. Among the insects, beetles are the most species-rich group, with almost 400 000 known species.

The number of individual insects thought to be alive today is impressive as well; the abundance of ants alone is estimated to be at least one million times higher than that of humans. Thanks to their small size, short generation times and high reproductive potential, insects are able to adapt quickly to changing conditions and survive catastrophic events. They have succeeded in colonizing virtually all terrestrial habitats. These range from grassland, steppes, forests, deserts, mountains, water bodies and glaciers, to hot springs and even human dwellings and settlements. Only the polar ice, the highest mountain peaks and the depths of oceans remain unoccupied. Their food is just as varied as their habitats. They feed on grasses, leaves, needles and other green plant tissue, fruits, sap, wood, bark, rotting plant material, invertebrates and vertebrates, faeces, carcasses, hair, fungi, bacteria and even leather, paper and wax. There is hardly a substrate that is not used in some way by a specialised insect species.

1.2 The forest habitat

In Europe, forest was the original and formerly most widespread habitat type. After the last Ice Age, at least three quarters of Central

The pinhole beetles (Platypodidae; above) enclosed in amber around 20 million years ago in today's Dominican Republic are very similar to the extant native oak pinhole borer (*Platypus cylindrus*; below).

Virtually all organic substrates can serve as food for insects. Even at the level of a single species, different diets are possible. The forest bug (*Pentatoma rufipes*), which lives mainly on maple and lime, sucks plant sap, but feeds also on living and dead insects.

Distribution of species numbers of presently known organisms (data basis: Chapman 2009)

The focus of this book is on the organisms known as insects. Occasionally, other arthropods with similar ways of life are also mentioned. In this book, the following nomenclature is used:

Invertebrates (Invertebrata)	Animals without a spinal column. Examples: arthropods, ringed worms, molluscs

Arthropods (Arthropoda)	Invertebrates with a segmented body, jointed limbs and an exoskeleton. Examples: insects, millipedes, crustaceans, arachnids

Insects (Insecta)	Six-legged arthropods with a tripartite body, antennae and external mouthparts. Examples: beetles, butterflies, dragonflies	Arachnids (Arachnida)	Eight-legged arthropods with bipartite body. Examples: spiders, harvestmen, scorpions, pseudoscorpions, mites (including ticks)

1 Diversity and functions

Europe was forested, mainly with broadleaf trees. Only bogs, extremely steep slopes, coastal areas and high altitudes above the climatic timberline were free of forests (Mantel 1990). It was not until humans began to exploit forests that larger and permanently forest-free areas developed. Most of today's forests have been influenced by humans. Their tree species composition and stand structure differ to a greater or lesser extent from those of the original natural forests. Nevertheless, forest areas are still much closer to nature than, for example, areas used for agriculture. Forest ecosystems, consisting almost exclusively of native plant species, are more stable because they have long-term cycles and are better buffered against disturbances. In addition, the use of any substances hazardous to the environment, such as pesticides and fertilizers, is restricted or prohibited in forests in many countries. The living conditions for organisms in a forest are therefore relatively constant, but this does not mean

Coniferous mountain forests are less diverse in tree and shrub species than the mixed deciduous forests of the lowlands. This usually also means less but often specialised insect species.

Light mixed broadleaf forests have a rich insect fauna.

that dramatic changes due to disturbances such as storms or fires cannot occur locally. Forest habitats are structurally very rich with varied microclimates and a pronounced third dimension in height. Although they are relatively stable, they also experience ecological disturbances, which have, in the course of millions of years, enabled very species-rich biocoenoses to form. The plant and animal species found in forests are often in a complex network of relationships with each other.

A forest does not, of course, consist only of trees. Although these constitute the largest biomass, their species number is negligibly small compared to that of other organism groups. Reliable data on the number of forest species, especially animal species, are scarce because forest biodiversity has only recently received much attention. Moreover, identifying what makes an organism a forest species is not so simple. Many animal species spend only part of their lifetimes in the forest.

Estimates of species numbers in Central Europe taken from various sources are roughly: 2000 vascular plants, 2000 lichens and mosses, 3000 to 4000 mushrooms and 300 to 400 vertebrates. For vascular plants, more precise figures are available for Germany, where there are thought to be around 1200 species (Schmidt et al. 2011), and Switzerland, where the estimate is 700 species (Brändli and Bollmann 2015). For animals, 114 vertebrate species (mammals, birds, amphibians and reptiles) are listed for Switzerland as at least occasional forest users (BUWAL and WSL 2005). In comparison, the number of European forest insect species is much higher and estimated to be about 30 000 species (Wermelinger et al. 2013a). Thus, insects are also dominant in the forest in terms even of weight, despite their small size. The biomass of insects in temperate forests weighs 30 to 50 times more than that of vertebrates (Schowalter 2013). Flies (Diptera) alone, whose

Plant- and structure-rich forest edges are also species-rich in terms of insects. There are species of open land and closed forest.

The tau emperor *(Aglia tau)* is a typical representative of beech forests. The males (photo) fly around restlessly in search of females shortly after leaf emergence.

larvae develop mainly in soil, are estimated to amount to 14 kilograms per hectare, and a mass outbreak of moth caterpillars can weigh as much as one ton per hectare (Duvigneaud 1974). The weight of tree biomass, however, is hundreds of tons per hectare, which is clearly much more than that of insects.

In Switzerland, for example, a total of 45 890 species of organisms, excluding slime moulds, low algae and protozoa, have been identified (Cordillot and Klaus 2011). Of these, 32 000 are regarded as forest species (Bollmann *et al.* 2009), although these include some that should be considered forest-edge species since they live in the transitional habitat between the forest and open land. This so-called ecotone is extremely diverse in terms of microclimates, structures, substrates and food supply, which benefits, in particular, many saproxylic (wood-dwelling) beetles as their larvae depend on wood for their development. Moreover, the adult beetles need pollen from flowering plants as food for egg production.

The number of insect species in a forest depends on climate and many biotic factors. Tree species composition normally plays an important role with broadleaf trees, in general, harbouring considerably more species than conifers. Oaks and willows are particularly rich in insects, while among the conifers, Scots pine has the lead (Kennedy and Southwood 1984). Oaks may host about 5000 to 6000 species and pines 1500 to 2000 species (Dajoz 1998). Only a few species colonize both coniferous and broadleaf trees.

The degree of light penetration into the forest also affects insect species numbers.

The caterpillar of the pine hawk moth *(Sphinx pinastri)* eats exclusively (monophagously) pine needles and wears a corresponding camouflage dress.

1 Diversity and functions

More open forests have a warmer microclimate and the ground vegetation of herbs and grasses is more diverse, resulting in a correspondingly more diverse insect fauna. Another crucial factor is the so-called 'habitat tradition', which denotes the fact that a habitat has existed for a long time and, as a consequence, has developed a specific insect fauna.

1.3 The most important insect groups in the forest

Taxonomic groups

Most representatives of the approximately 30 European insect orders also occur in the forest. Beetles (Coleoptera) are, according to the database 'Fauna Europaea' (De Jong et al. 2014), the most species-rich group with around 28 000 European species. Beetle lifestyles vary tremendously. In forests, they feed on all kinds of plant matter, mosses, fungi, and lichens, but also on excrement and carrion. Many species are predatory, eating other insects or other invertebrates. Beetles also include the principal insect pests in coniferous forests, namely bark beetles. Many groups of beetles, including again bark beetles, play a vital role in the degradation of dead organic matter, especially wood. They range from specialised species that colonize trees that have recently died to species that thrive in the rotten wood substrate.

The number of species and lifestyles of true flies (Diptera; 25 000 European species) are equally impressive. Many species feed on living plants or dead organic matter, while others live as predators or parasites. As pollinators of many flowering plants and decomposers of dead plant and animal matter, they play a significant and noticeable role in forest ecosystems. In addition, some flies parasitize important herbivorous insects, but they have little economic impact as potential pests.

Hymenoptera are among the most species-rich orders, with about 24 000 European species. In the forest, the many parasitoid wasp species and the wood ants are particularly important, as they regulate other insect populations. Numerous wild bee species are valuable pollinators of flowering plants. The larvae of some sawflies can cause damage in coniferous plantations. Among the woodwasps, *Sirex noctilio* causes significant damage where it has been accidentally introduced

◁ These almost identical looking species of jewel beetles are closely related. However, their larvae develop on completely different tree species: The larva of *Chrysobothris affinis* (above) lives under the bark of various broadleaf trees, while the larva of *Chrysobothris chrysostigma* (below) mainly feeds on spruce bark.

1 Diversity and functions

Among the many beetle species in the forest, *Lilioceris merdigera*, which belongs to the leaf beetles (Chrysomelidae), is a striking spot of colour in the sea of leaves of the bear's garlic. Its larvae feed on the underside of its leaves.

Tipula maxima is the largest species of craneflies native to Central Europe having a wingspan of almost 7 cm. It occurs in humid places along streams. Its larvae develop in the soil of swampy banks.

from Europe to other continents. Gall wasps form conspicuously shaped and colourful galls, but usually have little detrimental impact on their host plants.

The herbivorous larvae (caterpillars) of butterflies and, in particular, moths are important components of forest insect communities. They feed on herbs, grasses, leaves or needles. Moths include some typical forest pests, which, under certain conditions, have mass outbreaks and thus become detrimental. Among them are the tussock moths (Lymantriinae), the winter moths *Erannis defoliaria* and *Operophtera brumata,* the green oak leafroller *(Tortrix viridana),* and the pine beauty moth *(Panolis flammea).* The number of butterflies in the forest is rather modest. Some, however, such as the woodland brown *(Lopinga achine),* are on the Red List of endangered species.

Smaller groups, like true bugs and plant lice (aphids), are also well represented in the forest and along forest edges. They have sucking mouthparts and mostly feed on plant sap. Some bugs, however, are predatory on other insects. Springtails (Collembola) are species-poor but very abundant. They are an extremely important arthropod order for the formation of forest soil, as they feed on dead organic substances (detritus).

Feeding types

Insects can be classified into different functional groups (guilds) according to their diet. So-called folivores feed on living green leaves, needles, herbs or grass. They include, in particular, the larvae of moths and sawflies, many grasshoppers and various flies and beetles. Plant-sap suckers, such as plant lice, many true bugs, cicadas, thrips and spider mites, also feed on living plants. Xylophagous species eat bark or wood. They include many beetles, for example bark beetles (Scolytinae), jewel beetles (Buprestidae) and longhorn

While its larvae are herbivorous, the adult sawfly *Rhogogaster punctulata* is a predator. Here it has captured the brown lacewing *Hemerobius humulinus.*

beetles (Cerambycidae). Other xylophagous guilds can be found in the Hymenoptera, e.g., woodwasps, the Diptera and even some Lepidoptera, e.g., the European goat moth *(Cossus cossus)*. Specialised fungivorous beetles and flies feed on fungal tissue. Detritivorous insects colonize carrion and dung. They include many mosquitos, flies and springtails, as well as beetle and fly species. Predatory and parasitic species form two other important guilds. While the predators are taxonomically extremely heterogeneous (see Chapter 6), the parasitic species consist mainly of parasitoid wasps (Hymenoptera), flies and mites. Some of them are used for biological control, especially in agriculture, as natural enemies of harmful organisms.

Another categorisation can be made on the basis of a species' lifestyle. Galling insects, for example, developed in various taxonomic units, such as gall wasps (Cynipidae), gall midges (Cecidomyiidae), certain sawflies (Tenthredinidae), aphids, beetles and gall

The springtails are tiny animals whose food consists mostly of dead vegetable material and which are therefore important humus formers. However, the springtail *Ceratophysella sigillata* feeds on algae.

Of the diurnal butterflies, only few are regarded as forest species. The comma butterfly *(Polygonia c-album)* hibernates as an adult and is one of the first butterflies to appear in spring. Its caterpillars feed on elm, willow and hazel.

Caterpillars of moths are typical herbivorous insects in the forest. By feeding on green plant tissue, they accelerate nutrient turnover.

mites (Eriophyidae). Their galls are special plant excrescences, which are induced by the release of phytohormone-like substances by the gall formers. Social insects may form highly specialised groups with a division of tasks between different castes. In Central Europe, social insects include bees, wasps and ants, and in Southern Europe, termites.

1.4 Ecological functions and economic significance

Insects perform many important ecological functions as a result of their long evolution and their presence in almost all ecosystems. The following sections provide a general overview of their diverse functions in forest habitats, as well as their economic significance for humans. These aspects are described in more detail later in the corresponding chapters.

Ecological functions

Organisms can be grouped according to their ecological roles, e.g., based on their required resources, as herbivores, pollinators, predators or detritivores. A single species may be assigned to different functional groups at different stages in its development. Moths, for example, are herbivorous as larvae, but are often pollinators as adults.

One of the best-known roles of insects is as pollinators of flowering plants, especially of shrubs and herbaceous plants, which depend on insect pollination (see Chapter 2). Herbivorous insects accelerate the turn-over of plant energy sources and nutrients by eating or sucking (Chapter 3). Saproxylic insects promote the degradation of wood from dead trees or tree parts (Chapter 4). Specialised

Galls of the gall wasp *Cynips quercusfolii*. Gall wasps produce the most conspicuous galls. They induce their galls almost exclusively on oak. Their larvae develop inside the galls and feed on the continuously regrowing plant tissue.

groups of carrion and detritus feeders help decompose animal cadavers and excrement (Chapter 5). Insects, mites, woodlice and millipedes contribute to soil formation and fertility (Chapter 6). The invertebrates themselves serve as food for other organisms. It is mainly vertebrates, such as birds, bats and insectivores, as well as numerous microorganisms, that live directly from insects and other arthropods (Chapter 7). Insects are also important regulators; a vast number of predatory and parasitic species are natural enemies of potentially harmful herbivores, keeping the population densities of pests at 'normal', sustainable levels (Chapters 8 to 10). Certain fungi, mites, which are poorly mobile, and other invertebrates depend on flying insect species for transport within a habitat or to new ones (Chapter 11). The colonization of living trees by insects does not per se lead to damage. When insects colonize and kill diseased and weakened trees, the overall health ('vitality') of a forest is ultimately increased (Chapter 12). After large-scale outbreaks, some species are able to alter entire landscapes and initiate new forest growth (Chapter 13).

Economic significance

Only a few forest insects have direct economic significance for humans. From a human point of view, they are considered pests when they greatly affect important forest products and services. Such species include mainly bark beetles and moth caterpillars (Chapter 14). Not only may insects damage important resources, but certain insects and ticks may also directly

Not only dead plant material, but also animal carrion is processed by detritus-feeding insects. The picture shows the carcass of a chamois with different species of flies and carrion beetles.

Two functional groups in one picture: A wild bee (*Andrena bicolor*) as an important pollinator of shrubs and herbs falls victim to the predatory crab spider *Ozyptila atomaria*.

Bark beetles can have quite different significances. As pioneer colonizers, they initiate the degradation process in dead trees. However, they can also transmit fungal diseases or infest healthy trees under certain conditions, thereby changing the abundance of tree species. The picture shows the galleries of the small elm bark beetle (*Scolytus multistriatus*).

affect human health (Chapter 15). Conversely, insects supply products that humans can use directly as food, e.g., honey, or raw materials for a wide variety of applications, such as silk or wax (Chapter 16). Additional chapters deal with the impact of alien insects on the forest (Chapter 17), and with endangered species and nature conservation (Chapter 18). Other non-material or cultural aspects of forest insects are not considered in this book.

Bark beetles, especially the spruce bark beetle (*Ips typographus*), are among the economically most important pest organisms in the forest. A mass outbreak of this beetle can lead to large-scale mortality in spruce. This can mean an economic damage for the forest owners or a felt loss for residents and forest visitors. It can also impair the protective capability of a forest for a long time.

Functions of insects in the forest	Importance of forest insects for humans
Insects and other arthropods have manifold functions in the forest habitat, as they do in almost every other ecosystem. They are explained in more detail in the following chapters of this book. Insects play a role: − as pollinators and seed dispersers in flowering plants (Chap. 2) − in the turnover of plant mass (Chap. 3) − in the decomposition of wood (Chap. 4) − in the decomposition of animal waste (Chap. 5) − in soil formation and soil fertility (Chap. 6) − as a source of food and energy for other organisms (Chap. 7) − as natural enemies of potential pest organisms (Chap. 8-10) − as vectors for other organisms (Chap. 11) − in maintaining forest vitality (Chap. 12) − as 'ecosystem engineers' in shaping habitats (Chap. 13)	A few species may be directly significant for humans in affecting economics or health because they: − cause economic damage (Chap. 14) − impair human health (Chap. 15) − manufacture useful products (Chap. 16) − are newly introduced organisms (Chap. 17) − are specially relevant for nature conservation (Chap. 18)

1 Diversity and functions

Ecological functions

Insects and plant reproduction

2

In the course of evolution, manifold relationships between plants and insects have developed. Initially, plants were primarily food for herbivorous insects. About 100 million years ago, some plants began to capitalise on the abundance and diversity of insects, and used them to transport pollen between these 'modern' plants, thus pollinating their flowers. It is possible that as long as 300 million years ago insects were already pollinating some non-flowering plants, which are now extinct (Ollerton and Coulthard 2009). While in general plant seeds are dispersed rather randomly, some plants have concentrated in the course of time on having their seeds spread more efficiently by specific groups of insects.

Hoverflies are among the most frequent pollinators of forest plants. *Syrphus torvus* lives preferentially in forests. Since it already flies early in the year, this species is a frequent visitor of the early flowering Norway maple.

2.1 Pollination of flowers

Pollinating flowering plants is one of the most important ecosystem services that insects perform. This service is particularly important in agriculture, where, for example, 84 percent of all crops in Europe depend at least partly on insect pollination (Williams 1994). The pollination by bees and bumble bees of field and fruit crops, as well as of plants in greenhouses, has even been commercialised. However, these bees only perform about half of the crop pollination, while non-bee insects are responsible for up to 50 percent of pollination, and even produce a better fruit set (Rader *et al.* 2016). In contrast, 80 percent of all trees and shrubs as well as all grasses in forests are pollinated by wind (anemophily), which is the original form of pollination. Correspondingly, not only do the 'primitive' conifers with mostly unisexual flowers have their pollen spread by the wind, but so too do some common broadleaf trees, such as ash, beech, oak, alder, poplar and elm. Sweet chestnut may be pollinated by wind or insects. Hazel is one of the few shrubs to be pollinated by wind. Most of these woody plants bloom before or during budburst so that their foliage does not impede pollen spreading.

With wind pollination, the pollen only accidentally reaches flowers of the same plant species. Therefore, some tree species in the windless forest interior and, in particular, low-growing species along the forest edge, have specialised in insect pollination (zoophily). Insects visit specific flowers and thereby transfer the pollen. Insect-pollinated tree species include maple, cherry, willow, lime and mountain ash, as well as shrubs such as blackthorn, hawthorn, buckthorn and dogwood. Herbaceous plants on the forest floor are pollinated by insects as well. In the course of evolution, all these plants have managed to attract insects by producing colourful flowers, fragrant volatiles and nectar, thus gaining an advantage over their competitors. Almost all insect-pollinated plants therefore have large flowers with bright colours (often white or yellow) and fragrant scents. In addition, they direct assimilates (photosynthesis products) to the production of nectar. The pollinators use this nutritious carbohydrate source for 'operating energy'. The pollination relationship between plants and insects is considered a symbiosis: the plant provides pollen and nectar as food for pollinators and, at the same time, serves as a meeting place where insects can easily find mating partners. In return, insects transport pollen to flowers of the same plant species. Pollen is a very nutritious substrate of proteins, enriched with starch, fats and minerals. Female insects need more pollen than males because they produce eggs.

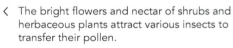

⟨ The bright flowers and nectar of shrubs and herbaceous plants attract various insects to transfer their pollen.

The marmalade hoverfly *(Episyrphus balteatus)* is one of the most common and widely distributed hoverflies, and therefore an important pollinator. Its larvae live predaciously on aphids. The overwintering females can also be seen on mild winter days.

Most flower-visiting insects, such as honeybees, beetles or flies, are generalists. This means that they visit flowers belonging to different plant species and transfer the pollen to flowers of other plant species, where it is, of course, useless. Pollen feeders like beetles visit flowers because they need pollen as a food source. Nectar suckers, such as flies or moths, frequent flowers in search of nectar and distribute pollen randomly. In the course of evolution, however, many plants have adapted the structure of their flowers to suit the best pollinators. They restrict access to the rewarding nectar to those insects that can efficiently gather, transport and transfer their pollen to conspecific flowers. This means that the plants do not need to produce so much pollen and can therefore invest less energy in producing it. This selection pressure has led to the development of specialised insect species with a longer proboscis, which enables them to reach the nectar hidden deep in the flower calyx and to outcompete other species with shorter proboscises. This is why some plants can be pollinated solely by very specific species of wild bees or moths with correspondingly long mouthparts.

Some orchids attract particular species of bees and bumble bees to pollinate their flowers by perfectly imitating the shape, colour and scent of the bees' sexual partners and seducing them to attempt mating. The insects then transfer the pollen between the orchids and bees without being rewarded with nectar.

2 Plant reproduction

Eristalis pertinax is a very common hoverfly and occurs in the forest and many other habitats. Its so-called 'rat-tailed maggots' develop in the mud of pools. The adult flies visit very different flowers.

The snout-hoverfly *(Rhingia campestris)* has the longest proboscis of all hoverflies. This enables it to tap nectar located deep in the flowers. While resting, it retracts its long proboscis to the extension of its head capsule.

A bee fly (*Bombylius* sp.) nibbling on pollen from a wood anemone. The herbaceous flora in forests and along forest edges are pollinated by insects.

Similarly, plants that smell of excrement or carrion attract specific flies and beetles as pollen vectors.

Hoverflies

The most frequent pollinators in the forest are hoverflies (Syrphidae), which mainly favour yellow flowers. These flies occur primarily in sunlit and warm places in open forests, as well as along the borders of forests and paths, or in clearings. There they live on nectar, pollen and honeydew. When visiting flowers, they passively transmit pollen. The length of their proboscis determines the type of flowers they can feed on. For example, the snout-hoverfly (*Rhingia* spp.) can exploit flowers of the mint family (Lamiaceae), whose nectaries (nectar-producing glands) are not accessible to other flies, thanks to its 12-millimetre-long proboscis. Some hoverflies have long, partly forked or curled hairs, which the pollen adheres to easily. The flies comb out most of the pollen with their legs and feed on it. Some of it, however, remains on their bodies and is stripped off on the stigma of the next flowers. In contrast, the lifestyles of hoverfly larvae vary greatly. They may develop in moist tree cavities, in rotting material or in excrement. Some predate on aphids, while others live parasitically in wasp and bee nests (see Section 8.1).

Bees

Honeybees, bumble bees and wild bees are very important pollinators because they need nectar and pollen not only for feeding them-

Wild bees such as the grey-backed mining bee *(Andrena vaga)* have furry bodies and are thus good transmitters of pollen. This species constructs its nest burrow in sandy soils.

selves, but also for nourishing their broods. A single bee visits and pollinates about 1000 flowers during a single day (Pimentel 1975). Honeybees *(Apis mellifera)* alone would not be able to pollinate all the flowers in our cultural and natural landscape. For this reason, the diversity and frequency of the almost 2000 European wild bee species are incredibly important for plant pollination (Nieto *et al.* 2014).

Most wild bees occur in open landscapes rich in flowers with variegated structures. In the forest they are limited to warm, sunny locations such as along paths and forest edges, where the flower supply is normally rich. They are largely absent in so-called high forests where little sunlight reaches the forest floor. Bees have developed special mechanisms for taking up nectar and harvesting pollen. Since the depths at which the nectaries are hidden depends on the plant species, bees have developed probosces of different lengths. Bee species with long probosces can reach nectaries lying deep in the flowers and thus visit this type of flower, while short-sucker bees head for plant species that have more easily accessible nectaries. The length of the suckers ranges from 1 millimetre (*Hylaeus* species) to 2 centimetres (bumble bees, *Bombus* spp.). Most wild bees and honeybees visit flowers of many different plant species and are thus called 'polylectic'. Some 'oligolectic' wild bee species specialise in just a few plant genera and are thus restricted to visiting only these plants.

The red mason bee *(Osmia rufa)* lives along forest edges and in clearings where flowers are abundant. It wipes off pollen from the flowers with its ventral pollen brush and transports it on the brush to the nest. The nest consists of a consecutive series of cells in hollows, such as abandoned beetle galleries in wood. The female deposits an egg in each cell and supplies it with pollen.

2 Plant reproduction

Buff-tailed bumble bee *(Bombus terrestris)* gathering pollen on goat beard flowers. The pollen sticks to its hind legs, with which it then carries it to the nest.

The pollen grains are gathered in many different ways. Depending on the species, wild bees collect it with their legs, mouthparts, heads or abdomens. The corresponding body parts are often intensely pubescent, with hairs similar to those of some hoverflies. The hairs are often twisted or hook-shaped so they can collect the pollen more efficiently. Bumble bees (*Bombus* spp.), carpenter bees (*Xylocopa* spp.) and other species can shake plant anthers by vibrating their wing muscles so that the pollen falls onto their bodies. In primitive species, the pollen is transported in their crops, while more highly developed species usually carry it in a hairbrush on their hind legs or their belly. Honeybees collect pollen with

‹ The domesticated honeybee *(Apis mellifera)* is also an important pollinator in open forests and along forest edges. Note the bee's proboscis extended into a maple blossom, the forehead powdered with pollen, and the pollen basket on the hind legs with the collected pollen clearly visible.

2 Plant reproduction

their legs and entire bodies, and transport it, moistened with nectar, in so-called 'pollen baskets' on the tibiae of their hind legs into the hive.

Other pollinators

In addition to bees, hoverflies and other flies, moths also suck nectar but transfer the pollen rather accidentally. Nocturnal species, such as hawk moths (Sphingidae) and owlet moths (Noctuidae), are especially likely to pollinate forest plants. The hawk moths hover in front of flowers like hummingbirds, and can even reach nectar situated deep in the flowers with their long proboscis. To get to the nectar, owlet moths need flowers that provide a landing platform where the moths can sit down while sucking. Some beetles are typical flower visitors, but they are considered rather primitive pollinators. They eat pollen and parts of flowers, thereby also incidentally transferring pollen.

Hawk moths are among the fastest insect fliers and can visit numerous blossoms within a short period of time. The privet hawk moth *(Sphinx ligustri)* sucks on the flowers of privet, honeysuckle and other species.

A pair of red-brown longhorn beetles *(Stictoleptura rubra)*, powdered with red pollen, feed on the flowers of a dwarf elder.

The larva of the bee beetle (Trichius fasciatus) develops in deadwood. The very pilose adults feed on various species of flowering plants.

2.2 Dissemination of seeds

After the flowers have been pollinated, the fruits ripen. For plant propagation, their seeds should be spread over as wide an area as possible. Light seeds or seeds with special flying devices are transported by the wind, as is the case with willow or maple. Heavy seeds, such as acorns, nuts and berries, are spread by birds and small mammals. A number of herbaceous forest plants have developed special features to encourage insects to spread their seeds on the windless forest floor. The rather large seeds of dead-nettles, violets, snowdrops and fumewort have so-called 'elaiosomes'. These

The conspicuous silver-washed fritillary (Argynnis paphia) is one of the few butterflies occurring in forests. It likes to suck nectar from hemp-agrimony growing along forest edges and in clearings with ample herbaceous vegetation.

The fumewort thrives in broadleaved forests, coppices and hedges. It is pollinated by bees with long proboscnes. Its pod-shaped fruits contain several black seeds, which have a white elaiosome that is extremely nutritious for ants.

A wood ant *(Formica polyctena)* worker transports a fumewort seed to its nest. On the way, it bites off the seed from the coveted elaiosome and leaves it behind.

appendages are rich in fat and sugar and very palatable for ants. The ants carry the seeds to their nest and bite off, on the way, the nutritious elaiosome from the seed, which is worthless for them. The seeds are left behind or are deposited in the ants' waste yards, thus getting to new areas. The spreading of seeds by ants is called 'myrmecochory'. A further advantage of myrmecochory is that the seeds germinate more easily because of the small injuries they receive when the ants bite off the elaiosome. The resulting seedlings also have a higher survival rate if they are close to an ant nest because herbivorous insects are fewer there. This interaction between plant and ants is called 'trophobiosis' (food-based symbiosis), whereby the ants obtain a nutritious food source and the plant can disperse more successfully.

2.3 Influence on plant competition

Insects may also change the competition between plant species (see also Section 13.2), which constantly compete with each other for nutrients, water and light. The various plant species mostly experience almost constant conditions, resulting in distinct plant species assemblages particularly of long-lived trees in a given area. Insects may limit the growth and reproduction of herbaceous and woody plants by reducing their leaf area or by consuming phloem sap. This temporarily diminishes the competitiveness of the infested plants and species, and may alter the abundance of the affected plant species locally or even regionally, thereby changing the species composition in the forest. In today's managed forests, however, tree species composition largely depends on the silvicultural measures implemented.

When gradual or abrupt abiotic or biotic factors affect the prevailing conditions, the plant species composition changes as well. This is most apparent when such changes occur abruptly. Ecological disturbances such as storms, forest fires or avalanches create gaps in the forest and eliminate the dominant trees, thus enabling other plant species to grow at least temporarily. Disturbances can also have biotic causes if, for example, certain tree species are selectively infested and killed by leaf- or bark-feeding insects (mainly bark beetles) (see Chapter 13).

In mountain forests, reforestation after ecological disturbances is particulary slow going. While disturbed areas are, in general, quickly colonized by fast-growing pioneer shrubs and trees with lightweight airborne seeds, the principal tree species take longer to establish. Their seedlings must assert themselves against the already established pioneer species. Large-leaved herbaceous plants, such as alpine sow-thistle, coltsfoot, alpine Adenostyles or butterbur, may cover the ground completely and thus inhibit the growth of the shaded tree seedlings. The dominance of such herbaceous flora can be locally reduced by leaf-feeding insects. In some years, leaf beetles (*Oreina* spp., *Chrysolina* spp.) of the family 'Chrysomelidae' occur in considerable numbers and perforate the large shading leaves extensively. As a result, the underlying tree seedlings receive more light and can gradually outgrow the inhibiting herb layer.

Leaf beetles of, for example, the genus *Oreina* feed on the foliage of tall forbs. The resulting perforation enables enough light to reach the ground for the tree seedlings to outgrow, with time, this regeneration-hostile layer.

2.4 Feeding on flowers and fruits

Although insects perform many positive functions for plant propagation as described above, insects and mites may also damage plants' flowers, fruits and seeds. Plants in a sense 'budget' for insects' consumption of pollen, which is more than compensated for by the positive effect of pollen transport. Nevertheless, some mites and insects can feed or suck on flower organs to such an extent that they impair fruit formation. When the cauliflower gall mite *(Aceria fraxinivora)*, which is only about 0.2 millimetres in size, sucks on the flowers of ash trees, galls (excrescences) form on their inflorescences. The flowers can then no longer be pollinated and do not form seeds. Depending on the severity of the infestation, a smaller or larger proportion of the seed production is lost.

Some beetle species, such as the weevils of the genera *Phyllobius* and *Polydrusus*, also feed on flower parts. Rose chafers (e.g., *Cetonia aurata*) like to feed on the reproductive organs of the white flowers of elder, guelder rose, mountain ash, hawthorn and other Rosacean plants. One of the most common beetles in windthrow or clear-cut areas is the raspberry beetle *(Byturus tomentosus)*. In spring the adults feed on the flowers of blackberries and raspberries, and their larvae develop in the fruit. By visiting the flowers, however, the beetles also contribute to the

All the flowers on this ash twig have been infested by the cauliflower gall mite *(Aceria fraxinivora)* and can therefore not form seeds.

The raspberry beetle *(Byturus tomentosus)* feeds on the anthers of raspberry blossoms, but without noticeably reducing reproduction. In contrast, when its larva develops in the berries, it damages them.

plants' pollination. The needle- and leaf-eating caterpillars of moths, such as the green oak leafroller *(Tortrix viridana)* and the winter moth *(Operophtera brumata)*, as well as sucking aphids, can also restrict the formation of flowers and fruit.

Some insects feed on plant seeds and fruit that are rich in carbohydrates and lipids. Many pest species live on seeds stored for human consumption, e.g., cereals and nuts, and destroy around five percent of the world's supplies (Boxall 2001). Forests are also home to many seed-devouring insects, but they rarely consume enough to jeopardize the reproduction of trees, shrubs and herbaceous plants. Such insects may, however, affect seed production in tree nurseries and that of so-called non-wood forest products, such as chestnuts or nuts. Many beetles, moths, flies, bugs and Hymenoptera feed or suck on

2 Plant reproduction

seeds, destroying them or removing enough energy to prevent them from successfully germinating. The larvae of various species of tortricid and pyralid moths, gall midges (Cecidomyiidae), anthomyiid flies, chalcid wasps (*Megastigmus* spp.) and anobiid beetles develop in conifer cones. In larch, for example, these seed-eaters can cause the loss of as much as 80 percent of seeds (Roques *et al.* 1984).

Beetles

Specialised weevils infest the fruits of oak, chestnut or hazel. These beetles have a characteristic head with a long protruding proboscis, at the end of which the mouthparts are located. The female uses these to gnaw a hole in the acorn, chestnut or nut, and usually deposits a single egg in the fruit with her equally long ovipositor (egg-depositing

A false oil beetle *(Oedemera nobilis)* with the huge hind thighs typical of males feeds on the anthers of a dog rose bush.

Many longhorn beetle species feed on pollen or the flowering parts of plants in forest clearings and along forest edges during their maturation, while their larvae develop in pieces of deadwood in the forest.

organ). A larva hatches from the egg and then develops in the fruit, making it unable to germinate (and inedible for humans). After the fruit has fallen to the ground, the larva leaves it and pupates up to 60 centimetres deep in the ground. To survive years with a poor fruit set, these species may go through a so-called facultative diapause (dormant stage). One example is the chestnut weevil (*Curculio elephas*), where about one-third to one-half of a population passes through such a diapausing stage (Dajoz 1998). This means that these beetles do not emerge before the second year after the eggs are laid. If hardly any chestnuts were produced in the first year after oviposition, the population of chestnut weevils would drastically decrease. However, since their remaining population are still diapausing in the ground, they can then benefit from the probably better conditions in the following year. In a Romanian study, acorns were regularly infested with the acorn weevil (*Curculio glandium*), which is related to the chestnut weevil, at a rate of more than 25 percent (Scutareanu and Roques 1993).

True bugs

Many true bugs like to suck on the nutrient-rich seeds of various coniferous and broadleaf trees, as well as of shrubs. Some bugs are specialised in feeding on certain tree species. The spruce cone bug (*Gastrodes abietum*)

◁ (a) The chestnut weevil (*Curculio elephas*) develops as a legless larva in chestnuts or acorns. (b) The larva then pupates deep in the soil. (c) In the following year, the beetle emerges, gnaws a hole in a growing nut with its long proboscis where it lays an egg. (d) Moth caterpillars may also develop in chestnuts. Here the larger hole was produced by a chestnut weevil larva, and the smaller one probably by a chestnut leafroller larva, i.e., by a moth.

2 Plant reproduction

sucks on spruce seeds and the birch catkin bug (Kleidocerys resedae) on the catkins (inflorescences) of birch and alder. The western conifer seed bug (Leptoglossus occidentalis), which originates from North America, is predominantly found on pine. The bug penetrates the cone scales with its proboscis and sucks on the developing seeds. In its home country, it causes up to 40 percent seed loss in Douglas fir (Ciesla 2011). The green shield bug (Palomena viridissima), the dock bug (Coreus marginatus) and many other species are less choosy about which seeds and fruits of herbaceous plants, shrubs and bushes they feed on.

Moths

Moths also include species that infest fruits and seeds. For example, the codling moth (Cydia pomonella) can be a very serious pest in commercial fruit growing. Species of the

The spruce cone bug (Gastrodes abietum) has fore thighs, which are thickened and armed with a tooth, characteristic for the genus. At all developmental stages it sucks on spruce cone seeds, and the larvae also suck on needles.

Both the larvae and adults of the birch catkin bug (Kleidocerys resedae) suck on the seeds of birch and alder seed heads.

34 Dock bugs *(Coreus marginatus)* suck on the shoots, leaves and fruits of various plants, including raspberries. The sucker attached to the bottom of the head is clearly visible here. It can be inserted deep into the berry.

A larva (recognizable by the still incompletely developed wings) of the green shieldbug *(Palomena viridissima)* sucks on the fruit of a rowanberry.

same genus also develop in the seeds of forest trees, such as spruce, larch, white fir, sweet chestnut, oak and beech. Besides chestnut weevils (see above), several other moth larvae may infest chestnut fruits. The slender larvae with thoracic legs and abdominal prolegs belong to the chestnut leafroller *(Pammene fasciana)* or the chestnut leafroller *(Cydia splendana)*. These two moth caterpillars may affect between 10 and 50 percent of chestnut fruits in Ticino, Switzerland (Müller 1957). If chestnut weevils are also included, well over half of all chestnuts may be infested. Among the pyralid moths (Pyralidae), the species with the most impact is the spruce coneworm *Dioryctria abietella*, which attacks the cones of various conifers such as spruce, fir or cedar. Its larvae eat their way through the infested cone, destroying all seeds and ejecting large amounts of boring dust, excrement and resin.

Insects can also cause galls on flowers and fruit and thus impair the formation of seeds. One of the most striking excrescences can be found on acorns. They are the creation of the knopper gall wasp *(Andricus quercuscalicis)*, which in Central Europe can only pass through the entire cycle if its second host, the Turkey oak *(Quercus cerris)*, is present. The generation reproducing sexually develops in small inconspicuous galls on the female catkins of Turkey oaks. It is from these catkin galls

One of the most conspicuous galls on pedunculate oak is formed during the development of the parthenogenetic generation of the knopper gall wasp *(Andricus quercuscalicis)*. The wasp lays an egg on the growing acorn. (a) When the larva feeds on it, a species-specific gall, which is first green or reddish, and later brown, develops. (b) The dissected gall shows the larva inside, (c) which will pupate in autumn after the gall has fallen to the ground. (d) In early spring, the wasp emerges to found the sexual generation on Turkey oak.

2 Plant reproduction

36 The larvae of the spruce coneworm *(Dioryctria abietella)* feed under the cover of a mixture of faeces and resin. Here the still green spruce cone shows the typical infestation symptoms.

that the parthenogenetic generation, which produces unfertilized eggs, then emerges. During their development, the wasp larvae from this generation produce galls on acorns, especially on pedunculate oaks *(Quercus robur)*. Several galls can form on one acorn, but each gall contains only one larva.

2 Plant reproduction

Turnover of green plant biomass

3

Green plants are the producers in the ecological cycle of organic matter. They store converted solar energy, water, carbon and inorganic minerals in the form of organic compounds. These energy sources and nutrients are the food basis for the numerous primary consumers (1st order consumers). With plant diversity increasing over millions of years, the diversity of herbivorous insects also increased. Today a huge number of leaf-, needle- and pollen-eaters, nectar-suckers, miners, gallers as well as phloem- and cell-sucking insects feed on green plant tissue or plant sap. Bark-, wood- and root-eating insects also colonize and degrade the woody supporting parts of plants (see Chapter 4). Herbivorous insects are thus the primary regulators of energy and

The larvae of the European pine sawfly (*Neodiprion sertifer*) feed exclusively on pine needles. They store the resin contained in the needle resin ducts in specific pockets in their foreguts. When attacked, they regurgitate the resin and smear it on the aggressor. Their droppings contain little resin and can be quickly degraded by microorganisms on the ground.

nutrient flows between the producers and the other food webs.

The availability of nutrients and water often limits plant growth. While a plant cannot influence the water supply much, there are some ways it can reinvest in its growth some of the nutrients bound in its tissue. In autumn, deciduous trees transfer part of the bound nutrients to the soil with the falling leaves or needles, where they are mineralised by microorganisms and, in inorganic form, made available for plant growth. This degradation may, however, be very slow depending on leaf composition. Under certain circumstances it can, therefore, be beneficial for a tree if insects consume some of its foliage and thereby accelerate the recycling of the leaf nutrients. This is especially true for many deciduous trees, which can flush new leaves in the same year, even after a complete defoliation, and replace the lost leaf mass. However, if several infestations occur in consecutive years, or if non-needle-shedding conifers are affected, certain insects can become pests for humans (see Chapter 14). The following examples illustrate how infestations by herbivorous insects do not always weaken, or even kill, a tree. Most plants have adjusted, in the course of evolution, to a certain loss of leaf surface and assimilates, which may even benefit their nutrient supply.

3.1 Caterpillar feeding

In the forest, it is mainly insects, in addition to the large ruminants, that feed on green plant tissue. Almost all butterfly and moth caterpillars, aphids, true bugs, cicadas and grasshoppers, as well as about one-third of all beetles live on plant food. Although this means a loss of leaf mass and assimilates for the trees, they have an amazing capacity to compensate for these losses by tapping their reserves. Usually 3 to 8 percent of the annual leaf mass in a forest is consumed by insects. Up to one-third of the leaf mass produced each year can be consumed by defoliators without affecting the overall production of a plant (Mattson and Addy 1975). Several examples show that the consumption of plant mass by insects can even increase the efficiency of a plant, accelerate nutrient turnover and improve the nutrient supply to trees. Leaf feeding also increases the translucence of the crown, promotes the leaching of nutrients from the bitten leaves into the soil and reduces competition among trees.

The leaves of many tree species (e.g., oak or sweet chestnut) contain high levels of tannins and other tanning agents, which increase as the leaves grow and senesce. In conifers, the needles contain large quantities of protective resins. All this makes the foliage difficult for microorganisms to degrade after leaf fall. In insect faeces, on the other hand, many plant constituents have already been extensively digested. The faeces' complete degradation on the ground, mainly through bacteria, therefore proceeds more easily and quickly.

Beech, oak and sweet chestnut are among the preferred tree species of gypsy moth (Lymantria dispar) caterpillars. These caterpillars are able to digest many complex leaf constituents that are difficult to degrade. The faecal pellets they excrete (bottom right) can then be mineralised more easily by bacteria.

3 Turnover of green plant biomass

The nitrogen, phosphorus and potassium levels are several times higher in the faeces than in the original plant tissue, and are also higher in dead insects when they fall to the ground at the end of their life. The nitrogen content in plant tissue is generally between 1 and 5 percent, but in animal tissue it is 7 to 14 percent (Mattson 1980). This explains why, for insects to grow, they have to consume such large amounts of plant material.

Faeces have a larger surface area per volume than intact leaves. They can therefore be colonized by more microorganisms and degrade more quickly. In addition, certain caterpillars are wasteful feeders, biting off bits of leaf that fall to the ground, where their gnawed edges can be easily colonized by bacteria. Insect feeding therefore enables the energy carriers and nutrients contained in the plant tissue to quickly reach the soil in considerable quantities, where they increase soil activity and thus quickly become available again for plant growth.

Moth caterpillars

Moth caterpillars, mainly from Lymantriinae and Geometridae, are among the best-known defoliators. Certain species can significantly influence the nutrient balance of a forest. This has been quantified for the gypsy moth (*Lymantria dispar*; see Section 14.1), which is known for its mass outbreaks (Szujecki 1987). During mass propagation, up to one-third of the organic material annually falling to the forest floor originates from these caterpillars, i.e., from their faeces, their exuvia (moulting remains) and their corpses. This corresponds to about 2.7 tonnes per hectare. Between outbreaks, this proportion decreases to almost zero, and the normal annual input of 9 tonnes of organic material is of plant origin. During an outbreak of the California oakworm (*Phryganidia californica*) in an oak stand in California, the flux of nitrogen and phosphorus from the tree crown to the ground doubled. Approximately half of this biomass consisted of faeces and dead caterpillars (Hollinger 1986). Winter moth (*Operophtera brumata*), mottled umber (*Erannis defoliaria*) and the oak leafroller (*Tortrix viridana*) likewise have caterpillars that may potentially defoliate broadleaf trees on a large scale.

Larch can, as a deciduous conifer species, produce new needles from its reserves. It also benefits from the enhanced nutrient conditions in the soil after an infestation by the nun moth (*Lymantria monacha*) or the larch budmoth (*Zeiraphera griseana*; see Section 13.2).

Outbreaks of leaf- and needle-eating caterpillars often lead temporarily to entire forest stands becoming completely defoliated. Solar

⟨ Gypsy moth caterpillars are wasteful feeders and drop many bitten bits of leaf onto the ground. These bits have relatively large surface areas and accessible feeding edges, which makes it easier for microorganisms to colonize and degrade them quickly.

If leaf-feeding caterpillars completely defoliate a stand during the vegetation period, the microclimate in the stand will be fundamentally altered. More incoming solar radiation will warm the forest soil and accelerate the degradation of organic matter, making nutrients more readily available for plants. This photo of a stand defoliated by gypsy moth caterpillars was taken near Bellinzona in Ticino (Switzerland) in mid-summer (1 July 1993).

Caterpillars degrade many substances – including some toxic ones – in their guts. Here the green faeces of the spurge hawk moth (Hyles euphorbiae) indicate that the nitrogen-rich chlorophyll is still intact and will only be degraded by soil bacteria. These faeces are formed in the rectum. They have a marked structure with a large surface area, which allows microorganisms to colonize them extensively.

irradiation is, as a result, more intense and the temperatures on the ground rise, thereby increasing soil activity. More organic matter is therefore converted, which increases the supply of nutrients to the plants. Nutrients are usually resorbed from the leaves into the wood in late autumn before they fall, with far fewer nutrients, to the ground. Insect infestations normally occur in the first half of the vegetation period, so that the soil receives an input of nutrients via faeces and leaf remains when its activity is high. These nutrients become available for a second flush of leaves in

3 Turnover of green plant biomass

the same year. In many cases, an insect infestation triggers increased plant growth in the years following an outbreak. For example, after an outbreak of the Douglas fir tussock moth *(Orgyia pseudotsugata)* in British Columbia, the annual tree ring growth declined in the first two years, but was, after five years, significantly higher than that of uninfested trees (Alfaro and Shepherd 1991).

Sawfly larvae

The larvae of certain sawflies may also undergo mass propagations, mainly on conifer trees, which, with the exception of larch, cannot resprout after defoliation, or only to a very limited extent. On deciduous trees, however, sawflies can have the same 'fertilisation effect' as moth caterpillars.

‹ Outbreaks of the nun moth *(Lymantria monacha)* provide an impressive example of how fast the turnover of plant biomass can be. When their caterpillars feed extensively on spruce, the trees are severely weakened or even killed. If, however, the outbreak affects a larch stand – a deciduous conifer species, the trees will benefit when they resprout in summer from a boost of nutrients in the centimetre-deep carpet of caterpillar faeces covering the ground.

A colony of birch sawfly larvae *(Craesus septentrionalis)* has consumed leaf after leaf on a hazel branch. But the nutrients contained in their droppings quickly become available again to the affected shrub.

The slug-like, legless larvae of the sawfly *Caliroa cinxia* feed gregariously on the underside of oak leaves, where they scrape off leaf tissue. The feeding tracks they share become wider as the caterpillars grow. In the end, only the upper epidermis and the leaf veins remain intact. The tannins in the oak leaves are broken down in the guts of the larvae, and soil bacteria can then easily decompose the nitrogen-rich faeces.

3 Turnover of green plant biomass

3.2 Other plant feeders

Beetles

Among the beetles, the cockchafer *(Melolontha melolontha)* can play the most important role in the nutrient cycle of green plants. After three years of development as grubs in the soil of meadows and fields, the beetles emerge from the soil and perform their maturation feeding on the leaves of trees. In high population densities, they can cause complete defoliation along nearby forest edges. However, they are feared because of the damage their grubs can do to field crops. For this reason, the beetle was officially excommunicated in the 15th century by the church in several regions in Switzerland!

In addition, a number of leaf beetles *(Chrysomelidae)* sometimes feed in masses on alders, willows and other deciduous trees. If a

During their maturation feeding, cockchafers *(Melolontha melolontha)* feed on various broadleaf trees and shrubs, but they prefer oak, beech and walnut.

Garden chafers *(Phyllopertha horticola)* can conspicuously defoliate willow trees, ferns, raspberries and other shrubs. This nutrient turnover is, however, only relevant for the individual plants.

certain degree of defoliation is exceeded, the trees resprout again.

Grasshoppers

The rare outbreaks of the Generoso mountain grasshopper *(Miramella formosanta)* on the north-western slopes of Lake Lugano in Switzerland are more anecdotal. The humid and cool slopes with mixed deciduous forests offer this grasshopper ideal conditions for sporadic heavy propagations of their populations. In years with normal population densities, the grasshoppers feed mainly in the herb and shrub layer. During a mass outbreak, however, they also spread into the treetops and may cause large-scale but non-recurring defoliation. Although the infestation restricts the growth of the trees in the year of infestation (Asshoff *et al.* 1999), the trees normally recover quickly. The short-term loss of leaves results in increased solar radiation, which promotes the rapid mineralisation of the nutrients stored in the faeces dropping to the ground and in insect corpses. Similar outbreaks are also known from other *Miramella* species.

In contrast to the defoliation caused by caterpillars, the heaviest defoliation by these grasshoppers occurs only in midsummer. This means the benefit of a new flush of leaves is rather uncertain because producing new leaves is energy-intensive, and they are available for photosynthesis for only a relatively short time. In addition, there is a risk that an early frost will kill the not yet fully matured leaves.

The mass propagations of the Generoso mountain grasshopper *(Miramella formosanta)* in 1964, 1988 and 1992 were almost like biblical locust plagues. By mid-summer, the broadleaf forests on the north-western slopes of Lake Lugano in southern Switzerland had become widely defoliated. (Photos in centre, bottom courtesy of Forest Entomology WSL.)

3 Turnover of green plant biomass

Springtails

Another unusual phenomenon can be observed in one particular springtail. Most species of springtails (Collembola) feed on dead plant material in the soil (see Chapter 8). In contrast, the springtail *Ceratophysella sigillata*, which is about one and a half millimetres in size, feeds on live algae. It is active during the winter half-year, which is why it is sometimes also called a 'snow flea'. After an aestivation in summer and autumn in the soil of humid forests, the creatures move to the soil surface in their thousands looking for tree stems and pieces of deadwood covered with algae. The springtails climb up in huge numbers to a height of several metres and graze on the algae cover. Their striking jumping abilities enable them to get past cracks and crevices between the bark scales. The vesicles on their antennae and abdomen help them stick to the bark after a leap and prevent them from falling. When wandering from one trunk to the next, they form grey-violet carpets with hundreds of thousands or even millions of individuals, which are easy to spot, especially on snow. Their aboveground activity only lasts for a short time and is mainly in December, February and March, when temperatures are between 3 and 10 degrees Celsius (Zettel 2007). Subsequently, they reproduce, and their offspring appear again at the beginning of summer. Surprisingly, these tiny primitive insects (strictly speaking, springtails are no longer classified as insects, but as Entognatha) can live for two years and reproduce in both years. Their colour indicates their age: the one-year-olds are violet, and the two-year-olds grey.

The contribution of the faeces and corpses of these springtails to nutrient turnover is moderate and local. The 'snow flea' phenomenon does, however, illustrate how insect turnover of green plant biomass is not only limited to the foliage of trees, but also affects herbaceous plants and even algae.

The springtail *C. sigillata* lives on algae, from which it absorbs antifreezing substances and stores them in its own body. In the bottom photo, the grey-violet cover on the tree stump and on the ground consists of hundreds of thousands of tiny springtails.

One local phenomenon is the mass accumulation of *Ceratophysella sigillata*. These so-called snow fleas, which belong to the springtails, are active in winter and graze on the algae deposits growing on tree stumps and stems. This green biomass thus returns to the soil through the snow fleas' excrement.

3 Turnover of green plant biomass

3.3 Plant-sap-sucking insects

Sucking insects such as aphids and cicadas can also influence the energy balance and nutrient turnover of a tree or even a stand. Although part of their liquid faeces (the so-called honeydew) adheres to the foliage or is harvested by ants, considerable amounts of honeydew reach the ground during periods of extensive colonization. A study on the energy budget of linden aphids *(Eucallipterus tiliae)* on lime trees revealed that 90 percent of the energy absorbed by the aphids is excreted in the form of honeydew (Llewellyn 1972). This resource is low in nitrogen but very rich in carbohydrates (see Section 7.4). On the ground, it can stimulate the activity and propagation of nitrogen-fixing soil microorganisms. This leads to a higher nitrogen supply in the soil, which is of great importance for plant growth, especially in nutrient-poor soils (Owen 1980).

Accumulation of honeydew droplets on a leaf underneath a colony of woolly honeysuckle aphids *(Prociphilus xylostei)*.

A colony of ash leaf-nest aphids *(Prociphilus bumeliae)* powdered with wax wool. Clearly visible are the honeydew droplets excreted by the sucking aphids before dropping to the ground. The droplets serve as an energy source for the soil bacteria.

During the summer months, millions of linden aphids *(Eucallipterus tiliae)* can live on a single lime tree. Their honeydew promotes the nitrogen-fixing bacteria in the soil.

3 Turnover of green plant biomass

Decomposition of wood

Compared to green plant mass, wood and bark are poor in nutrients and more difficult to digest for consumers. Wood consists essentially of cellulose, hemicellulose and lignin; the phloem (inner bark) also contains pectin. These components are primarily degraded by fungi and bacteria. The few insects that can digest cellulose include some cockroaches, termites, woodwasps (Siricidae), anobiid beetles and longhorn beetles (Cerambycidae). To digest the cellulose, they are often assisted by symbiotic fungi and bacteria in their guts, which can provide their hosts with additional vitamins and sterols (e.g., cholesterol). The nitrogen required for the development of their larvae comes only partially from the wood. Most wood insects have bacteria in their guts that can fix nitrogen from the air (Ulyshen 2015). A large number of insects are involved in the decomposition of a tree. Species that depend, during any phase of their lives, on living or dead wood, or on organisms living in the wood are called 'saproxylic' insects. These include the true xylophages ('wood-eaters'), as well as predatory and parasitic species and

A timberman beetle *(Acanthocinus aedilis)* emerging from a dead pine stem. Its larva feeds and pupates underneath the bark. Food remains and frass of decomposers can easily be colonized and degraded. Exit holes and larval tunnels provide wood-decomposing fungi access to the interior of the wood.

Beetles that have developed inside the wood need strong mouthparts to gnaw their way out. Those of the large poplar longhorn (*Saperda carcharias*), which is up to three centimetres long, are ideal.

those living on wood fungi. The xylophages penetrate the bark and wood and render this substrate accessible to the decomposers. After industrialisation, little deadwood was to be found in European forests until the middle of the 20th century, which is why many insects living in deadwood are still rare and endangered today (see Section 18.2).

During the lifetime of a tree, the bark prevents fungi and other pathogens from infecting it with its stored resin and tanning agents. These components make it difficult for fungi to access the sapwood even after the tree has died. When insects colonize the tree, they create galleries and holes in its bark and wood through which the fungal spores can enter and colonize the wood. Towards the end of the decay process, fungi and bacteria become more important in the decomposition process, although insects and other invertebrates are still involved. It takes decades or even centuries for a dead tree to be transformed into soil organic matter, depending on the tree species and exposure of the stem. If insects did not play a role in this process, it would take approximately twice as long (Dajoz 1998).

In woody substrates, it is not only the true xylophages that develop, but also their natural enemies, decomposers feeding on detritus, and specialists living on the wood-decomposing fungi. During the decomposition of deadwood, a specific sequence of species communities occurs. The sequence depends, among other things, on the tree species, the degree of decomposition, the volume of the wood, its moisture content and the degree of insolation. In general, the species in coniferous wood are most diverse at the beginning of the decomposition, while in broadleaf wood diversity peaks in later decomposition stages (Stokland et al. 2012).

The decomposition of a dead tree from the intact wooden body into soil organic matter passes through several stages. A short insect colonization phase after tree death is followed by a long decomposition phase during which the bark and wood decay, until, in the humification phase, the disintegrated organic substance becomes mineralised in the soil. Diverse microhabitats are created during the decay process and populated by characteristic insect fauna (Möller 2009). In this chapter, the general role of insects in the decomposition of wood to soil organic matter is described, while their role in the actual process of soil formation is discussed in Chapter 6.

4.1 Colonizers of living trees

Only a few insects are capable of infesting and eventually even killing vital trees. A number of bark-breeding insects, such as various bark beetles (Scolytinae), some jewel beetles (Buprestidae) and longhorn beetles, colonize weakened but still living trees and initiate or accelerate their death. In addition to the most

The oak splendour beetle (*Agrilus biguttatus*; above) normally colonizes newly dead oaks. Under certain conditions, however, it can also infest living trees and become a pest. Another oak specialist, the rare jewel beetle *Anthaxia hungarica* (below), develops exclusively in dead oak branches.

The endangered great capricorn beetle *(Cerambyx cerdo)* is an oak specialist. It is one of the few beetle species that can digest cellulose. It mostly develops in age-old moribund, but still living trees. The galleries of the gigantic larvae are clearly visible on the stems after the bark has fallen off. Numerous generations of this beetle often develop over decades in such habitat trees.

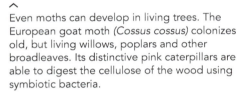

Even moths can develop in living trees. The European goat moth *(Cossus cossus)* colonizes old, but living willows, poplars and other broadleaves. Its distinctive pink caterpillars are able to digest the cellulose of the wood using symbiotic bacteria.

famous bark beetle in Central Europe, the European spruce bark beetle *(Ips typographus)* (see Section 14.3), other bark beetle species, such as the pine bark beetle *Ips acuminatus*, the two pine shoot beetles *(Tomicus minor* and *T. piniperda)*, and the silver fir bark beetle *(Pityokteines curvidens)*, are able to overcome the defensive features of living conifers. The steelblue jewel beetle *(Phaenops cyanea)* may attack living pines, and some *Agrilus* species (*A. viridis, A. biguttatus*) colonize still living broadleaves. The large poplar longhorn *(Saperda carcharias)* develops in living poplars or willows. If such beetles infest valuable individual trees or entire stands, they become, from a human perspective, economic pests. Even some moth caterpillars thrive in the bark and wood of living trees, such as those of the

On a cool rainy day, a musk beetle *(Aromia moschata)* is waiting for warmer conditions (above). It even colonizes living willow trees in urban areas. The larval feeding and the gnawing activity of emerging adults produce large quantities of boring dust (bottom).

goat moth (*Cossus cossus*), the leopard moth (*Zeuzera pyrina*) or the hornet clearwing moth (*Sesia apiformis*). Certain ants like the carpenter ant (*Camponotus herculeanus*) also occasionally construct their nests in trunks of still living spruce trees.

4.2 Pioneers on dead trees

For the decomposition of deadwood, the pioneering colonizers of newly dead trees or tree parts are more important than those of living trees. As mentioned before, most insects do not possess any cellulases (enzymes for the degradation of cellulose), which is why the first colonizers mainly feed on the phloem, which is rich in starch and energy. During this colonizing phase, the small shoots and branches of the dead trees are still present, the bark is still intact, the phloem soft and full of carbohydrates, and the sapwood firm and rich in water. The phloem is easily exploited by insects and fungi and quickly degrades. In a study on dead oak wood, the phloem lost 80 percent of its original biomass during the first two years (Schowalter 1992). This pioneer phase lasts only about one to two years, by the time the bark and wood will have become too dry for the early colonizers. The substrate during the colonization phase is short-lived, which is why pioneer insects are mobile species that respond to chemical cues to quickly find potential host trees.

If no weakened living trees are available, fresh deadwood can also serve as the substrate for the pioneer bark and jewel beetles mentioned above. The extensive feeding of bark beetle larvae and the subsequent maturation feeding of the teneral adults, in particular, detach the bark from the tree. On humid soil, the nutrient-rich bark is quickly decomposed and the nutrients are released. During this stage, the wooden body is no longer protected by the bark and wood-decomposing fungi can access it more easily.

Pioneer insects must be able to overcome the partially intact physical and chemical defences of a newly dead tree. Bark beetles are the most important initial colonizers, especially in conifers, as the resin compounds in the dead bark and wood do not prevent these beetles from breeding. Pioneer insects are often restricted to specific tree species. Unlike most other insects, they can overcome the defences of a particular tree species, but in return they also depend on it as a host tree. An exception is the black timber bark beetle (*Xylosandrus germanus*), which was introduced into Europe in the mid-20th century. It colonizes the fresh stems of a number of different coniferous and broadleaf trees.

In order to exploit not only the bark but also the fresh, nutrient-poor wood, some insect species inject fungal spores into the wood when laying their eggs. These then germinate, and the mycelium of these so-called ambrosia fungi serves as food for the larvae.

The introduced black timber bark beetle (*Xylosandrus germanus*) has become one of the most frequent bark beetle species at lower elevations. It can develop in almost any tree species. The females extrude characteristic small boring dust cores out of their entrance holes when boring into the wood. These remain well visible until the next rain or strong wind. The beetles, like other pioneer sapwood insects, also introduce a fungus into the wood. This is fed on by the larvae and further degrades the wood.

Such a symbiosis between insects and fungi can be found in some bark beetles, timberworm beetles (Lymexylidae) and woodwasps (Siricidae) (see Section 11.2).

Various jewel beetles, longhorn beetles, weevils (Curculionidae), timberworm beetles and woodwasps are also pioneer insects. A prime example is the black fire beetle *(Melanophila acuminata)*, which colonizes immediately after a forest fire the still partially glowing stems. Its larvae can only develop in the phloem of trees killed by fire. The beetles can detect smoke fumes several kilometres away with the chemical sensory receptors in their antennae. In addition, they have sensitive sensors in their abdominal organs, where the electromagnetic infrared radiation of a fire is converted into a mechanical sensory stimulus by heat-induced volume changes (Schmitz and Bleckmann 1998).

Among the many *Anthaxia* species on broadleaf and coniferous trees, the metallic wood-boring beetle *(Anthaxia quadripunctata)* is one of the most frequent pioneers on fresh dead branches and stems of spruce, fir and larch. Among the longhorn beetles, the spruce longhorn beetle *(Tetropium castaneum)* and the large *Monochamus* species are typical early colonizers. Their larvae tunnel a few centimetres into the wood to pupate. The coarse woody shreds they expel are clearly visible on the bark surface and easily accessible for fungal decomposition.

Many bark beetles are typical pioneers on newly dead trees. If you know the tree species, you can easily identify several bark beetle species from their galleries: (a) large larch bark beetle *(Ips cembrae)* on larch, (b) lesser pine shoot beetle *(Tomicus minor)* on pine, (c) small spruce bark beetle *(Polygraphus poligraphus)* on spruce, (d) six-toothed spruce bark beetle *(Pityogenes chalcographus)* on spruce, (e) olive bark beetle *(Hylesinus toranio)* on ash, (f) birch bark beetle *(Scolytus ratzeburgii)* on birch. The maternal beetles excavate the larger galleries, while the developing larvae produce the smaller side tunnels.

While the larvae of phloeophagous bark beetles excavate long tunnels during their development (see left page), the xylophagous bark beetles (so-called ambrosia beetles) only need short galleries. Inside the galleries, their larvae feed on fungi whose spores were introduced by the maternal beetles during oviposition. The striped ambrosia beetle *(Trypodendron lineatum)* produces a typical gallery in conifers consisting of the maternal gallery along the annual tree rings (horizontal in this photo) and the short larval side galleries (vertical).

A larva of a spruce longhorn beetle *(Tetropium castaneum)* has constructed its typical L-shaped pupation tunnel in the wood. In the colonization phase, many longhorn beetles feed first under the bark and then penetrate into the wood for pupation. Their abandoned tunnels are later colonized by wood-decomposing fungi. (Photo courtesy of Forest Entomology WSL.)

4 Decomposition of wood

The large timberworm (*Hylecoetus dermestoides*) is another typical pioneer in freshly dead conifers and broadleaves. The tunnels of its characteristic larvae penetrate deep into the wood. They are colonized by a symbiotic fungus, which is grazed by the beetle larvae. The feeding larvae eject large quantities of light boring dust.

Bark beetles and longhorn beetles consume less than one percent of the actual wood mass during their first year of colonization (Zhong and Schowalter 1989). Through their feeding galleries and exit holes, however, they create entry ports for wood-decomposing fungi and improve the oxygen supply inside the wood, which is necessary for further wood-decomposition.

Besides beetles, woodwasps (or horntails) are also typical pioneering colonizers of newly dead trees. The females of these large wasps have a long ovipositor with which they lay their eggs up to one centimetre deep in the sapwood. Three of the four genera occurring in Europe develop in coniferous wood, the fourth in broadleaves. The larva takes, on average, three years to develop into an adult

The metallic wood-boring beetle (*Anthaxia quadripunctata*) is one of the most common jewel beetles in fresh coniferous wood. Its spoon-shaped larvae (left) leave behind the typical frass of many jewel beetles. The boring dust produced by the larval feeding in the border zone between the bark and wood is arranged in clouds that are alternately light- or dark-coloured.

⌄

4 Decomposition of wood

The eight-spotted jewel beetle *(Buprestis octoguttata)* develops mainly in newly dead pine and spruce trees in warmer areas.

The males of the timberman beetle *(Acanthocinus aedilis)* hold the record for having the longest antennae among the European longhorn beetles. They are more than eight centimetres long and can extend to up to five times the beetles' body length. The timberman larvae develop in the bark of fresh pine.

The genus *Monochamus* comprises typically large species of longhorn beetles with long antennae: Above: a *Monochamus sartor* adult. Below: a sawyer beetle larva (*Monochamus galloprovincialis*). Their larvae use their strong mandibles to feed first in the bark and then in the wood of conifers. Their exit holes are round, unlike the oval holes most other longhorn beetles make.

woodwasp. Like the ambrosia beetles, woodwasps also transport specific fungi, which thrive in the wood and greatly improve the nutritional basis for the woodwasp larvae (see Section 11.2).

The giant woodwasp (*Urocerus gigas*), which occurs mainly in mountain forests, is a typical pioneer on newly dead conifers. For oviposition, the female first searches with her ovipositor for a suitable place and then slowly, using great effort, forces it into the wood. During the extraction of the ovipositor, she deposits about five eggs inoculated with a symbiotic fungus in the wood. This fungus serves as a food source for the larvae and initiates the decomposition of the wood.

After spending three years developing in the wood, two larvae of the giant woodwasp eat their way back towards the bark. They pupate about one centimetre below the surface, from where the adult wasp then gnaws its way out. (Photo courtesy of Forest Entomology WSL.)

Various anobiid beetles develop in wood that is still solid, but whose bark has already detached. Only the entrance and exit holes are visible on the surface (on the far left in the photo). Immediately below, the larvae have completely eaten away the wood.

The blue longhorn beetle *Callidium violaceum* is a typical insect found in dry coniferous wood. Its larvae feed extensively under the dry bark, causing it to detach from the wood. For pupation, the larvae tunnel into the wood. This species, like some other beetles, often emerges from firewood when it is brought into warm rooms in winter. They are, however, harmless for processed construction wood.

4.3 Insects of the decomposition phase

The decomposition of a tree involves very different stages and takes decades to centuries, depending on the tree species, the stem's position (standing or lying), size, soil contact and exposure to sunlight. At the beginning of the decomposition phase, desiccated bark remains may still be present. Fallen trees are still supported by their branches and have little soil contact. Their wood is firm and dry and still contains easily degradable assimilates. In the course of decomposition, the supporting branches decay, the fallen stems settle on the ground in full contact with the soil, and

The longhorn beetle *Ropalopus clavipes* develops in various species of dead, dry broadleaf trees. Its larvae feed in the boundary layer between the bark and sapwood, producing fine boring dust. They pupate in the sapwood.

the humidity from the soil infiltrates into the wood. The sapwood is the first to become soft and spongy before, finally, the heartwood decays. At any given point in time, a lying tree stem may show quite different decay stages with correspondingly different fauna. During the long decomposition process, the range of arthropods that colonize the deadwood substrate is broad and very heterogeneous.

The larvae of the striking longhorn *Saperda scalaris* develop under the bark of dead broadleaf trees.

These pupal chambers underneath the bark of dead conifers are made of wood shavings. They are unmistakable signs left by ribbed pine-borer larvae *(Rhagium inquisitor)*. After emerging from the pupa, the teneral beetle remains in the chamber until next spring. Other *Rhagium* species in broadleaf trees behave similarly.

Beetles

Beetles are particularly rich in species in the decomposition phase. Roughly 30 percent of all beetle species in forests are thought to be saproxylic (Speight 1989). In the still dry, hard deadwood, insects such as anobiid and powderpost beetles (Lyctidae) process the wood into fine, easily degradable meal. One of the most species-rich saproxylic groups is that of the longhorn beetles. The females usually lay their eggs in bark or wood cracks, where

The larvae of the capuchin beetle *(Bostrichus capucinus)* feed on the easily degradable carbohydrates still contained in the wood of oak and other broadleaf trees that has been sun-exposed and rapidly desiccated, but is still solid.

the neonate larvae hatch and bore into the substrate. Many species associated with the early decomposition phase first feed on the bark and then gnaw their way into the wood to pupate. Species associated with later decay stages, however, develop in the wood from the beginning. Among the species associated with the early wood decomposition phase are, for example, the tanbark beetles (*Callidium* spp., *Phymatodes testaceus*), the wasp beetles (*Clytus* spp.) or the ribbed pine borer (*Rhagium inquisitor*). The pupal chambers of the pine borer are made of wood shavings and remain visible for some time even after the bark has fallen off.

As the complex wood components are progressively degraded by fungi into digestible sugars, more and more species of beetles and other insects can develop in the wood. Their frass (excrement) is quickly colonized and degraded by microorganisms. Later, as the wood softens and rots, other species of longhorn beetles remain present and further disintegrate the substrate. In coniferous wood, typical species associated with this stage are *Oxymirus cursor* and *Anastrangalia sanguinolenta*. In broadleaf wood colonized by white-rot fungi, the wasp longhorn (*Rutpela maculata*) or the four-banded longhorn beetle (*Leptura quadrifasciata*) develop. While 52 percent of all saproxylic beetles prefer broadleaf and 23 percent coniferous wood (Stokland *et al.* 2012), the tree species becomes less relevant for them as the wood decay progresses. Instead, the wood's humidity and the associated fungal flora are decisive.

The longhorn beetle *Oxymirus* cursor lives in humid spruce forests, where its larvae develop in rotten tree stumps and stems.

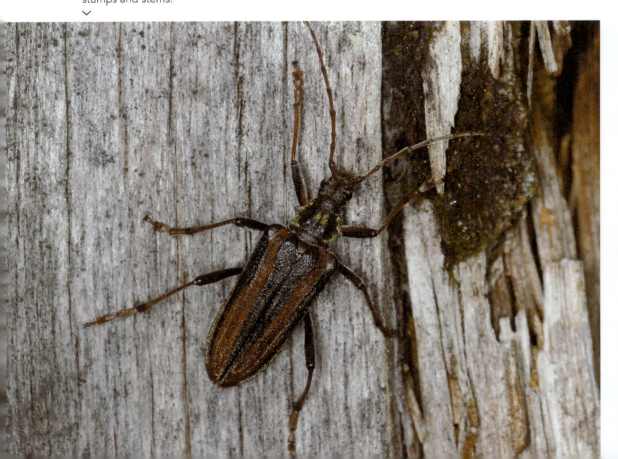

The wasp beetle (*Clytus lama*) can often be found on the bark of stored coniferous wood, whereas the almost identical congener, the wasp beetle proper *(Clytus arietis)*, develops in dry branches of broadleaf wood.

65

The wasp longhorn *(Rutpela maculata)* is one of the most common longhorn beetles. Its larvae undergo several years of development in damp and rotten broadleaf wood.

The frequent red-brown longhorn beetle *(Stictoleptura rubra)* shows a sexual dimorphism: While the female has red-brown elytra, the male is yellow-brown in colour. The larvae develop in white-rotten stems, stumps and roots of spruce and pine.

A stem riddled with tunnels made by longhorn beetle larvae. Through these, other organisms can get into the wood.

A pupa of the longhorn beetle *Exocentrus punctipennis* in a dry elm branch.

The larvae of the speckled longhorn beetle *(Pachytodes cerambyciformis)* develop in decaying roots of broadleaf and coniferous trees.

The Rosalia longicorn *(Rosalia alpina)* is one of the most beautiful longhorn beetles and is protected throughout Europe. This rare species needs sun-exposed beech stems weakly colonized by fungus for its three-year development.

The larvae of the strikingly coloured, four-banded longhorn beetle *(Leptura quadrifasciata)* live in wood of various broadleaf tree species colonized by fungi. The photo illustrates the way many longhorn beetles in their adult stage depend on flowers. They need their pollen to sexually mature.

The two-to-three-year development of the larvae of the two-banded longhorn beetle *(Rhagium bifasciatum)* with its unmistakable markings takes place in rotten wood of broadleaf or coniferous trees.

Like many other species of the fungus weevil family (Anthribidae), *Platyrhinus resinosus* develops in dead, but still solid wood of different broadleaf trees.

For example, the two-banded longhorn beetle *(Rhagium bifasciatum)* and the common black-striped longhorn beetle *(Stenurella melanura)* develop in the rotten wood of almost all tree species. Most xylophagous beetles live in the aboveground tree parts. An exception is, among others, the tanner beetle *(Prionus coriarius)*, whose larvae spend three years developing underground in the rotting roots of broadleaf trees.

Beside longhorn beetles, there are many further groups of saproxylic beetles. The fungus weevils (Anthribidae) live in the wood of broadleaves that, although infected with fungi, is still solid. Such rotten but still compact wood is also a habitat for stag beetles (Lucanidae) and many click beetles (Elateridae). The stag beetle proper *(Lucanus cervus)* is well known. Its larvae feed belowground for 5 to 8 years on thick dead roots or large

The stag beetles (Lucanidae) have grub-like larvae. The photo shows the larva of a lesser stag beetle *(Dorcus parallelipipedus)* in woody substrate that is already very degraded. The larvae take around four years to develop, which indicates that wood at this stage of decomposition is already poor in energy and nutrients.

4 Decomposition of wood

The male of the rare, approximately 15-millimetre long least stag beetle (*Sinodendron cylindricum*) has a conspicuous horn on its head.

pieces of wood, preferably oak, lying on the ground. The other stag beetle species, such as the lesser stag beetle (*Dorcus parallelipipedus*) and the least stag beetle (*Sinodendron cylindricum*), develop aboveground in the white-rotten wood of dead broadleaf trees.

In the final stage of decomposition, the wood decays into a crumbly, amorphous substrate called 'wood mould' or tree humus. Wood mould can also be found in the cavities of old, but still living trees, where flower chafers (Cetoniidae) are typical inhabitants. Of these, the rose chafer (*Cetonia aurata*) is the best known. It can also be found in com-

The beetle *Valgus hemipterus* belongs to the family of flower chafers (Cetoniidae). Its larvae develop in rotten but still compact wood of broadleaf trees.

The stag beetle (*Lucanus cervus*) is an endangered species in many regions. South of the Alps, however, it is quite common and it can sometimes be seen and heard flying at dusk. The huge, antler-like mandibles are characteristic for the up to 85-millimetre long males, which use them to fight male competitors.

4 Decomposition of wood

The larvae of the false darkling beetle *Melandrya caraboides* (Melandryidae) live in decaying wood of oak, beech, birch and other broadleaf trees.

post heaps or even in flowerpots. Another frequent chafer is the bee beetle (*Trichius fasciatus*), but some flower chafer species (*Protaetia* species) are much rarer. The grub-like larvae of certain flower chafers and stag beetles are known to ingest bacteria with their food, which break down the cellulose in the guts of the larvae. The quaint-looking European rhinoceros beetle (*Oryctes nasicornis*) also needs heavily degraded rotten wood for its development, which takes several years, but, it can, like the rose chafer, switch to substitute substrates such as fermenting wood chips or compost heaps.

< The larvae of the click beetle *Ampedus sanguineus* (Elateridae) take several years to develop in rotten wood of broadleaf and coniferous trees. The click beetle larvae – colloquially also known as wireworms – live both on decaying wood and predatorily on insect larvae.

4 Decomposition of wood

Other insects involved in the decomposition phase

In addition to beetles, many hymenopteran and dipteran insects also feed on bark, wood or the waste products from other wood dwellers. The main Hymenoptera involved are ants, such as the carpenter ants (*Camponotus* spp.) or – in later decay stages – ants of the genus *Lasius*. They build their nests under the bark, in old beetle galleries and in the wood, processing the wood into powdery dust and wood mould. In a tree stem,

The larvae of the bee beetle *(Trichius fasciatus)*, which belongs to the flower chafers, need heavily degraded wood mould for their development. The adult beetles can often be observed as flower visitors in gardens.

The rare flower chafer *Protaetia aeruginosa* takes three years to develop in cavities in old trees.

The larvae of all flower chafers are grub-like. This larva of the rose chafer *(Cetonia aurata)* developed in an oak knothole filled with wood mould. However, this flower chafer species also uses surrogate habitats such as compost heaps or flower boxes.

The female of the European rhinoceros beetle *(Oryctes nasicornis)* has, unlike the male, only a small horn on her head. The length of this species' larvae is an impressive 12 centimetres.

the carpenter ants' nest can extend up to ten metres aboveground, and also have an underground nest in the soil. Carpenter ants, however, live mainly on honeydew and insects.

While most wood-dwelling wild bees depend on existing holes and galleries for breeding (see Section 4.4), some species gnaw their own tunnels into the wood. For example, the bumblebee-like, bluish black and shiny carpenter bee *(Xylocopa violacea)* burrows its breeding nests into still firm deadwood, lays an egg in each cell and provides it with pollen and honey pulp. They separate the individual cells with walls of wood shavings and saliva.

Many species of flies and mosquitoes also develop in wood. The most important families are craneflies (Tipulidae), which, like some beetles, employ bacteria to digest cellulose, as well as hoverflies (Syrphidae). The cranefly larvae of the conspicuously coloured genus *Ctenophora* live in moist wood colonized by fungi. Among the hoverflies, the *Brachyopa* species, for example, develop under the bark of dead branches and stems, while the larvae of the hoverfly *Myathropa florea* live in small tree cavities, knotholes or rotting tree forks that are intermittently filled with water (so-called dendrotelms). Other saproxylic dipteran species include March flies (Bibionidae), black fungus gnats (Sciaridae) and gall midges (Cecidomyiidae).

In the final stage of the decomposition process, the wood decays and disintegrates into small pieces. The contours vanish and the substrate becomes crumbly and soft. The wood loses its solid structure and disintegrates into formless components that become part of the soil. Rich soil fauna and microflora then decompose these further and mineralise them (see Chapter 6).

The large carpenter ants (*Camponotus* spp.) occur in warm mixed forests and usually nest in dead tree stems, where they erode large amounts of the wood.

The jet ant *(Lasius fuliginosus)* constructs its nests in already rotten stems, ejecting large quantities of wood dust. This substrate is readily colonized and degraded by microorganisms.

The carpenter bee *(Xylocopa violacea)* gnaws its galleries into still solid wood. A single larva develops in each cell. When their development is complete, the bees emerge one after the other. They feed on flower pollen and nectar. (Photo on left courtesy of Forest Entomology WSL.)

4.4 Secondary dwellers in feeding galleries

The holes and galleries in the wood caused by feeding of xylophagous insects may be used by other insects for their development. Various wild bees, which are not able to gnaw such cavities themselves, are dependent on these pioneer insects. In the pioneers' tunnels, especially those of beetles, the bees construct brood cells, which they provide with plant nourishment (nectar, pollen, and

The cranefly *Ctenophora festiva* (Tipulidae) develops, like other true craneflies, in wet wood mould. The males have comb-like antennae. (Photo courtesy of Forest Entomology WSL.)

bits of leaf) before depositing an egg in each cell.

Bees of the genus *Hylaeus* and the leafcutter bees (*Megachile* spp.) use holes and crevices in wood, plant stems, rock or soil. The leafcutter bees line their brood cells with bits of leaves, which they also use to separate the brood cells from each other. Various representatives of the wasp family Crabronidae have a similar biology. Certain species such as *Trypoxylon figulus* use existing beetle tunnels, while others such as *Ectemnius* spp. make their tunnels themselves by gnawing into wood or plant stems. Unlike the bees, crabronid wasps do not supply their offspring with nectar and pollen, but rather with paralyzed insects as prey. Other insects, spiders and mites also make use of wood cavities. The wood is further decomposed through the feeding activity of all these larvae and adults, whose faeces, moulting and food residues degrade easily.

Austrolimnophila ochracea (Limoniidae) is closely related to the craneflies. Above: the pupa; below: the emerged adult insect.

The larvae of the rarely found hoverfly *Chalcosyrphus valgus* live in damp rotten wood.

A *Temnostoma bombylans* hoverfly. Its larvae develop in decaying wood.

Myathropa florea has a typical pattern on its thorax and is one of the most common species of hoverflies. It deposits its eggs in rotting tree knotholes or forks filled with water.

< The strikingly coloured hoverfly *Brachyopa vittata* develops in beetle galleries in the wood and underneath the bark of dead conifers.

4.5 Colonizers of tree fungi

As mentioned before, many beetle and other insect species live on decaying wood colonized by fungi. Thus, the transition from xylophagous to fungivorous species is continuous. Several species, such as flat bugs (Aradidae), live on the fungal mycelium that grows under the bark of dead trees. The larvae of some specialised insects develop in the fruiting bodies of tree polypores. Fungal spores often also serve as food for adult beetles whose larvae develop elsewhere. Since these fungi

< An egg clutch of black fungus gnats (*Cratyna* sp.; Sciaridae) developing under the bark of a dead beech tree. The maggots feed on waste products and fungal mycelia.

4 Decomposition of wood

Pupae of the wasp *Trypoxylon figulus* (Crabronidae). This species builds its nests in cavities in wood, plant stems or the abandoned belowground nests of yellowjackets. The female lays an egg in each cell, supplies it with several paralyzed spiders, and then separates the cell from the next cell with a clay wall.

The red mason bee (*Osmia rufa*) nests in a wide variety of cavities. Here it is closing up a nest populated with eggs in an artificially constructed so-called bee hotel. The bee uses a mixture of soil, clay and saliva as mortar.

A leaf cutter bee *Megachile willughbiella* transporting a piece of leaf. She uses it to line her breeding cells in, for example, beetle tunnels in wood.

Flat bugs like *Aradus conspicuus* are very flat and suck on fungal mycelium under the bark.

are dependent on wood, the insects that colonize them are also called saproxylic. The fungi are able to break down not only cellulose and lignin, but also resins and toxins. For many insects, the fungal mycelium is more readily digestible than the original wood and is therefore a rich source of food. The assemblage of fungivorous insect species is largely determined by the type of fungi that colonize the wood. The beetle fauna associated with brown-rot wood is completely different from that associated with white-rot wood. Brown rot is the name given to a fungal attack that primarily degrades the light cellulose and gives the wood a brown colour and a cubical structure. With white rot, on the other hand, the dark lignin is broken down (as well) and the wood appears white and fibrous.

Among the tree fungi, the brown-rot sulphur polypore and the two white-rot fungi, tinder fungus and *Trametes*, provide particularly valuable substrates for beetles that are fungivorous specialists. In sulphur *polypores*, various species of click and darkling beetles (Tenebrionidae) develop such as *Diaperis boleti*. Typical colonizers of the tinder fungus are certain anobiid or ciid beetle species. Anobiid beetles are also numerous in *Trametes* fungi and in the red belt conk. Generally, however, few species can be found in a red belt conk. Not only does the species of the fungus influence which insects live on it, but so too does its consistency, degree of decomposition and climatic factors (Möller 2009). Other fungivorous beetle species include rove beetles (Staphylinidae), hairy fungus beetles (Mycetophagidae), the handsome fungus beetles (Endomychidae) and other families. In addition to the beetles, other fungivorous insect species are, for example, the Mycetophilidae,

The fruiting bodies of the sulphur polypore serve as habitats for a particularly rich variety of insect fauna.

4 Decomposition of wood

The hairy fungus beetle *Mycetophagus quadripustulatus* (Mycetophagidae) develops in sulphur polypores.

The larvae of the darkling beetle *Diaperis boleti* (Tenebrionidae) live in the fruiting bodies of sulphur and birch polypores.

gall midges and the craneflies. The yellow flat-footed fly (*Agathomyia wankowiczii*) is associated with an unusual phenomenon: it induces the formation of tower-like galls protruding downwards from *Ganoderma* polypores in which their larvae develop.

4.6 Natural enemies of deadwood insects

Xylophagous deadwood insects are the food source for a higher trophic level of consumers, namely their natural enemies. These include predatory, parasitoid and parasitic species (see Chapter 8). These species are, via their prey and hosts, also dependent on deadwood and are therefore considered saproxylic spe-

‹ The tinder fungus serves as a habitat for a large number of insect species, some of which depend exclusively on this fungus species.

4 Decomposition of wood

The minute tree-fungus beetle *Rhopalodontus perforatus* (Ciidae), only two millimetres in size, is a specialist in tinder fungi growing on dying or dead beech trees.

This *Mycetina cruciata* beetle is representative of the handsome fungus beetles (Endomychidae), whose larvae develop in decaying wood colonized by fungi. Adult beetles can also be found on fungal fruiting bodies.

The yellow flat-footed fly (*Agathomyia wankowiczi*; Platypezidae) has a special characteristic. It induces tower-like galls on the *Ganoderma* polypores in which its larvae develop.

cies as well. Among them are highly specialised species that are able to detect their prey or hosts even when they are concealed deep inside the bark or wood and are thus difficult to access. The natural enemies of xylophagous insects do not contribute directly to wood decomposition, but their faeces and exuvia, as well as the remains of their prey, are quickly colonized and degraded by bacteria. In this way, the former wood components are fed back into the nutrient cycle via sometimes multiple trophic levels.

Predators mainly consist of a large number of beetle species. Some ground beetles (Carabidae) mainly live underneath the bark, where they prey on the larvae of bark, jewel and longhorn beetles. The larvae of cardinal beetles (Pyrochroidae) feed on the larvae of longhorn and other beetles, but also on decaying wood and waste materials present under the tree bark. Certain click beetles such as the genus *Ampedus* also have a mixed diet. In addition to these groups, many more saproxylic predators from different beetle families develop in the woody substrate as well as in tree fungi. The groups specifically considered as natural enemies of bark beetles are described in Chapter 9.

Among the Diptera, predatory saproxylic species can be found as well. The larvae of long-legged flies (Dolichopodidae) and lance flies (Lonchaeidae), in particular, live predatorily under the bark (see Section 9.2). Many robber flies (Asilidae) also develop in wood colonized by fungi and live on other insect larvae.

Xylophagous larvae living in or immediately underneath the bark are readily para-

The larvae of the golden net-wing (*Dictyoptera aurora*) feed on various insect larvae in rotten wood of broadleaf and coniferous trees.

4 Decomposition of wood

^
The larvae of the characteristically coloured malachite beetle (*Malachius bipustulatus*; Malachiidae) develop under bark, in wood or in wood fungi. There they feed on other saproxylic larvae. The adult beetles consume insects as well as flower pollen.

While the adult cardinal beetle *(Pyrochroa coccinea)* lives on honeydew and tree sap, its larvae feed on longhorn beetle larvae.
˅

sitized by various species of parasitoid wasps. The wasps either penetrate the bark with their ovipositor and lay an egg on their host or, in the case of bark beetles, may access the bark beetles' breeding systems through the entrance holes of the colonizing adults (see Section 9.3). In order to reach the larvae of woodwasps or longhorn beetles deeper in the wood, a parasitoid wasp must have a correspondingly long ovipositor. The giant ichneumon *(Rhyssa persuasoria)* possesses one of the longest egg-laying organs, and is thus able to reach woodwasp larvae that live deep inside coniferous wood. Other wasp species from the family of the true ichneumonid wasps as well have specialised on wood insects (see Section 8.3).

Bumblebee robber flies (*Laphria flava*; Asilidae), which are very hairy, copulating. The female then lays her eggs in holes and tunnels in deadwood, where the larvae feed on other insects.

The larva (top) of the fly *Xylophagus ater* (Xylophagidae) has a characteristically pointed head (left) and lives on other insect larvae. The life of the adult flies (below) is very brief.

4 Decomposition of wood

The rubytail wasp (*Chrysis ignita*; Chrysididae) lays its eggs, in an unguarded moment, in the brood cells of wild bees or wasps, which in turn use abandoned beetle tunnels to deposit their eggs. The larvae of the rubytail wasp then feed on the host larvae and their food supply.

Parasitoid wasps (here *Dolichomitus mesocentrus*; Ichneumonidae) with a long ovipositor (the black shaft extending below the abdomen to the wood) can reach beetle larvae living deep inside the wood and parasitize them.

Exploitation of animal waste

5

Both herbivorous and carnivorous animals produce organic waste in the form of excrement or waste products, and of carcasses when they die. Insects play a decisive role in recycling these organic substances. They consume and disintegrate the firm tissue, excrete the ingredients in the form of readily degradable faeces, and their feeding galleries facilitate access to the substrate for other invertebrates and microorganisms.

This chamois carcass is full to bursting with fly maggots (below), which have developed in its decaying tissue. Burying beetles (Silphidae), such as *Nicrophorus vespilloides* (above), are other typical scavengers.

5.1 Colonization of carrion

When vertebrate animals die due to disease, accident, hunger or old age, their carcasses become a valuable source of food and breeding places for a large number of so-called necrophages (scavengers). These convert the energy stored in the carrion into their own growth and pass on, as part of the material cycle, the nutrients via their faeces. In addition to carrion-eating vertebrates, insects are also involved in this process.

Insects often colonize and degrade carcasses extremely rapidly. In an experiment with dead piglets in a mixed forest, insects devoured 90 percent of the carcass biomass within six days (Payne 1965). When, on the other hand, the insects were excluded, the carcass remained intact for months and slowly mummified. During the decomposition of cadavers, different insect species are successively active. Their assemblage is also determined by the type of carcass (Watson and Carlton 2003).

Flies

Blowflies (Calliphoridae) are among the best-known and most frequent scavengers. They are often the first to colonize a dead animal, attracted within minutes to a carcass by the volatiles produced during the bacterial degradation of proteins. After a few days, a carcass will be already teeming with fly larvae. Typical representatives of blowflies are the genera *Lucilia* and *Calliphora*. The adult flies lick the developing fluids and start laying eggs immediately on the surface or in wounds. The hatched fly larvae – so-called maggots – feed

The blowfly *Calliphora vicina* has a bluish shimmer and is one of the earliest and most frequent colonizers of carcasses. Its larvae feed on rotting flesh.

↑
This common greenbottle *(Lucilia caesar)* (Calliphoridae) is laying eggs on a dead vole.

The 'fly of the dead' *(Cynomya mortuorum)* lives along forest edges and in meadows. It mainly colonizes the carcasses of small mammals, but also dead fish.
↓

Adult flies and their larvae (Muscidae) on exposed carcass tissue.

on the decomposing tissue. Since many species primarily feed on necrotic tissue, some species were formerly used in human medicine for wound cleansing – as they have been again recently (see Section 15.4). Different fly species are attracted at different times by the scents emitted from a carcass. Thus fly maggots are also used as an indicator of the time and place of death in a criminal investigation when a corpse is found. Fly maggots can completely colonize and exploit a whole carcass within a very short time. Bacteria alone would break it down very slowly and the dead body would begin to mummify, or the bacterial toxins it produces would make it unusable for other organisms.

Other important necrophagous fly species are the flesh flies (Sarcophagidae), cheese flies (Piophilidae), black scavenger flies (Sepsidae) and house flies (Muscidae). Many of them develop not only in carrion, but also in excrement.

Beetles

After the flies have settled, beetles gather on the carrion. They are also attracted by the decaying smell of the animal corpse, but get to it a few days later. Burying beetles (Silphidae) are typical carrion colonizers with some frequent and conspicuous species, although not all live on dead animals. Those of the genus *Nicrophorus* feed not only on decaying tissue, but also on the larvae of flies and beetles developing in the carcass. When they reproduce, these burying beetles show parental care for their young, which is very rare

The burying beetle *Nicrophorus vespilloides* feeds not only on decaying flesh, but also on the larvae of other carrion dwellers. For breeding, it buries the carcasses of smaller vertebrates (here a mole) for the beetle larvae to feed on. The mother beetles provide a distinctive form of parental care.

among solitary insects. The couple that wins the battle against other competing burying beetles buries the carcass of, e.g., a mouse, mole, bird or some other small vertebrate, in the ground with their strong legs. In the process, they free the cadaver from hairs and feathers and compact it into a ball. The female then deposits her eggs in a lateral tunnel in the ground and prepares the carrion as food for the larvae that will soon hatch. It gnaws funnels into the flesh ball and repeatedly vomits digestive fluids into them. After the larvae have hatched, they gather around their mother, who initially nourishes them with regurgitated food pulp before they later feed themselves on the decomposing carrion. During this time, the mother also defends her brood against possible predators. Another common carrion beetle is the red-breasted

Adult red-breasted carrion beetles *(Oiceoptoma thoracicum)* and larvae live predominantly on dead vertebrates and insects.

5 Exploitation of animal waste

carrion beetle *(Oiceoptoma thoracicum)*. This species feeds not only on carrion, but also on excrement and mushrooms. Another important group of carrion beetles that feed on dead animals is the genus *Silpha*.

Other beetle families also have some species that develop in carrion, for example the checkered beetles (Cleridae) *Necrobia* spp., the rove beetles (Staphylinidae) *Creophilus* spp. and the skin beetles (Dermestidae) *Dermestes* spp. Skin beetles also feed on other animal waste products (see Section 5.3).

Other carrion exploiters

Wasps usually fulfil the protein requirements of their queen and brood by providing live insects (see Chapter 8), but also utilise the flesh of vertebrate carcasses. Carpenter ants *(Camponotus* spp.), wood ants *(Formica* spp.) and the widespread moisture ants *(Lasius* spp.) also exploit animal corpses. Other invertebrates, such as woodlice, mites and spiders, do not arrive until later to feed on carrion that is already dry and mummified.

Of course, insects not only exploit the carcasses of vertebrates, but also of insects and other invertebrates. Many predatory beetles use dead animals as well as living prey. The common scorpionfly *(Panorpa communis)*, for example, feeds on dead and living insects, as well as on animal excrement and plant substrates, such as nectar and fruit.

5.2 Processing faeces

Irrespective of an animal's diet, it produces digestive residues, which it excretes as faeces

Social wasps (Vespidae), such as the *Vespula species*, usually capture living insects, but may also use other protein sources such as dead vole.

The larvae of some burying beetles (Silphidae) resemble woodlice.

A common wasp *(Vespula vulgaris)* gutting the thorax of a dead dark bush-cricket *(Pholidoptera griseoaptera)*.

95

Ants *(Myrmica* sp.) feeding on the flesh of a dead mouse.

The common scorpionfly *(Panorpa communis)* sometimes avails itself of dead prey trapped in spider webs (left), but it does not despise bird droppings either (right).

and urine. Mammals' urine is essentially composed of water and urea, and is quickly decomposed by soil bacteria into nitrogen available to the plants. However, their faeces consist of undigested tissue components and degraded products. This makes them a nutritious food resource for adult insects and their larvae, which break down the excrement and recycle the nutrients. The quantities of faeces produced are considerable: roe deer deposit about 20 piles per animal per day, and red deer up to about 50 (Mitchell et al. 1985; Rogers 1987). A large pile of deer manure can attract thousands of dung beetles. Dung beetles alone have been estimated to bury up to 100 kilograms of manure per hectare and year in West African forests, and as much as one ton in open savannah (Cambefort 1984).

Solid excrement is consumed by specialists with chewing mouthparts, whereas thin and moist excrement, like bird droppings, also serves as food for sucking insects. As in the decomposition of wood (see Chapter 4), bacteria can degrade faeces already colonized by insects more quickly because the tunnels insects make in them provide bacteria with access to a larger surface.

By far, the majority of excrement colonizers are beetles or flies. Several of the insect groups that decompose carrion also feed on faeces. Blowflies, flesh flies, and house flies are frequently found on vertebrates' excrement, but various other flies and mosquitoes may be present as well. The adults lick on the fluids, and their maggots develop in the dung. Dung piles provide rapidly changing, short-lived habitats. They tend, therefore, to be colonized within hours as the surface becomes encrusted quickly, making it unsuitable for the egg deposition of certain fly species.

Firebugs *(Pyrrhocoris apterus)* live mainly on plant seeds, but can also suck fluid from dead insects or vertebrates.

5 Exploitation of animal waste

Since dung dwellers develop very rapidly, colonizing dung a few hours earlier than their competitors can give them a decisive advantage (Hanski 1987).

The three functional groups of dung beetles have fundamentally different strategies (Cambefort and Hanski 1991). They are classified into 'dwellers', 'tunnelers', and 'rollers'. The dwellers develop directly in excrement piles. For example, the genus *Aphodius* (Aphodiidae), most of whose species are grassland inhabitants, lay their eggs directly in the excrement piles of ungulates. In contrast, earth-boring dung beetles (Geotrupidae) belong to the tunnelers. They do not breed directly in the excrement pile, but on separate smaller balls of excrement, which they bury in a safe place where their larvae can develop without competition. This precautionary measure to provide food for their offspring represents a type of parental care.

The most well-known and common earth-boring dung beetle in forests is the dor beetle (*Anoplotrupes stercorosus*), which deposits its eggs in the chambers at the end of the tunnel it excavates in the soil together with a supply of small excrement pellets. The larvae then take a year to develop into adult beetles. *Onthophagus* beetles, which also belong to the earth-boring dung beetles, feed mainly on manure from cattle and game. The females dig tunnels directly under the excrement pile, supplying each with a ball of faeces in which they lay an egg.

The rollers include scarab beetles (Scarabaeidae), for example the *Sisyphus* beetle, which makes small balls out of the pieces of excrement it separates from the dung piles of various mammals. It then rolls and pushes the balls backwards and forwards over a distance of several metres until it finds a suitable place to bury them and deposit one egg

Adult flesh flies (*Sarcophaga* sp.) also like to suck on fresh faeces rich in nutrients.

The yellow dung fly *(Scathophaga stercoraria)* predates on other flies. Its larvae develop mainly in cattle dung.

The lower part of the abdomen of the widespread dor beetle *(Anoplotrupes stercorosus)* is shining blue-violet in colour. Its larvae develop in vertebrate excrement, which the parental beetles have transferred into self-dug tunnel systems.

Each dung beetle couple *(Sisyphus schaefferi)* rolls balls of mammal excrement to a suitable place for burial, where their larvae develop in the balls.

The scarab beetle *Aphodius fimetarius* occurs in virtually all habitats and at all elevations. Its larvae develop directly in excrement piles.

in each ball. Their tireless struggle to move their balls over obstacles or up steep slopes is reminiscent of the futile efforts Sisyphus proverbially made according to Greek mythology. The most famous scarab species is the sacred scarab *(Scarabaeus sacer)*, which was considered a sacred animal and lucky charm in Ancient Egypt. Other scarab beetles and beetles with similar biology from other families can be found outside the forest.

5 Exploitation of animal waste

5.3 Other animal waste products

Insects exploit and degrade not only animal carcasses and faeces, but almost any substance of animal origin. Fur, bones, horn, remnants of flesh, exuvia, blood, feathers, silk, hair, and skin scales serve as food for various specialised insect groups. Birds' nests and the dens of mammals contain considerable organic waste, such as faeces, skin and feather remains. These are therefore colonized by, among others, the beetles and flies that use them as substrate for food. Typical exploiters of such animal remains are the skin beetles and their very hairy larvae. The carpet beetle *Anthrenus pimpinellae* often develops in the nests of sparrows, where its larvae feed on the keratin from feathers and hair. The beetles and larvae of the genus *Dermestes* may live in mammal dens or the nests not just of birds, but also of wasps and bees. They can also be found in the fur of carcasses, where they feed on various animal remains. In houses,

A male of the taurus scarab *(Onthophagus taurus)* with its typical horns pointing backwards. The larvae of this genus feed on dung, which the parental beetles have shifted from a pile of excrement into a tunnel directly underneath.

The adult skin beetle *Anthrenus pimpinellae* (Dermestidae) eats pollen and nectar. Its larvae, in contrast, live in birds' nests, where they feed on bits of hair and feather.

A typical skin beetle larva, which feeds on animal and vegetable waste.

skin beetles may damage furs, down-filled cushions or even insect collections. Certain rove beetles are specialised in the nests of hornets or ants, where they feed on dead animals, waste products as well as living larvae.

In hoverflies, the grand flies of the genus *Volucella* rely on the nests of wasps and bumble bees for their development. The larvae of the pellucid hoverfly *(Volucella pellucens)* feed on waste products and dead insects, but may also predatorily feed on the larvae of their host colony. Surprisingly, female hoverflies can 'wander' through the entrance of the otherwise well-guarded wasp nest to lay their eggs without being bothered. The lesser hornet hoverfly *(Volucella inanis)*, however, may face wasp stings when entering a wasp's nest despite its wasp-like camouflage (Schmid 1996). Bumblebee and wasp nests seem to serve as good habitats because they contain a rich food supply and probably also provide safe and constant environmental conditions. Some moth species have a similar lifestyle to that of *Volucella* flies, such as the bee moth (*Aphomia sociella*; see Section 8.2).

In addition to the insects mentioned above, several other insect groups also feed on faeces and animal remains. These include mostly beetles, but true bugs (Heteroptera) and silverfish (Zygentoma) also process animal waste.

5 Exploitation of animal waste

Skin beetles of the genus *Dermestes* (left: *D. undulatus*, right: *D. lardarius*) live in the nests of birds and insects and feed on animal waste.

The pellucid hoverfly *(Volucella pellucens)* is a common species along forest edges and in forest clearings. Its larvae feed primarily on cadavers in the nests of wasps and bumblebees.

5 Exploitation of animal waste

Maintaining soil fertility

6

Approximately 90 percent of the biomass produced by plants is returned to the soil in the form of dead organic matter (Coleman *et al.* 2004). This corresponds, in a Central European broadleaf forest, to 11.5 tonnes of plant waste per hectare and year (Swift *et al.* 1979), which are processed by specialised macro-, meso- and microfauna (see Glossary). The macrofauna mainly includes earthworms, snails, millipedes, woodlice and insects. The mesofauna consists mostly of mites and springtails, and the microfauna of, e.g., protozoa. The composition of the soil fauna largely depends on the composition of the litter layer. In fine litter that has already been thoroughly degraded, the macrofauna predominates in the form of earthworms and mosquito larvae; while in coarser, less degraded material, the mesofauna is the most abundant.

Soil organisms are important for soil fertility in many different ways: they transport

The tiny springtails feed on bits of organic waste in the litter and soil layers. They are important members of the soil mesofauna.

Various slugs and snails, such as the grove snail, recycle dead plant material and excrete easily degradable faeces.

organic waste, and they break down dead plant and animal matter, thereby increasing the surface area accessible to bacteria and fungi. The organic substance is digested in the soil dwellers' guts, chemically modified and converted into humus. The breakdown of the material and the excretion of faeces improve the soil's structural properties and increase its organic matter content. Without the detritivores (waste consumers), it would take much longer for waste materials to degrade and organic material would accumulate.

The faeces excreted by the soil fauna are rapidly colonized by fungi and bacteria. It is these colonizers that are responsible for mineralizing the organic matter and making the nutrients available to plants. They are responsible for almost the entire CO_2 released from the forest floor.

In this chapter, other invertebrate animal groups besides insects (see box on page 15) are also included as they play just as important a role as insects in degrading dead plant matter and in maintaining soil fertility.

6.1   Improving the soil structure

The macrofauna actively helps to displace organic matter spatially. It spreads the material on the soil surface and works it into the forest soil. The biomass of the macrofauna is usually larger in broadleaf than in coniferous forests. Earthworms pull dead leaf material down into the soil to feed on it. Their nutrient-rich excrement then stays in or on the soil. Ants transport large quantities of organic material over considerable distances and accumulate it in

6 Maintaining soil fertility

the belowground part of their nests. Dung beetles incorporate dung into the soil, as has already been described in Chapter 5.

The feeding, digging and tunnelling activities of the macrofauna loosen the soil and thus improve its porosity and density. Shifting the soil improves the oxygen supply and facilitates the infiltration of rainwater. The macrofauna's activities, in particular those of earthworms, but also of nesting wood ants (*Formica* spp.; see Chapter 10), improve the physical, chemical and biological properties of the soil. When constructing their nests, ants loosen and aerate the soil, and mix it with organic matter, thereby raising its pH-value by one to two units, and improving its aggregation structure. The increased soil quality benefits earthworms and other soil organisms.

Soil respiration is higher in both inhabited and abandoned ant nests, which indicates more biological activity, especially of bacteria. Ant nests also improve the water balance in the soil because they increase its water-retention capacity. In wet soils, the belowground nest parts sealed against humidity provide other organisms with drier conditions (Gösswald 2012).

The macrofauna also mixes mineral soil with organic matter, which it excretes as faeces. This process takes place on a larger scale in, for example, the digestive tract of March flies (Bibionidae). The faeces they produce not only physically improve soil quality, but also serve as an important food source for the meso- and microfauna, as well as for fungi and microorganisms.

Earthworms are among the most important soil organisms. Their tunnelling works dead plant material into the soil and improves oxygen availability and water infiltration.

6.2 Decomposing organic matter

The soil fauna's contribution to soil fertility is very important as it breaks down dead needles, whose resin contents make them particularly difficult to decompose, as well as dead leaves and decayed wood mould. After digesting this material, the soil fauna excretes it in the form of nutrient-rich faeces. This improves the conditions for bacteria and fungi. For example, the soil fauna's processing of an intact pine needle that has fallen to the ground and has a 180 mm² surface area may yield tiny particles with a total surface area of 1.8 m² (Dajoz 1998). In this case the resulting surface area is a thousand times larger and can be efficiently colonized by microorganisms. The macrofauna also plays an important role in the passive spread of microorganisms in the soil, as an exclusion experiment with detritivores in a forest soil demonstrated. When macro- and mesofauna were excluded, the leaves of herbaceous plants and of ash and maple took about five times longer to become degraded (Wise and Schaefer 1994). In another experiment, birch seedlings produced 70 percent more leaf mass in soils with soil fauna than in those without (Setälä and Huhta 1991).

The large quantities of faeces that earthworms produce not only improve the physical properties of the soil, as already mentioned, but also the nutrient supply for numerous other organisms. Woodlice and millipedes have a similar function; with their strong mandibles, woodlice efficiently break up larger plant parts. They are able to degrade toxic plant constituents, such as phenols, in their digestive tracts, and some species can even digest cellulose. Millipedes are vigorous decomposers of dead plant material, especially in broadleaf forests, and play a very important role in recycling calcium.

Important detritivorous insects include, in particular, some fly and mosquito species (Diptera). The larval biomass present in a

Wood ant activities improve the soil's physical, chemical and biological properties near the belowground parts of their nests.

Worm faeces contain nutrient-rich organic material that has not yet been completely degraded. It serves as a food basis for various other soil organisms. The nutrients from the organic material are eventually converted into a mineral form available for plants by fungi and bacteria.

hectare of forest soil has been estimated to amount to 14 kilograms (Duvigneaud 1974) and may account for up to 90 percent of the soil fauna. The most relevant insects in soil formation are March fly and cranefly larvae (Tipulidae). Gall midges (Cecidomyiidae), fungus gnats (Mycetophilidae) and black fungus gnats (Sciaridae) can also be abundant. March fly larvae alone can double the decomposition rate of broadleaf litter (Karpachevski et al. 1968), and may be responsible for turning over the entire annual leaf production in certain forests. The best-known March fly in our forests is St. Mark's fly *(Bibio marci)*. Its larvae develop in the boundary layer between soil and litter, and feed on humus and leaves. In broadleaf forests they are sometimes very abundant. Cranefly larvae are known to degrade up to one kilogram of leaves per year and square metre (Szujecki 1987). Moreover, click beetles (Elateridae), featherwing beetles (Ptiliidae) and earwigs also feed on organic waste.

Wood ants also contribute to the degradation of organic waste. They gnaw at the rotten rootstocks inside their nests (see Chapter 10), and thus accelerate their degradation. The mesofauna is significantly richer in the vicinity of ant nests than in the surrounding

Glomeridans (*Glomerida*; above) can roll into a ball when facing danger. They belong to ball millipedes, while the woodlice (below: *Oniscus asellus*) are related to the crustaceans. Many species of these two groups live in the forest, where they feed on dead plant material and convert it into nutrient-rich faeces.

6 Maintaining soil fertility

Millipedes (Diplopoda) are other important representatives of the litter-degrading macrofauna. As their scientific name suggests, millipedes have two pairs of legs on each body segment.

forest soil. In addition, the ant mounds provide a good climate for mineralizing fungi and bacteria. As a result, more nutrients become available, and the soil structure is improved (see Section 6.1), which is why the surrounding trees preferentially let their fine roots grow into ant nests. In Finland, the nitrogen content in the leaves of birches growing in the nests of wood ants *(Formica aquilonia)* was 20 percent higher than in neighbouring trees (Karhu and Neuvonen 1998).

The mesofauna consists mainly of mites and springtails. The most numerous representatives are the moss mites (Oribatida), which, in pine forests, reach densities of over 400 000 individuals per square metre (Coleman et al. 2004). The approximately 0.5 to 2-millimetre long animals live on fungal mycelia, plant remains, algae and microorganisms. The springtails (Collembola) are almost as frequent as the moss mites. In the upper soil layer, they feed on a wide variety of food, such as fungal mycelia, plant remains, roots, faeces, microbes or nematodes. The springtails living in the soil generally do not have a furcula (fork-like organ for propelling themselves in the air), unlike their relatives living in the

The larvae of the St. Mark's fly *(Bibio marci)* sometimes occur in densities of several thousand individuals per square metre (above). They are significant converters of dead organic matter. The adult flies (below) are sluggish flyers, which can often be found in April on shrub leaves along forest edges.

The striped millipede *(Ommatoiulus sabulosus)* occurs in various habitats, including the litter layer of forests.

6 Maintaining soil fertility

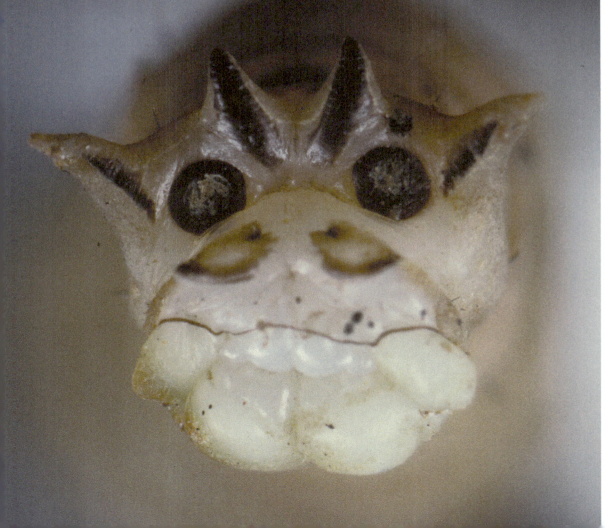

Nephrotoma crocata is a conspicuously coloured species of cranefly. Some other species, however, have similar colouring.

litter layer (see Section 3.2). Their population density can amount to tens, or even hundreds, of thousands of individuals per square metre of land (Werner and Dindal 1987). They promote the mineralisation of nitrogen and soil respiration, and thus plant growth. They are extremely important for soil fertility, especially in mountain forests, where the humus may consist almost exclusively of springtail faeces.

The organic substances in dead plant material passes through the guts of the macrofauna and especially of the mesofauna several times before they are completely mineralised. Their faeces are the most important food source for fungi and bacteria, which finally mineralise the organic matter, in particular lignin, cellulose

Orchesella flavescens, which lives in the litter layer of forests, is up to 5 millimetres long and thus one of the largest native springtails. Springtails are important members of the mesofauna as they prepare organic waste for mineralization by microorganisms.

Craneflies belong to the largest dipterans. Their larvae, called leatherjackets, recycle dead plant material and rotten wood. This larva's 'head' is, in fact, its rear end. Its 'eyes' are the rearmost spiracles surrounded by appendages. (Photo on bottom courtesy of Forest Entomology WSL.)

6 Maintaining soil fertility

The brown centipede *(Lithobius forficatus)* is a predator on insects, spiders, and other arthropods on the ground and under the bark of trees.

and other wood components. The inorganic, nitrogen- and phosphorus-rich nutrients then become available for plant growth again.

All soil organisms – especially mites – also serve as food for a large number of predatory soil dwellers such as beetles, ants, two-pronged bristletails (Diplura), spiders, harvestmen and centipedes.

Food for other organisms

Insects, spiders and other arthropods are an important food source particularly for birds, but also for many mammals, amphibians, reptiles and fish. Thousands of insect and spider species also eat their own kind and play an important role in the regulation of potentially harmful organisms (see Chapter 8). In addition, various parasitic worms, fungi and microorganisms depend on insects for their development and reproduction. Insects and spiders are a premium food source because of their high protein, lipid, glycogen and vitamin contents. Their exoskeletons, which consist of chitin, are the only parts that are indigestible and low in energy. The chitinous compounds make it even more difficult for digestive enzymes to access the proteins in the rest of their bodies. Nevertheless, even dead insects are a valuable food and energy source for vertebrates, necrophagous insects and bacteria. In addition, insect products serve as food for other organisms.

Tit parents feed their nestlings with large quantities of moth caterpillars.

7.1 Food for birds

Birds are probably the best-known predators of forest insects. They have adapted in different ways to cope with the high chitin contents in their prey. Certain species specifically select insects with low chitin contents. Others remove the highly chitinous parts like wings or legs before consuming them or dismantle the whole insect body and pick out only the soft entrails. Some birds even have chitinases (enzymes) that enable them to break down and process the chitin (Klasing 1998).

Songbirds and cuckoos

Birds contribute greatly to the regulation of potential pests by consuming large quantities of forest insects, as several studies have shown (e.g., Dickson et al. 1979; van Emden and Rothschild 2004). Most songbirds depend on insects as a protein-rich energy source for their offspring when rearing their young. Tits, finches, thrushes, warblers, sparrows, nuthatches and many other bird species search vegetation tirelessly on the lookout for caterpillars, aphids, flies, mosquitoes, beetles and spiders. They can detect even tiny insect forms barely visible to the human eye. The composition of their diet depends on the season, the insect supply and the weather. Blue tits, for example, not only eat the prey they can find easily on plant surfaces, such as moth caterpillars, aphids, scale insects, small beetles and spiders, but also peck at plant galls to get to the larvae of galling insects. Tits even pick mining insects out of their tunnels in leaves or wood, and they also detect caterpillars in densely woven webbings, such as the caterpillars of the brown-tail moth (*Euproctis chrysorrhoea*). Most of the caterpillars they catch belong to the families of the geometer moths (Geometridae), noctuid moths (Noctuidae) and leafrollers (Tortricidae). In a 24-hour experiment, three marsh tits, one coal tit, one long-tailed tit and two goldcrests consumed 1876 pine looper (*Bupalus piniaria*) caterpillars, weighing a total of 97 grams (Rörig 1903). The breeding onset and clutch size of great tits have been shown to depend strongly on the availability of the larvae of the winter moth (*Operophtera brumata*), which make up the principal food for their young (Perrins 1991; van Noordwijk et al. 1995).

Both adult birds and their young may adapt their diets flexibly to the available supply. For example, abundantly propagating aphids could become the principal food of young marsh tits. During one of the regularly recurring outbreaks of the larch budmoth (*Zeiraphera griseana*) in the Upper Engadine (see Section 13.2), its caterpillars contributed to about a quarter of the coal tit nestlings' diet (Glutz von Blotzheim and Bauer 1993). If the supply of green oak leafroller larvae

< Winter moth (*Operophtera brumata*) larvae live secretively hidden between spun-together leaves, but this does not prevent songbirds from using them as the most important food source for rearing their young in spring.

(*Tortrix viridana*) is ample, nuthatch nestlings have been found to rely on them for up to three-quarters of their diet. Nevertheless, insectivorous birds generally have little impact on the density of caterpillars during a mass outbreak, partly due to the birds' territorial behaviour. They regulate insects at normal low endemic densities and help to prevent their populations from reaching epidemic levels. Birds can thus extend the intervals between insect outbreaks. Interestingly, there is evidence that birds avoid feeding on caterpillars parasitized by wasps (Otvos 1979). This behaviour presumably even increases the effect of parasitoids.

Many bird species feed on huge numbers of arthropods not only when breeding, but also during wintertime. In a Swedish study, birds reduced the number of spiders on spruce by two- to three-quarters during wintertime, and the number of barklice (Psocoptera) and aphids by as much as 99 percent (Jansson and von Brömssen 1981).

The cuckoo, similar to the songbirds, likes to consume a wide variety of insects such as beetles, grasshoppers and caterpillars. It also eats large hairy moth caterpillars, such as those of the gypsy moth (*Lymantria dispar*), which other birds tend to despise.

Woodpeckers

The larvae of bark-, anobiid and longhorn beetles, as well as of wood wasps and other wood insects, form part of the specialised diet of woodpeckers even though they live hidden away under bark and in wood. It is not yet fully understood how woodpeckers manage to track down the insect larvae hidden deep in the wood they pick out with their powerful beaks. They may notice the feeding sounds the larvae make. Given the size of the expec-

The larvae of the bedeguar gall wasp (*Diplolepis rosae*) in the so-called Robin's pincushion they form have been attacked by a bird, with the gall's branched filaments providing little protection.

ted larva and the current degree of wood decomposition, woodpeckers can judge whether it would be worthwhile digging it out. They often hack open rotten parts and pull out the larvae living in the firmer wood with their long and sticky barbed tongues. While the large and sturdier species frequently use this strategy, the lesser spotted woodpecker prefers aphids in summer and for feeding its young. In autumn and winter, however, it has to rely on insects and spiders living on the bark surface.

Woodpeckers are generally not considered very effective in regulating harmful insects living inside wood, as it is impossible for them to detect all larvae. They play, however, an important role in controlling harmful wood insects that occur frequently for a longer time. Thus, well over half of all wood wasp larvae in

7 Food for other organisms

The great spotted woodpecker, one of the most common woodpeckers, has wide-ranging tastes. Beside wood-dwelling insects, it also feeds on insects and spiders on the surface and even on the nestlings of other birds. In winter it is known to also eat seeds and berries.

an infested tree stem can fall victim to woodpeckers (Spradbery 1990). Larvae of longhorn beetles, weevils and clearwing moths can also suffer from mortality rates of up to 90 percent (Otvos 1979). The great spotted woodpecker is considered the most efficient natural enemy in the native range of the Asian longhorn beetle *(Anoplophora glabripennis)*, which was introduced from East Asia to Europe and North America (Jiao *et al.* 2008). The three-toed woodpecker is an important natural enemy of bark beetles, as discussed in more detail in Section 9.4.

Some woodpecker species have specialised to varying degrees in feeding on ants.

Black woodpeckers, which live in almost all types of forest, feed in winter on wood ants (*Formica* spp.) and on the larvae of anobiid beetles living just below the wood surface. In the warmer seasons, they feed mainly on the wood-dwelling carpenter (*Camponotus* spp.) and moisture ants (*Lasius* spp.). The Eurasian wryneck occurs predominantly in open cultivated landscapes, but also lives in light forests and wetlands. It collects the adult ants and brood directly from the nests of *Lasius*, *Myrmica* and other ant species.

In semi-open landscapes, such as light forests and along forest edges, green and

7 Food for other organisms

↑
This stem had obviously been heavily colonized by large insect larvae and extensively exploited by woodpeckers.

↑
This Scots pine was colonized by wood insects after a forest fire. Woodpeckers subsequently lifted away the charred bark plates and hacked out the larvae of jewel and longhorn beetles living underneath.

119

Aphids like these conifer aphids *Lachnus longirostris* are the main food for the lesser spotted woodpecker in summer.
∨

Anobiid beetles often densely colonize dead trees that have already lost their bark. One of the most common species is the fan-bearing wood-borer (*Ptilinus pectinicornis;* left). Although its larvae are only up to seven millimetres long, they are a welcome winter food for woodpeckers, which tend, therefore, to work particularly intensively on densely colonized stems (right).

grey-headed woodpeckers search the ground for food in summer and live predominantly on moisture ants (*Lasius* species). The grey-headed woodpecker in particular also consumes other insects such as caterpillars, grasshoppers, wood beetles and spiders. In winter, both woodpecker species look for wood ant (*Formica* species) mounds even when they are hidden under the snow. They dig deep holes into the mounds and extract the stiff defenceless ants overwintering deep inside the mounds with their long sticky tongues. A green woodpecker's tongue may be up to ten centimetres long!

One phenomenon that is not yet fully understood is the so-called 'anting' of woodpeckers, jays and other birds, whereby they sit on ant mounds and let themselves be sprayed with formic acid. Alternatively, they may grab an ant and rub their plumage with it. Possible explanations range from fighting parasites, cleaning their plumage to stimulating erotic effects.

7.2 Food for other vertebrates

Mammals

Insects are also on the menu of many mammals. As their name suggests, insectivores, i.e., hedgehogs, shrews and moles, feed on insects and other arthropods. Rodents, in particular dormice and mice, regularly supplement their vegetarian diet with various invertebrates. Shrews and mice can have an important function as regulators of harmful moth and sawfly larvae because they feed

Black woodpeckers chop away large chips of wood when searching for ants living in the wood. The ants' nutritious pupae are the most important food-source for this woodpecker species.

121

The green woodpecker feeds mainly on ants living in the soil.

on their pupae overwintering in the soil. Correlations have been found in studies in the USA between the population size of small mammals, the seed production of oaks and the outbreaks of the gypsy moth. While many small mammals rely on acorns as their main food source, they also feed on caterpillars and pupae of the gypsy moth and other moths. In years in which none of the different oak species produce many acorns, these mammals produce fewer offspring. As a result, they consume fewer gypsy moth caterpillars and the caterpillars' survival rate increases (Liebhold et al. 2000).

All native bats feed on insects and other arthropods. Every night they capture mainly flying insects, such as moths, beetles and flies, in quantities amounting to about half their own body weight. The common noctule, a typical inhabitant of tree hollows, weighs around 40 grams and therefore needs to catch several hundred or even a thousand insects every night. When hunting, bats usually locate their prey with echolocation. They emit calls in the ultrasonic range, which are reflected by the prey and detected by the bats with their sensitive ears. The closer a bat gets to the prey

Certain tiger moths like the garden tiger moth (*Arctia caja*) emit clicking sounds to warn bats that they are inedible. The moths move their forewings forward when threatened during daytime. Their vividly coloured rear wings then indicate that they are inedible.

insect, the more frequently they emit these calls to obtain precise information on the size and position of the prey. A bat does not capture its prey with its teeth, but with its wings or its tail membrane, which it bends down to form a kind of scoop. It then fishes the insect out of the scoop and eats it. Numerous moth species have developed strategies to escape these natural enemies. They can also detect the ultrasonic sounds. As soon as they get into the sound sector of the aggressor, they accelerate their flight, flying in zigzags or dropping down quickly. Many tiger moths (Arctiidae) even launch a kind of counteroffensive by making clicking noises with their hind legs, which make the bats veer off. This has clear advantages for both: the tiger moths escape

Wild boars are omnivores and dig for acorns, roots and invertebrates in the soil, rootstocks and ant mounds. Their favourite insect food tends to be beetles and their larvae, for example the grubs of rose chafers, cockchafers and dor beetles.

Hedgehogs live along forest edges, in hedges and coppices. As typical insectivores, they mainly consume beetles, caterpillars and earwigs, but also millipedes, worms and even carrion. (Photo by Doris Hölling.)

death and the bats avoid catching something they find repulsive. When bats start to eat such an unappetising moth for the first time, they spit it out again immediately. From then on, they associate the clicking sounds with inedible prey and leave it alone (Surlykke and Miller 1985). Other related but edible moths take advantage of this and emit the same sounds as their unappetising relatives to avoid being caught (Barber and Conner 2007).

Larger mammals, such as martens, weasels, badgers, foxes, and wild boars, eat insects more or less regularly as well. Badgers and wild boars in particular like to dig into ant mounds in search of the rose chafer grubs living there, and sometimes severely damage the ant nests. Finally, in some human cultures, the larvae of certain forest insects are valued as food (see Section 16.3).

Amphibians, reptiles and fish

Among the amphibians, salamanders and newts feed, both as larvae and as fully grown adults, on insects and spiders, in addition to other food sources. The diet of yellow-bellied and other toads as well as frogs also includes a wide variety of insects, in addition to worms and slugs. Among the reptiles, slowworms occasionally and lizards almost exclusively feed on beetles, caterpillars, flies, ants and grasshoppers, in addition to other arthropods such as spiders and woodlice.

In the water in alluvial forests and in streams and rivers going through forests, many fish species feed on insects that either develop in the water (e.g., mayflies, stoneflies, caddisflies and mosquitoes) or that fall onto the water surface. In a study on streams in Alaska,

Lizards feed on insects, spiders and other arthropods. In this photo, a common wall lizard has captured a large horsefly.

about half of the food of young salmon consisted of aquatic insects, and the other half of terrestrial insects and spiders that had fallen into the water from the vegetation along the shore (Allan *et al.* 2003).

7.3 Hosts for microorganisms, fungi and parasitic worms

Dead insects are either fed on by scavengers (see Section 5.1) or colonized and degraded by fungi and microorganisms. In addition to these saprobiontic organisms, numerous viruses, bacteria, fungi and parasitic worms may also infect and kill living insects. They therefore can have an antagonistic, regulatory effect on insect populations. Certain viruses and bacteria are used to control insect pests bio-technologically in agriculture and forestry. For example, the naturally occurring NPV virus is used in Europe and the USA to combat the caterpillars of the gypsy moth. The same virus also infects the nun moth *(Lymantria monacha)*, a congener of the gypsy moth. The virus makes the infected caterpillars on a tree climb to the top before dying. The viral body fluid then drips down from the dead animals onto the caterpillars feeding below and infects them, providing a perfect way for the virus to spread.

The main insect-pathogenic bacterium is *Bacillus thuringiensis*, which produces a toxin that is lethal for many insects. It has also been successfully used commercially to combat harmful moth caterpillars and mosquitoes. After its spores have infected an insect, the hyphae of the insect-pathogenic fungus

< This dead gypsy moth *(Lymantria dispar)* caterpillar is infected with the NPV virus and is hanging on a branch in a characteristic inverted V-shape

penetrate the insect's living body. The fungal mycelia then proliferate throughout the insect's whole body and kill it within a few days. Under humid conditions, fruiting bodies grow out of the insect's dead body and the spores are dispersed by the wind. Two well-known fungus species used for biological control are *Beauveria* and *Entomophaga* species: *Beauveria brongniartii* is used to control cockchafer grubs *(Melolontha melolontha),* and *Entomophaga maimaiga* to combat the gypsy moth.

Roundworms, or nematodes, live parasitically. The insect-pathogenic species among them predominantly attack soil insects. Some are also used commercially against harmful insects in agriculture and in private gardening, for example against the larvae of *Otiorhynchus* weevils. Horsehair or Gordian worms (Nematomorpha), whose larvae mainly parasitize insects, belong to another taxonomic group. They have a diameter of about one millimetre, but grow to be several times as long as their host, which they leave when they are adult. The infested insects migrate to water, where the adult horsehair worms leave the insect bodies to mate. The worms are called horsehair worms because people used to believe that they were horsehairs that had fallen into the water and come alive. Horse-

< These fungus-infected dead dung flies (Scathophagidae) are clinging to a plant. The white mycelium of the fungus *Entomophthora scatophagae* fills their bodies full to bursting and has grown over the abdominal segments.

7 Food for other organisms

This devil's coach-horse beetle *(Ocypus olens)* has fallen victim to a fungal disease.

hair worms are often found in or near the drinking spots of horses or cattle.

7.4 Insect products

It is not only the insects themselves that are a source of food and energy for other species, but also some of their products. Honey produced by honeybees and bumble bees is a delicacy not only for bears and humans (see Section 16.1), but also for insects. The adult death's-head hawk moth *(Acherontia atropos)*, which is not a forest insect, but an inhabitant of open scrub landscapes, is known to enter bee nests, where it broaches the honey-filled

Horsehair worms develop parasitically in insects. After reaching sexual maturity, they leave the dead host (right) and mate in a watercourse. A fully grown native horsehair worm (left) can grow several decimetres long. (Photo on bottom right courtesy of Forest Entomology WSL.)

cells with its short, firm proboscis and sucks out the honey. The moth is well protected from bee attacks by its dense hair and especially by its odour, which imitates that of bees.

A much more important insect product in the forest is honeydew. Aphids and scale insects insert their long and fine stylets into the phloem of the host plants and ingest the plant sap, which is under pressure. The phloem sap is relatively poor in amino acids (nitrogen source), but rich in various sugars (mainly sucrose) and, of course, in water. In order to gather sufficient amino acids, the insects have to absorb large amounts of plant sap, but do not use all the water and sugar themselves. The excess is converted into melezitose, which they then excrete in the form of droplets. To prevent a colony from sticking together, the aphids kick the honeydew droplets away with their hind legs or encapsulate them in a waxy covering. Sooty mould quickly colonizes the sticky substrate that accumulates on the plant's leaves below, covering the surface of the leaves with a black coating. The energy-rich droplets are also a valuable source of food for many insects, including not only honeybees (see Section 16.1), but also many wild bee species, as well as bumble bees, lacewings, and parasitoid and paper wasps.

Certain aphids and ants have developed a symbiotic relationship (trophobiosis). Honeydew is an important source of energy for the workers especially among wood ants ('operating energy'). In return, the ants prevent

128

Honeybees (*Apis mellifera*) produce their honey reserves from pollen and nectar. Modern breeding methods and beekeeping measures have led to far fewer bee colonies swarming today than in the past. A honeybee queen in the wild will, however, leave her nest in summer with a large part of the colony to establish a new one in a suitable tree cavity.
⌄

The adult death's-head hawk moth (*Acherontia atropos*) feeds on honey from bee hives.
⌄

the aphids from sticking together and ward off their natural enemies such as ladybirds, hover flies or parasitic wasps. The ants may even stroke the aphids with their antennae to stimulate them to suck more and thus produce more honeydew ('milking'). Ant-tended aphid colonies can thus cause greater damage than untended ones (Piñol *et al.* 2012). When aphids no longer supply enough honeydew, the ants sometimes eat them or transport them to more productive sites where they can become productive again. Some ants collect aphid eggs in autumn and overwinter them in their nests, where they are cared for and are more likely to survive. In spring, the ants move the hatched aphids back onto plants (Matsuura and Yashiro 2006).

The umbrella wasp (*Polistes* sp.) here is visiting an aphid colony to pick up honeydew.

The elder aphid (*Aphis sambuci*) is one of the larger aphids. It uses its strong proboscis (visible under its head pointing backwards) to puncture the bark and tap the sap-conducting cells. The juice is under pressure and flows into its gullet without the aphid having to actively suck.

△
Lachnid aphids (Lachnidae) are among the most productive suppliers of honeydew, not only for ants, but also for beekeeping. Honeybees convert it into honeydew honey.

△
This carpenter ant (*Camponotus* sp.) is stroking a colony of large walnut aphids *(Panaphis juglandis)* with its antennae to stimulate them to excrete more honeydew.

The ant (*Myrmica* sp.) here is taking a honeydew droplet from an aphid.

7 Food for other organisms

Natural enemies

8

It is not only higher animals that feed on insects (see Chapter 7). Insects also eat each other and play an important role as natural enemies or so-called 'antagonists' of herbivorous arthropods. They act as 'top-down agents' in regulating herbivorous insects, in contrast to the host plants, which have physiological properties that may regulate herbivores 'bottom-up'. The interactions between prey and their natural enemies have developed and have been fine-tuned over millions of years, with the antagonists adapting to overcome the new defence strategies their prey develop. For example, there is evidence that predators are less likely to prey on insects living hidden inside plant tissue (e.g., leaf miners) than on others. These insects, however, then run a higher risk of being parasitized. The insects with the best protection against natural enemies are those that form galls, as well as those dwelling in wood and roots.

The majority of insects, spiders and mites live predatorily or parasitically. Worldwide, about 54 percent of all insect species are

A seven-spot ladybird (*Coccinella septempunctata*) feeding on a winged aphid.

zoophagous, i.e., predatory, parasitic or scavenging, and 46 percent are phytophagous (Strong *et al.* 1984). Parasitic insects account for 10 percent of all known animal species (Askew 1971). Studies on phytophagous insects and their antagonists, which have mostly been performed in forests and on agricultural crops, indicate that parasitism causes much higher mortality than do predators or pathogens, especially in temperate latitudes (Hawkins *et al.* 1997).

Natural enemies can be divided into three categories according to the amount of prey they require to develop and their way of life at different developmental stages. Predators are usually larger than their food, i.e., their 'prey'. Predatory insects need several prey to complete their larval development. Ground beetles are well-known representatives of this group. Unlike predators, parasitic species are often much smaller than their food, i.e., their 'host'. In addition, a single host is generally sufficient for them to complete their development. Parasitic species may be further subdivided into so-called parasitoids and true parasites. While true parasites, such as mites, live parasitically in both their larval and adult stages on or in insects and usually only weaken their hosts, parasitoids, such as parasitic wasps, live parasitically only in their larval stages and always kill their hosts. Adult parasitoids, however, usually live on nectar, honeydew or pollen.

The two categories cannot always be clearly separated, and some species have a hybrid lifestyle.

8.1 Predatory insects

Predators hunt for their prey, ambushing or capturing it in different ways (e.g., spiders, see Section 8.2). They afterwards consume their prey within a short time. Since the prey is of-

---

Natural enemies (antagonists)

Predators
- larger than their prey
- need several prey for development

Parasitoids
- smaller than their hosts
- need a single host for development
- parasitic only in their larval stages
- kill their hosts

Parasites
- smaller than their hosts
- need a single host for development
- parasitic in all stages
- do not kill their hosts

Example: ladybirds

Example: parasitoid wasps

Example: mites

ten much smaller than the predator, predatory insects need several prey for their larval development and the adult insects for their survival and reproduction. Most use their mandibles to crush and eat mainly the muscles, fat reserves and internal organs of their prey, i.e., the softer and nutritious parts. Others pierce their prey and suck out the haemolymph. Sometimes they first inject digestive enzymes into the prey's body to liquefy the body contents. The most common and most important predatory insects are beetles, especially ladybirds, ground beetles and rove beetles.

Ladybirds (Coccinellidae)

Ladybirds belong, together with hoverflies and lacewings, to the most important enemies of aphids and scale insects. Aphidophagous insects are attracted to aphids by their honeydew excretion and lay their eggs next to aphid colonies. Honeydew is the sugar-rich liquid excreted by these sucking insects. It consists of the excess water and carbohydrates taken up from the plant's phloem sap. Both the larvae and adult beetles of the approximately 70 Central European ladybirds feed almost exclusively on aphids. The seven-spot ladybird (*Coccinella septempunctata*) consumes several thousand aphids during its lifetime. This species, which is considered to bring luck in many cultures, is an ubiquist, i.e., it occurs in a wide variety of habitats such as forests, meadows, hedges or gardens. Since the beginning of the 21st century, native ladybirds have faced increasing competition from the harlequin ladybird (*Harmonia axyridis*), imported from Asia to Europe. This beetle is exceptionally variable in its colouring and has spread to almost all habitats in Europe within a few years. While it kills aphids very effectively, it also feeds on the larvae of competing

The seven-spot ladybird, our best-known ladybird species, is an important consumer of aphids. This plant's shiny leaves are covered with honeydew from aphids.

This harlequin ladybird (*Harmonia axyridis*) is taking off, revealing the two pairs of wings that beetles have: the hard forewings (elytra) for protection and the membranous hindwings for flying.

8 Natural enemies

A harlequin ladybird larva devouring an aphid.

Harlequin ladybirds not only feed on aphids, but also on other ladybird larvae. This has led to the composition of ladybird fauna changing.

native ladybirds. Ladybirds often spend the winter as adult beetles clustered into groups in sheltered sites, which, in the case of the harlequin ladybird, can sometimes be annoying when they collect on the walls of buildings or inside rooms. Certain ladybird species, such as the two-spot ladybird, which may be very variably coloured as well, are used for biological control of agricultural pests. Forest edges and hedges are, in general, both the source and major overwintering habitats for important antagonists of agricultural pests.

Among the ladybirds, typical forest species are, for example, the pine ladybirds (*Exochomus quadripustulatus*), which can be found on coniferous and broadleaf trees, the eyed

‹ The colouring of the two-spot ladybird (*Adalia bipunctata*) is very variable. Here, a red male with black spots is copulating with a black female with red spots on an elder leaf.

ladybird *(Anatis ocellata)*, which occurs in coniferous forests up to the upper timberline, and the *Scymnus* species, which live on coniferous trees and whose larvae characteristically camouflage themselves with waxy excretions.

Ground beetles (Carabidae)

The majority of Central Europe's almost 800 ground beetles are nocturnal predators on insects, worms and slugs. Some also feed on carrion or vegetable matter. Ground beetles' daily food consumption is roughly equivalent to – or even several times more than – their own body weight. Their diet is usually not restricted to certain prey species, and their food varies mainly according to size. They are often large and metallic, with long legs. Most are flightless, but they are agile hunters on the ground. They use their large and strong mandibles to capture and pin down their prey. Rather than crushing and devouring their prey, they often spit out secreted digestive juices onto them and then consume the resulting pulp. Such behaviour is called 'extraintestinal digestion'. The larvae are completely different from the adult beetles and are strongly segmented. Most species produce only one generation per year.

The two- to four-centimetre-long *Carabus* species often dwell in forests, and feed mainly on worms and slugs. The largest species, *Carabus coriaceus*, is a predominantly nocturnal predator that lives mainly in humid broadleaf and mixed forests, as well as in gardens and meadows. When threatened, the beetles can eject a foul-smelling secretion from their abdominal glands towards the aggressor. Numerous other *Carabus* species

The almost one-centimetre long eyed ladybird *(Anatis ocellata)* is one of the largest ladybirds. It lives in coniferous forests, where it feeds on aphids and sawfly larvae.

Frontal view of a blue ground beetle's *(Carabus intricatus)* head. Clearly visible are its large eyes, sickle-like mandibles for catching prey, and downward protruding palps carrying sensors for physical and chemical sensing.

8 Natural enemies

Larva of a *Carabus* species.

are associated with forest ecosystems. *Carabus problematicus* lives beneath stones and deadwood in coniferous and broadleaf forests and hunts insects at dusk. Other conspicuous *Carabus* species are *C. auronitens*, *C. irregularis*, and *C. violaceus* (violet ground beetle). They are mainly found in humid areas in forests at higher elevations and remain during daytime hidden underneath the bark of dead trees.

Cychrus species live in forests or along forest edges in humid places where their exclusive food source – slugs and snails – are normally numerous. With their long heads and protruding mandibles, they can reach their prey even when they are retracted deep inside the snail shell.

One of the largest and most beautiful European ground beetles is the forest caterpillar hunter (*Calosoma sycophanta*). This beetle, measuring up to 28 millimetres in size and active during the daytime, even climbs trees to capture the large caterpillars of such notorious forest pests as the gypsy moth (*Lymantria dispar*) and the nun moth (*L. monacha*). As adults, the beetles live for two to four years, but are only active for about two months in summer. According to studies where gypsy moth larvae were provided as food, one adult forest caterpillar hunter can kill up to 400 gypsy moth caterpillars every year (Scherney 1959). For a larva to develop, it needs around 40 to 90 caterpillars, depending on the size of the caterpillars (Burgess 1911). Surprisingly, given this insect is quite large, its larval development takes only four weeks (Weseloh 1985). During the occasional outbreaks of the gypsy moth in Central and Southern Europe, when its caterpillars severely defoliate broadleaf forests, the conspicuous forest caterpillar hunter and its larvae can easily be spotted. It

The elytra and pronotum of the blue ground beetle are bright blue. This species may be found in various forest types at medium elevations. It likes to hide in tree stumps or under loose bark.

The ground beetle *Carabus depressus* lives in mountain forests.

is amazing how quickly this otherwise rare, and therefore in many countries protected, beetle can benefit from the sudden, abundant supply of caterpillars. This large carabid predator is an important regulator of caterpillar populations. During certain phases in gypsy moth outbreaks, it may eliminate as many as three quarters of the caterpillars (Weseloh 1985). *Calosoma sycophanta* was successfully exported from Europe to North America at the beginning of the 20th century to fight gypsy moth there. Several thousand of the first beetles to be released in New England originated from Switzerland (Burgess 1911).

In addition to the genera described above, dozens of other ground beetle species live in forests, especially representatives of the genera *Pterostichus*, *Amara* and *Abax*. Some *Dromius* species feed on bark beetles and are listed among their natural enemies (Chapter 9).

The shiny ground beetle *Carabus auronitens* occurs in various types of forests, as well as in gardens close to forests.

This snail-killing ground beetle *(Cychrus caraboides)* has captured a slug.

Rove beetles (Staphylinidae)

Rove beetles are less well-known predators, but nevertheless represent a very species-rich family with approximately 2000 species in Central Europe alone. Almost all of them can fly. When resting, they fold their membranous hind wings in a most complicated way under their short elytra with the help of their abdomens. Some members of the species are very tiny (0.5 millimetres long). They can be found in various habitats, including forests, living under bark or in moss, the litter layer or fungi. The majority feed as diurnal predators on maggots and other prey that is easily accessible. A number of species live in the nests of birds and mammals, while others prefer those of social insects like wasps or ants.

A forest caterpillar hunter *(Calosoma sycophanta)* larva feeding on a gypsy moth caterpillar *(Lymantria dispar)*.

8 Natural enemies

There they live either on waste products or feed directly on the wasp or ant brood. Some smaller species can be found underneath the bark of trees, where they feed on bark beetles, for example (see Section 9.2). Some of the larger predatory forest species belonging to the genus *Staphylinus* feed, similar to ground beetles, on snails and insects. The devil's coach-horse beetle *(Ocypus olens)* is the largest rove beetle in Central Europe and is more than three centimetres long. It occurs not only in forests and along forest edges, but also in gardens, where it occasionally falls into light wells and gets into cellars. When threatened, it bends its abdomen up like a scorpion in danger, which, together with its powerful mandibles and large size, makes it quite impressive, as its common name suggests. Its pinch is strong, but despite its scorpion-like appearance, it cannot sting.

Threat display of a devil's coach-horse beetle *(Ocypus olens)*.

Other beetles

The many other predatory beetle species in addition to the three large predatory families already described include the family of burying beetles (Silphidae), which mainly feed on dead animals. Some also eat live prey such as insects and slugs. The four-spotted carrion beetle *(Dendroxena quadrimaculata)* lives mainly in oak forests. It climbs up into tree crowns to capture the caterpillars of, for example, geometer moths and sawflies, while its larvae eat insect larvae and carrion. Some of the predatory species among the cardinal beetles (Pyrochroidae), checkered beetles (Cleridae), soldier beetles (Cantharidae), click beetles (Elateridae), and bark-gnawing beetles (Trogositidae) are presented in Chapters 4 and 9.

The rove beetle *Dinothenarus fossor* is nocturnal and hides during the day under rocks or deadwood.

This forest caterpillar hunter has captured a gypsy moth caterpillar on a tree trunk. Note the larva's stomach, where the leaf parts it has consumed are clearly visible.

8 Natural enemies

Some burying beetles, such as the four-spotted carrion beetle *(Dendroxena quadrimaculata)*, also feed on living insects.

Wasps

The order 'Hymenoptera' comprises, among others, sawflies and wasps. Wasps are divided into parasitic wasps and stinging wasps (Aculeata). Stinging wasps include bees as well as predatory wasps and ants. Wood ants play a very important role in forests and are therefore dealt with separately in Chapter 10. Some examples of the taxonomically heterogeneous predatory wasps are described in the following sections. In addition to the well-known nest-forming social paper wasps, there are other predatory families of wasps that live solitarily.

Paper wasps (Vespidae)

Paper wasps form social colonies organized according to clear rules. As with other social insects such as bees and ants, they have so-called castes with different tasks. The queen starts the nest and founds the colony in spring. She is the only one in the whole colony that lays eggs. The majority are workers. Although they are female, like the queen, and develop from fertilized eggs, their ovaries remain undeveloped. The workers are responsible for building the nests, procuring food and nursing the brood. The reproductive caste consists of the female queens, who develop from fertilized eggs, and male drones developed from unfertilized eggs. The drones' only duty is to mate with the young queens during their swarming flight.

The yellowjackets with their yellow–black warning coloration (aposematism) use their stingers both for defence and for capturing large prey, such as bees that can defend themselves. Paper wasps rely on two types

Predator feeding on predator. This hornet *(Vespa crabro)* has captured a European garden spider *(Araneus diadematus)* in the spider's web and is hanging upside down eating it.

8 Natural enemies

of food. Juices rich in carbohydrates from flowers, berries, fruit, honeydew or wounds in trees provide the operating energy for the workers. The wasp larvae feed on insects, which are also the source of the protein the queen needs to produce eggs. Flies make up most of their diet, but they also catch grasshopper, cicada, moth and sawfly larvae. The wasp nest is made of wood fibres mixed with saliva. This paper pulp is spread out into a thin layer of paper that then hardens. Nests with several cell layers, e.g., those of the *Vespula* species, are surrounded by a multi-layered paper envelope.

Hornets *(Vespa crabro)* are the largest paper wasps in Europe. They are rather shy when outside the immediate range of their nests and are erroneously considered dangerous. The annual life cycle of a hornet colony described here is similar to that of many other social paper wasps. The fertilized queen, who may be up to 35 millimetres long, emerges from overwintering in March or April and then searches for a suitable place to build her nest.

She prefers to construct her nest in old tree hollows or in other dark and protected places in parklands, light mixed forests, orchards or even in people's houses. There she produces the first brood-cells and deposits an egg in each. Not only is she busy with constructing the nest and laying eggs, but soon also with procuring food for the hatched larvae and with feeding them. This is a delicate phase in the colony's life because if the queen dies or long phases of bad weather prevent her from foraging, the whole colony may perish. Once the first workers have developed, they take over constructing the nest, foraging and feeding the larvae, while the queen remains in the nest and devotes herself entirely to producing offspring. In summer, the population of the colony reaches its highest level with several hundred insects. In late summer, the queen deposits the eggs from which the reproductive caste emerges. Unfertilized eggs develop into drones, while the larvae hatching from fertilized eggs receive some special food and become queens. The colony then slowly

This *Dolichovespula wasp* is crushing and eating its prey.

European paper wasps *(Polistes dominula)* rarely occur in forests, but are more frequent in open terrain. The photos illustrate the two main food types exploited by paper wasps: protein-rich insects for feeding their brood (left) and carbohydrate-rich juice for the workers (right).

disintegrates. First the mother queen leaves the nest and dies. Then, at the end of the summer, the virgin males and queens leave the nest to mate. Eventually, the drones and workers die as well. Only the young queens that have mated remain and spend the winter in sheltered hiding places.

Most of the workers live on plant juices, nectar and honeydew. They capture flies, caterpillars, wasps, bees and spiders mainly to

What distinguishes hornet workers from almost all other paper wasp species is their size as well as the extensive red colouring on their thorax and head.

A hornet has two main weapons: its strong, chewing mandibles and its stinger, which it uses to defend itself against aggressors and to overwhelm large prey.

feed the brood and the queen. The only parts of the prey they use are its flight muscles, which they process into small meatballs and then take to the nest to feed the queen and her larvae. Watson (1922) noted that about 60 workers could capture around 230 flies in an hour. Extrapolated to a colony of 600 hornets and a 20-hour working day, this yields a theoretical catch of 46 000 flies. Assuming the average weight of a fly to be 2 milligrams,

Interactions between spiders and wasps vary. Hornets may eat spiders (page 143) and spiders may eat wasps (page 161). Wasps may steal spiders' prey as in this photo, where a *Vespula* wasp is stealing a honeybee caught in the web of a European garden spider.

Paper nest of a median wasp (*Dolichovespula media*, left). This wasp species lives in light forests and shrubs, as well as in residential areas. Paper wasps rasp wood to obtain the fibres they use as material for building their nests (right).

this means they catch almost one kilogram of prey in 10 days. Hornets thus play an important role in the regulation of potential insect pests. Nevertheless their reputation is unjustly bad. They are not aggressive, nor are they a nuisance to people. Moreover, they do not compete for the food on our dining tables. People often destroy their nests, which together with a lack of breeding facilities, has led to hornets becoming rare. They are now protected in many European countries.

Solitary wasps

Paper wasps include not only social wasps, but also various kinds of solitary wasps. They do not build their nests out of paper, but may make them from mortar or nest in, for example, deadwood. When depositing their eggs, they add insect prey (often caterpillars and beetle larvae) for their offspring. This is similar to the way wild bees supply their offspring with pollen and nectar.

In some other wasp taxa, differentiating between predators and parasitoids (cf. Section 8.3) is not so easy. Most digger wasps (Sphecidae) and spider wasps (Pompilidae) supply their offspring with living, but paralyzed hosts. Spider wasps feed their young exclusively spiders. They deposit them, each with an egg attached, in individual nests. Even though spider wasps transport their hosts to a specially prepared nest, this behaviour corresponds, by definition, to that of parasitoids, which is why the family is discussed with the parasitoids.

The food range of digger wasps is much broader than that of spider wasps, and includes caterpillars, grasshoppers, spiders and cockroaches. The female wasp stings her prey to paralyze it and then takes it to her nest, which may, depending on the wasp species, be located in the ground, in cracks, deadwood or plant stems. A digger wasp nest has several cells, each containing an egg and several prey, and thus its way of life corresponds more to that of a predator. Digger wasps may be found in open terrain on warm sites. Only a few species live in the forest, wich is also true for several other wasp families.

8 Natural enemies

Solitary paper wasps (here *Ancistrocerus* sp.) nest in, for example, old beetle tunnels in wood.

True bugs

In contrast to the predators described above, true bugs (Heteroptera) suck on their prey. They include not only plant sap-suckers and some blood-suckers, but also a number of predatory species that suck on their prey. They sting their prey to paralyze or kill them, and then inject salivary gland secretions into them to predigest them. Some examples of predatory species, distributed over very diverse families, that live in forests or along forest edges are *Troilus luridus*, *Arma custos* and the spiny shieldbug *(Picromerus bidens)*, with its typical impressive lateral projections. All of them belong to the shield bug family (Pentatomidae). They live mainly on broadleaf trees or shrubs, where they capture caterpil-

A brood of a digger wasp in a small hollow branch. The glossy wasp larva in the middle has an ample supply of paralyzed mosquitoes to feed on.

lars, beetles and their larvae, bugs, aphids and other insects.

One of the most frequent true bugs is the common flower bug *(Anthocoris nemorum)*, which lives not only on stinging-nettles but also on broadleaf trees, where it sucks aphids, mites, small flies and caterpillars. The pretty plant bug *Dryophilocoris flavoquadrimaculatus* lives on oaks and feeds on plant sap, as well as on aphids, insect eggs and small caterpillars. Assassin bugs (Reduviidae) and damsel bugs (Nabidae) are two families with only a few species living in forests. However, the *Rhynocoris* species, which are quite frequent in some areas, like to colonize warm, sunny forest edges, where they prey on insects on flowers and on the ground.

This larva of the tree damsel bug *(Himacerus apterus)* is sucking out the larva of a ladybird, i.e., of another predator.

Bronze shieldbug *(Troilus luridus)* sucking on the caterpillar of a nun moth *(Lymantria monacha)*.

The common flower bug (*Anthocoris nemorum*) is often found on trees as well as on stinging-nettles.

Predatory flies

What is less well known is that some flies also belong to the major predatory species. In the hoverfly (Syrphidae) family, the adult flies live on nectar and pollen. They received their name from their hummingbird-like flight as they can stay hovering in sunlight. The larvae of some of these fly species feed predatorily on aphids and are significant consumers of aphids in open landscapes and forests. The larvae of the genus *Heringia*, for example, feed predominantly on the economically im-

This assassin bug *Rhynocoris iracundus* has captured a beetle and is sucking it out.

8 Natural enemies

The plant bug *Dryophilocoris flavoquadrimaculatus* lives on oak trees and feeds on both plants and insects.

portant balsam woolly adelgid (Dreyfusia piceae). In forests, the heliophilous hoverflies can be found mainly in clearings and along forest edges and paths. The females are attracted by aphids' honeydew, and deposit their eggs near aphid colonies. This ensures that, when the larvae hatch, they can find food for their development. The eyeless larvae (maggots) find their prey through touch, and lift it up so they can slurp its haemolymph.

The sturdy lesser hornet fly (Volucella inanis) chooses a very special habitat for its larvae to develop – the nests of hornets and other paper wasps. There they feed predatorily on the wasp brood, before pupating outside the wasps' nest in the ground. Other species of the genus *Volucella* feed merely on waste material they find in wasp nests.

The hoverfly *Syrphus torvus* occurs in a range of habitats. Its larvae feed on aphids.

In addition to hoverflies, there are several other predatory fly groups. The large robber flies of the genus *Laphria* can often be observed sitting on tree trunks or stumps waiting for a prey insect to pass by. They have very flexible heads and with their large eyes can closely follow possible prey or potential enemies. They catch their prey in flight with their forelegs and then, after they land, stab and suck on them. A robber fly can also overwhelm a well-armoured beetle, piercing it with its short but solid rostrum. Some robber fly larvae feed on the larvae of wood-eating jewel and longhorn beetles they find under bark.

The marsh fly (Sciomyzidae) larvae live predatorily or parasitically on snails, sometimes even in water. Adult *Coremacera marginata*, which are typical representatives of this dipteran family in forests and along rather shady

Adult *Eupeodes lapponicus* hoverflies live on nectar while their mottled larvae feed on aphids.

8 Natural enemies

↑
This hoverfly larva has detected the larva of a linden aphid *(Eucallipterus tiliae)* on the underside of a lime leaf and is sucking on it.

Hoverfly larva feeding in an aphid colony.
↓

Although ants normally protect aphids from enemies, this hoverfly larva remains undisturbed.
↓

∧ A robber fly *Choerades fuliginosa* sucking on a captured *Phyllobius* weevil.

forest edges, live on nectar. Other predatory flies are discussed in the section on the natural enemies of bark beetles (Section 9.2).

Net-winged insects

Net-winged insects (Neuroptera) live, at least in their larval stages, as predators on, e.g., booklice, aphids, mites and beetle larvae. Most species are typical forest dwellers, and often depend on specific tree or shrub species. Lacewings (Chrysopidae) are among the most frequent and important net-winged insects. *Chrysopa* species can be found in almost all habitats. Both adults and larvae feed on mites and insects, especially aphids, but they also eat pollen and nectar. In agriculture, *Chrysoperla carnea* s.l. plays an important role as an aphid feeder and is used for

< Lesser hornet fly *(Volucella inanis)* larvae develop in hornet and wasp nests, where their larvae suck on larvae of the wasp brood.

8 Natural enemies

biological control of pest insects. According to laboratory experiments, one larva consumes about 400 aphids or 12 000 spider mite eggs during its development (Wachmann and Saure 1997). In autumn, the insect changes its colour from green to brown, regaining its original green colour in spring after overwintering. Lacewings of the genera *Nineta* and *Nothochrysa* are other typical forest dwellers. Their adults live mainly on honeydew. The *Nothochrysa* species occur primarily in the forest canopy and are therefore often not noticed. Like ladybirds and hoverflies, green lacewings are attracted by the honeydew of aphids. They deposit their eggs in a special way – sitting on stalks – near the aphid colonies. The stalks protect them from predators such as ants. The newly hatched larvae find the aphids by touch, piercing them with their

This robber fly of the genus *Machimus* has caught a honeybee.

The larvae of the strikingly marked marsh fly *Coremacera marginata* prey on slugs and snails.

Lacewing larvae inject a digestive enzyme with their sickle-shaped mandibles into aphids and then extract their body juices. Photo on left: *Peyerimhoffina gracilis*. The common green lacewing (*Chrysoperla carnea* s.l.; photo on right) overwinters as an adult insect in a protected place and becomes active again in spring when the trees flush their leaves.

dagger-like mandibles and sucking them out. Some species put the empty aphid shells on their backs as camouflage.

Net-winged insects include not only lacewings, ant lions (Myrmeleontidae), with their well-known sand pit traps, and the inconspicuous dustywings (Coniopterygidae), but also some even more typical forest species belonging to the brown lacewing family (Hemerobiidae). Both adults and larvae feed preferably on aphids and scale insects. *Drepanepteryx phalaenoides* is, with a wingspan of more than 30 millimetres, the largest member of this family. As a larva, it lives on broadleaf trees and shrubs, and as an adult inhabits light broadleaf forests. Other brown lacewings are found exclusively on coniferous trees. In contrast, the common *Hemerobius humulinus* has no particular preference for any forest type and may also be found in gardens and parks.

Snakeflies, which are closely related to the net-winged insects, are discussed in the sec-

Their long stalks protect the eggs of the lacewing *Chrysopa pallens* from predators and cannibalistic siblings.

Left: This larva of the brown lacewing *Hemerobius humulinus* has grabbed an aphid and is sucking it out.
Right: The wing venation of *Drepanepteryx phalaenoides*, another brown lacewing species, is in perfect imitation of a dry leaf. If its camouflage is 'blown', the lacewing drops to the ground where, with its legs retracted, it resembles a beechnut.

tion on the natural enemies of bark beetles (Section 9.2).

Other predatory insects

Other predatory insects include some quite unusual predators, in addition to the various predators already described and other orders not typically occurring in forests, such as dragonflies. Many laypeople do not know that quite a few crickets are at least partially carnivorous. The bush-cricket *Tettigonia viridissima*, for example, feeds on grasshoppers and flies. The dark bush-cricket *(Pholidoptera griseoaptera)* is vegetarian as a young larva but in later instars and as an adult it has a mixed plant–animal diet, while the oak bush-cricket *(Meconema thalassinum)* lives exclusively on small insects such as aphids, flies and caterpillars. All three species are found mainly along forest edges and in light forests, but also in parks and gardens.

Earwigs generally feed on plants, but some species also feed on insects. The European earwig *(Forficula auricularia)* is a synanthropic species and occurs in various habitats. It eats aphids, scale insects and butterfly caterpillars, as well as vegetable material. It lives nocturnally and hides under moist leaves or in crevices during the day. The female produces her brood in the soil, where she looks after her eggs and protects them, and even feeds the larvae. Such parental care is very rare in insects.

Some butterfly species have predatory caterpillars, but these are very much the exception. In the family of blues (Lycaenidae), caterpillars of the genus *Phengaris* (= *Maculinea*) live predatorily in the nests of *Myrmica* ants, but they are not actual forest insects. Caterpillars of the satellite moth *(Eupsilia transversa)* feed on aphids on broadleaf trees. The lifestyle of the bee moth *(Aphomia sociella)*, which belongs to the pyralid moth family, is interesting. The female deposits several hund-

The predatory southern oak bush-cricket *(Meconema meridionale)* has spread from the Mediterranean to the North in recent years. South of the Alps, it can be found in light forests and along forest edges, and North of the Alps in the milder climates of residential areas.

red eggs on a bumble bee or wasp nest. The hatched caterpillars feed on waste material in the nest, but also on bumble bee or wasp larvae. They cover more and more parts of the nest with webbing so they can feed on the brood without being disturbed by the defensive workers. As a result, the whole nest is usually destroyed.

8.2 Predatory spiders and mites

In contrast to insects, a spider's body is only divided into two sections: a fore-body (prosoma) and a hind-body (opisthosoma). They lack an insect's middle thorax section, which supports the insect's wings and three pairs of legs. Spiders have four pairs of legs emerging from the prosoma. They also differ from insects in having small and simple eyes (ocelli) and no antennae. The silk fibres that spiders produce with their spinneret glands have different structures and functions: the adhesive and structural silk fibres are for their webs, while other silk types are used for immobilizing their prey, producing egg cocoons or for "ballooning", i.e., being passively displaced by the wind.

Forest habitats harbour an extremely rich range of spider species. Spiders are among the most important natural enemies of insects, and use many different strategies to catch their prey. Most species rely on orb-webs, funnel webs or irregular tangle webs made from silk threads. Others stalk their prey or lie in ambush and attack it when it is close

The European earwig *(Forficula auricularia)* lives on plant and animal substrates, including aphids.

enough. Spiders have no chewing mandibles to bite off bits of their prey. Instead, they have long jaws (chelicerae), with which they inject a paralyzing or lethal poison into their prey – either before or after wrapping it up in their silk threads. They then inject digestive juices into their prey or spit them on it to liquefy its body contents, before absorbing their prey's entire body contents. Spiders are thus similar to ground beetles and true bugs in having an extraintestinal digestive system.

About 60 to 80 percent of the prey of European orb-weaver spiders (Araneidae) consists of true flies (flies and mosquitoes), as well as aphids and hymenopterans (Nentwig 1985). Spiders that construct their webs on the ground and hunting spiders, among others, feed mainly on ground-dwelling prey.

Top: an adult of the bee moth *(Aphomia sociella)*. Bottom: cocoon webbings in which the moth caterpillars spend the winter before pupating.

8 Natural enemies

Such elaborate orb webs last only a few days and then have to be reconstructed from scratch. They are particularly clearly visible with backlighting or dew.

The best-known spider, the European garden spider (*Araneus diadematus*), which occurs in almost all habitats, also catches larger prey, such as venomous bees and wasps.

Sheet weavers or money spiders (Linyphiidae) spin irregular silk webs rather than uniform orb webs. They are the most species-rich spider family with over 400 species in Central Europe alone. They usually construct, as collectors, horizontally aligned sheet webs. Their prey trip over the irregular tangles of silk thread above the sheets and fall down onto them. The spider waiting underneath the sheet then bites its prey through the sheet web and paralyzes it.

Jumping spiders (Salticidae) or crab spiders (Thomisidae) lurk waiting for their prey and then pounce on them. A common species is the goldenrod crab spider (*Misumena vatia*), which occurs in very different colours. The female can adapt its colouring according to the plant it is sitting on. On a yellow flower, it has a yellow body. If, however, the spider moves to a white flower, the yellow pigments are transferred inside its body and the spider turns white within just a few hours. It may also take on one of many transitional shades between these two colours.

Even predatory species such as this venomous wasp fall victim to the European garden spider (*Araneus diadematus*). Note the spider's chelicera in the middle of the photo.

8 Natural enemies

Mites are also arachnids. Some live predatorily and suck on other invertebrates. The mite *Trombidium holosericeum* is just four millimetres long, which is huge for a mite. It searches on the ground for insect eggs and other small prey and pierces them with its rostrum. Its larvae live parasitically on insects (see Section 8.4).

Enoplognatha ovata is a tangle-web spider frequently found along forest edges, where its web stretched between twigs or stalks may trap even large, aggressive insects.

Here the prey has been immobilized with poison, wrapped in silk and stored as live food.

This cucumber green spider *(Araniella cucurbitina)* has caught a fly in the simple net it stretched across two oak leaves.

8.3 Parasitoids

The phenomenon of parasitism has long been known. Initially, however, the famous German entomologist Julius T.C. Ratzeburg thought that only insects that were already sick, and therefore doomed to die, would be attacked by ichneumons (Ratzeburg 1844). He therefore considered parasitoids to have only limited use since they just, he thought, convert the "juices [of the sick larvae], which are close to polluting the air with their exhalation and stench", into "living and healthy animal matter". He did realise, however, that high parasitism rates in harmful forest insects (caterpillars and bark beetles) indicate the imminent end of an outbreak. Today the important role of parasitoids – together with predatory agents – in the regulation of herbivorous insects is undisputed (see Section 9.6).

In parasitoids, only their larvae live parasitically, while the adults feed on, for example, honeydew or pollen. The female oviposits an egg in or on the host's body. The egg hatches into a larva, which then feeds on the host. Depending on whether the larva feeds inside the host body or on its surface, the species is classified as an endo- or ectoparasitoid.

8 Natural enemies

Left: sheet weaver *Neriene radiata* in waiting position under its sheet web. Right: the tripping threads of the sheet weaver spider are clearly visibly above the sheet web.

This goldenrod crab spider *(Misumena vatia)* with its attractive colouring is waiting for prey on the edge of a leaf.

Wolf spider females carry their egg sacs attached to their spinnerets (left: *Pardosa lugubris*). After hatching, the spiderlings remain for a while on the back of their mother (right: *Pardosa amentata*).

165

This white goldenrod crab spider has retreated with a captured fly beneath a flower to extract the prey's haemolymph.

Jumping spiders (here: *Marpissa muscosa*) do not build any webs, but stalk their prey and then leap to attack them. They can, nevertheless, produce silk threads, e.g., to secure as 'safety ropes' before they leap.

This moth caterpillar is caught in the silk fibres of the tangle-web spider *Enoplognatha ovata*.

Velvet mites *(Trombidium holosericeum)* are widespread and suck out, for example, insect eggs.

Parasitism may be in the form of single parasitism (with just one parasitoid per host), superparasitism (multiple parasitoids belonging to the same species), multiparasitism (multiple parasitoids belonging to different species) and hyperparasitism (where a primary parasitoid parasitizes a secondary parasitoid). Since a host must serve as food for a longer period of time, it is not killed during the parasitization act (oviposition). Initially, the parasitized host continues to live apparently undisturbed, but it is then gradually eaten (koinobiont parasitoid). Haemolymph (body fluid) and less important tissues such as their fat bodies are consumed first, and only towards the end are the main organs also devoured. Successful parasitism, however, inevitably leads to the death of the host.

Host larvae are not completely at the mercy of their enemies. If a parasitoid attacks a host outside its usual species range, the eggs or larvae are often encapsulated and killed by the host's defence cells. If, on the other hand, a parasitoid species has co-evolved with its host, this immune reaction of the host is suppressed by, for example, viruses co-injected by the parasitoid during egg deposition (Vinson 1990). The adults of numerous species also engage in so-called 'host feeding', i.e. they pierce a host with their ovipositor and lick up the exuded body fluid without depositing an egg.

Parasitoid insects are particularly common in forests because plants with a complex architecture, such as trees and shrubs, harbour more species than herbaceous plants or grasses. This also increases the range of potential hosts.

Parasitoid wasps

Parasitoid wasps include, in the broadest sense, numerous hymenopterans such as the ichneumonid wasps (Ichneumonidae), braconid wasps (Braconidae), and chalcid wasps (Chalcidoidea). Parasitoid wasps account for almost one-tenth of all insects worldwide. There are over 5000 species of braconid wasps in Europe alone. The size of a parasitic wasp is adapted to the body size of its host, and varies from a few tenths of a millimetre to a few centimetres.

Some of the most conspicuous and largest ichneumonid wasps parasitize wood-dwelling insects, especially the larvae of longhorn beetles (Cerambycidae), jewel beetles (Buprestidae), and woodwasps (Siricidae). The

A female giant ichneumon (also called a sabre wasp; *Rhyssa persuasoria*) on a spruce stump. The long ovipositor, which is necessary for parasitizing hosts living deep in the wood, is clearly visible.

8 Natural enemies

largest species, the giant ichneumon *(Rhyssa persuasoria)*, has a body length of up to four centimetres (without ovipositor). It specializes in parasitizing woodwasp larvae that develop in the wood of freshly dead coniferous trees. The giant ichneumon is mainly guided in its search for woodwasp larvae that feed deep in the wood by volatile substances emanating from the larvae's excrement and from the associated symbiotic fungi (Spradbery 1977). The wasp locates a larva's position beneath the wood surface with the help of the sensory cells on its long antennae and at the tip of its ovipositor. When it has detected the exact position, it drives its up to five-centimetre-long ovipositor into the wood, thus reaching larvae hidden as far down in the wood as the length of its ovipositor. The parasitoid larvae hatch from the eggs deposited on the woodwasp larvae and slowly begin to consume their host. After one year, the adult giant ichneumons emerge and gnaw their way out of the wood.

Dolichomitus species are typical parasitoids of longhorn beetles. They detect and parasitize their hosts in a similar way to the giant ichneumon. Other parasitoids of wood-dwelling insects are listed among the natural enemies of bark beetles (Section 9.3).

In addition to the large parasitoids of wood insects, many small, inconspicuous species from different parasitoid wasp families parasitize the leaf- and needle-feeding larvae

A giant ichneumon female parasitizing a woodwasp larva hidden in some wood. While drilling, the ovipositor sheath gradually bends into a loop and only the actual drilling device, i.e., the ovipositor, penetrates the wood (a to c) until the female's abdomen reaches the wood with the sheath stretching out behind her (d).

An ichneumon wasp *Dolichomitus mesocentrus* looking for a longhorn beetle larva on a standing dead tree. It palpates the wood surface with its antennae (a) before placing the ovipositor exactly between its antennae tips (b) and starting to drill (c). It uses the ovipositor sheath initially to direct the needle-like ovipositor into the wood and then bends it back. The ovipositor is visible in (c) as a thin needle running along the body into the wood.

of moths and sawflies. These wasps play an important role in the regulation of potential pest populations during their mass outbreaks. The ichneumonid wasp *Phobocampe unicincta* (= *P. disparis*) and various braconid wasps (genus *Protapanteles*) are typical parasitoids of gypsy moth caterpillars. However, they can themselves be parasitized to a high degree by hyperparasitic parasitoids. Other

A parasitoid pupa and the remaining head capsule of its host, a longhorn beetle larva (lower right). (Photo courtesy of Forest Entomology WSL.)

8 Natural enemies

important parasitoid antagonists of leaf-feeding pests may be found in the genus *Bracon* and in the chalcid wasps.

Even small insect eggs are not safe from the tiny parasitoid chalcid wasps, which are a mere few tenths of a millimetre in size. These wasps are among the smallest insects worldwide. The wasp *Anastatus japonicus*, for example, lays its eggs in those of the gypsy moth. Subsequently, the entire development from larva to adult takes place in the parasitized egg.

Spider wasps (Pompilidae) are not related to the actual parasitoid wasp group (Terebrantes). These specialists paralyze spiders with a sting (idiobionts) and deposit each spider individually, together with an egg, in a hidden place. A few spider wasps (*Dipogon* spp.) build nests with several cells one behind the other, each containing an egg provided with one paralyzed crab spider.

The colourful, metallic cuckoo wasps (Chrysididae) parasitize the nests of various solitary bees and wasps. They deposit their eggs in the freshly constructed breeding cells of their hosts. The hatching larvae then feed on the host larvae and the stored food.

Several braconid wasps, such as *Atanycolus genalis*, parasitize longhorn beetle larvae.

This geometer moth larva has probably been parasitized by braconid wasp larvae, which bore out of the still living host and pupate directly on the body. The larva is freely hanging as it has lowered itself on a silk thread.

Parasitoid braconid wasp larvae have left a gypsy moth (*Lymantria dispar*) caterpillar and pupated next to it forming white cocoons. From each, an adult wasp (right: *Protapanteles porthetriae*) will eventually emerge.

An ichneumonid wasp *(Eridolius hofferi)* waiting beside a colony of birch sawfly *(Craesus septentrionalis)* larvae for a chance to parasitize a larva. The way they position their bodies and flip their abdomens synchronously in rhythm keeps deterring the wasp.

A hawk moth caterpillar infested with unidentified ectoparasitoid larvae.

This horse fly egg mass has been almost completely parasitized by scelionid wasps. The tiny wasps are just emerging.

Parasitoid flies

In addition to the predatory species, there are also parasitoid taxa among the dipterans. In contrast to parasitoid wasps, the ovipositor of parasitoid flies does not form a stinger. They deposit their eggs on the host's body surface. However, the larvae usually penetrate into the host's body after hatching and develop endoparasitically. How the larvae living in the haemolymph of their host acquire oxygen is interesting: They dock their spiracles (stigmata) to a spiracle or to a large tracheal branch of their host, or use the penetration hole through which they entered the host's body.

The most important parasitoid flies for regulating potential forest pest insects are

^
Cuckoo wasps (*Chrysis* sp.) develop parasitically in wild bee nests.

the tachinid flies (Tachinidae). The larvae of these endoparasitoids develop mostly in butterfly and moth caterpillars, but also in other insects, while the adult flies feed on nectar and honeydew. About 900 species of tachinids have been identified in Europe. Some of them, such as *Compsilura concinnata*, are extremely polyphagous and can develop in over 100 different host species. Others parasitize only very few, closely related species.

Some tachinid flies, such as *Tachina fera*, parasitize larger moth caterpillars. The main hosts of this species, which occurs in light forests and along forest edges, are owlet moths (Noctuidae), tent caterpillars (Lasiocampidae) and tussock moths (Lymantriinae), i.e., moth taxa that include potentially harmful pests for forestry. *Blepharipa pratensis* and

Dipogon species are among the few spider wasps found in forests. This female has supplied her larvae with crab spiders *(Diaea dorsata)*. The parasitoid larvae are clearly visible on the abdomens of the two spiders.

8 Natural enemies

> Several tachinid flies *(Exorista grandis)* emerging instead of the adult moth from the cocoon of a parasitized small emperor moth *(Saturnia pavonia).*

Parasetigena silvestris are powerful parasitoids of the above-mentioned gypsy moth. The female flies can lay thousands of eggs. The hatched larvae penetrate the caterpillars and feed on them from the inside, sometimes causing a gypsy moth caterpillar mortality exceeding 50 percent (Hoch et al. 2001). *Parasetigena silvestris* alone can account for more than two-thirds of total parasitism (Bogenschütz and Kammerer 1995). Like the forest caterpillar hunter (see Section 8.1), these tachinid flies have been exported to the USA to control the gypsy moth.

A representative of another dipteran family, the Bombyliidae, provides a classic example of hyperparasitism. The bee fly *Hemipenthes maura* parasitizes the pupae of some of the parasitoid tachinid flies mentioned earlier. Hyperparasitism can have a negative effect on the ability of tachinid flies to regulate outbreaks of harmful moth caterpillars.

174

A small emperor moth caterpillar with tiny white tachinid fly *(Exorista grandis)* eggs attached to its front (right) and on top of its middle.

8.4 True parasites

True parasites, such as lice on vertebrates or mites on butterflies or beetles, are always much smaller than their hosts. Parasites do not normally kill their host, but weaken it and make it more susceptible to disease. In general, both the larvae and adults of parasites live parasitically.

> The abdomens of tachinid flies are often heavily bristled at the end. This fly *(Leskia aurea)* has emerged from a yellowlegged clearwing moth *(Synanthedon vespiformis).*

8 Natural enemies

The larvae of the tachinid fly *Cylindromyia brassicaria* develop endoparasitically in shield bugs.

The development of a tachinid fly *(Blepharipa schineri)* in a gypsy moth caterpillar: (a) The fly egg is deposited on the surface of the caterpillar; the hatched larva develops endoparasitically in the caterpillar body. (b) At the end of the larva's development, it leaves the now shrunken host and (c) pupates in litter. (d) The fly emerges the following spring after overwintering.

These parasitoid tachinid larvae *(Phryxe erythrostoma)* have left the pupa of a hawk moth *(Sphinx pinastri)* and pupated next to it. Right: one of the emerged tachinid flies.

The bee fly *Hemipenthes maura* parasitizes the pupae of tachinid flies, which in turn develop parasitically in moth caterpillars.

While predatory mites may have a significant effect on the population dynamics of their prey (e.g., of bark beetles), parasitic mites play a minor role in regulating their hosts. The red or pale-coloured arachnids are often seen on butterflies, beetles, grasshoppers or harvestmen. Varroa mites, which can cause great damage in honeybee colonies, are the most well-known mites. The castor bean tick *(Ixodes ricinus)* is another notorious mite that infects not only animals, but also humans. It can transmit serious diseases such as encephalitis or Lyme disease (see Section 15.1).

The conspicuous larvae of the velvet mite *(Trombidium holosericeum)* attach themselves to and suck on various insects. However, their nymphs and adults live predatorily (see Section 8.2).

Among the insects, lice (Phthiraptera) and fleas (Siphonaptera) suck blood from mam-

8 Natural enemies

Ticks *(Ixodes ricinus)* between the bristles of a curled-up hedgehog (above the muzzle). A tick's body weight may increase by up to 200 times when it is sucking.

An adult tick female lying in wait for a mammal on the edge of a leaf.

Parasitic velvet mites *(Trombidium holosericeum)* larvae sucking on (above) a weevil *(Otiorhynchus apenninus)*, (left) a butterfly *(Melanargia galathea)*, and (right) a harvestman *(Phalangium opilio)*.

The introduced Varroa mite *(Varroa destructor)* sucks on adult bees and their brood.

↑
Some biting midges do not suck on warm-blooded animals, but on other insects. Here, *Forcipomyia eques* has attached itself to the wing veins of a lacewing *(Chrysopa perla)*. For its egg to mature, the parasite needs the host's haemolymph.

mals and birds, and they often specialize in certain host species. Lice eggs are called nits, such as those occurring as head lice on humans. Twisted-wing insects (Strepsiptera) live endoparasitically in the abdomen of cicadas, wasps and bees. So-called stylopized bees are those infected by *Stylops melittae* or other twisted-wing insects. Such an infection can be easily detected when the anterior part of the parasite's body protrudes between the segments of its host.

Among the Diptera, the flattened louse flies (Hippoboscidae) live as ectoparasites on the blood of mammals and birds. They cling, with their robust claws, to the fur or feathers of their host. Wingless species are transmitted via body contact. Louse fly larvae develop in the body of the female fly (viviparity). A common species in forests is the deer ked *(Lipoptena cervi)*. It attacks wildlife like roe deer and red deer, but also wild boar and badgers, attaching themselves to their skin to suck blood. Once established on a host, deer keds shed their now useless wings. Occasionally, they also attack and sting humans.

Flies and mosquitoes that suck blood mostly from warm-blooded animals form another dipteran category of parasites. In this case, the blood is not needed for larval development, but serves as a source of protein for females to produce eggs. This group includes well-known nuisance pests, such as

8 Natural enemies

mosquitoes (Culicidae), no-see-ums or biting midges (Ceratopogonidae), black flies (Simuliidae) and horseflies (Tabanidae).

Some fly species develop parasitically in wounds on vertebrates. The toadfly *(Lucilia bufonivora)* lays its eggs near the nostrils of toads and frogs. The hatched larvae then feed their way into the head of their hosts. Unlike with most parasites, this infestation inevitably leads to the death of the host.

This deer ked *(Lipoptena cervi)* is waiting for a wild animal. Right: this deer ked on a human arm has already shed its wings. (Photo on left courtesy of Forest Entomology WSL.)

8 Natural enemies

Antagonists of bark beetles 9

Predators and parasitoids of insects are described in general in the previous chapter. This chapter focuses on the natural enemies of bark beetles, which are considered to be the principal pest organisms in coniferous forests not just in Europe, but worldwide (see Section 14.3).

One enemy known already in the 19th century is the woodpecker, which can kill bark beetle broods. People also knew about the way of life of parasitoid wasps. However, it was not until the middle of the 20th century that specific studies revealed the importance of predatory and parasitic insects and mites in regulating bark beetle populations. Meanwhile, about 300 invertebrate bark beetle antagonists have been identified in Europe alone. The most recent information about the natural enemies of bark beetles is compiled in Wegensteiner et al. (2015).

In this chapter, the emphasis is on the antagonists of the most important bark beetle in Europe, the European spruce bark beetle *(Ips typographus)*. However, the same, or closely

This checkered beetle *Thanasimus formicarius* has caught a European spruce bark beetle *(Ips typographus)*. Both the larvae and adults of these predators feed on bark beetles.

related natural enemies, may also attack further bark beetle species that colonize coniferous and deciduous trees.

9.1 Prey and host location

How do predatory and parasitoid insects discover trees that have been colonized by bark beetles? How do parasitoid wasps locate the exact spot on the bark surface to put their ovipositor to parasitize a bark beetle larva hidden under the bark? They orientate themselves exclusively on the basis of chemical-olfactory cues. Predatory insects, in particular beetles and flies, are attracted to infested trees by volatiles produced by the tree, such as ethanol and α-pinene, as well as by pheromones. Pheromones are species-specific volatiles, namely monoterpenes such as cis-verbenol or ipsdienol, which are produced by the bark beetles to attract their conspecifics. The beetles produce so-called aggregation pheromones, i.e., volatiles that attract other beetles of their species, especially at the beginning of the colonization of a tree. These volatiles also serve predators as kairomones – substances that also attract predators. This is why they often arrive almost concurrently with bark beetles at freshly infested trees to lay their eggs. Right from when they hatch, the predators' larvae have a supply of bark beetle eggs and young larvae. These primary antagonists include, for example, checkered beetles and long-legged flies.

In contrast, most parasitoid wasps do not react to the pheromones the bark beetles produce during the early colonization phase. Instead, they rely on volatiles (oxidized monoterpenes) produced by fungi and microorgan-

When a checkered beetle catches a bark beetle (here a spruce bark beetle), it turns its prey's belly towards itself, cuts the prey in two between chest and abdomen, and then folds its head and thorax back. Afterwards, it eats the inside of the fore part before consuming the abdomen, leaving behind only the empty body shell.

The conspicuous, pink-coloured larvae of checkered beetles browse through bark beetle galleries feeding on their larvae and pupae.

isms in the bark beetles' feeding galleries. These substances occur in the beetles' excrement and the waste materials they produce. Thus parasitoids only arrive at a beetle-infested tree when their hosts are in the right instars for parasitism, i.e., when they are mainly older larvae or pupae. In contrast to larval parasitoids, adult parasitoids must arrive at the same time as their hosts, i.e., the adult bark beetles. Therefore, like the predators, they use the bark beetle pheromones as kairomones to find the trees when the beetles are just arriving and starting to bore into the bark.

Once larval parasitoids have detected an infested tree, they have to locate exactly where to insert their ovipositor so that they can lay an egg on a larva underneath. To this end, they probably use the same volatiles they use for identifying an infested tree, relying on tiny differences in the volatile concentrations.

Within a stem infested by bark beetles, the distribution of predatory and parasitoid insects differs: the predatory beetles and flies prefer to colonize the lower parts of the bole, while parasitoids are often confined to the thinner bark in the upper part of the stem or to branches because their ovipositors are relatively short. This separation is not strict, but it does reduce the competition between predators and parasitoids.

9.2 Predators

Checkered beetles

The colouring of the beetle *Thanasimus formicarius* from the checkered beetle family (Cleridae) is a striking black, white and red. It is undoubtedly the most conspicuous species among the almost 70 beetles that predate on bark beetles. It feeds on various bark beetle species when a larva and as an adult beetle, and includes more than 20 different bark beetle species, mainly on coniferous trees, in its diet (Gauss 1954). The adult beetle overpowers adult bark beetles when they are landing on the bark surface and starting to penetrate the bark or when just emerging from it. The predator reacts mainly to its prey's movement. It dissects its caught prey between the thorax and abdomen, and thrusts its head into the two body halves to feed, leaving behind just the empty shell of its prey.

Adult checkered beetles live for four to ten months, which is quite a long time for insects. The female lays 100 to 300 eggs in bark crevices in spring and summer. The hatched larvae enter the bark beetle galleries and, depending on the instar, feed on the eggs, larvae or pupae of their prey. After one to two months, they leave the bark beetle galleries to pupate. For most, this involves migrating down along the bark surface to the base of the stem, where they pupate in the outer bark or in the soil. Others pupate in the bark close to where they developed. The majority of adults emerge in autumn, but some do not emerge before the following spring. A checkered beetle larva consumes about 50 prey (Mills 1985), while the adult beetle – devouring up to five adult bark beetles per day – consumes many times more. This makes checkered beetles very effective natural enemies for bark beetles. These colourful beetles include several different species.

Development of a checkered beetle: After mating (a), the female lays her eggs in bark crevices, where the larva hatches in the bark beetle galleries. When fully grown, it produces a pupal chamber (b) lined with white secretion, where it pupates (c). The mature beetle then emerges one to two months later (d).

Other predatory beetles

While the family of bark-gnawing beetles (Trogositidae) in North America includes several important bark beetle predators, only two species are known in Europe. The most common is *Nemozoma elongatum*, which is known to be an antagonist of 16 bark beetle species that occur on coniferous and deciduous trees (Kenis et al. 2004). It plays a particularly important role as a natural enemy of the beech bark beetle *(Taphrorychus bicolor)*, as well as of the six-toothed spruce bark beetle *(Pityogenes chalcographus)*, which develops in fresh coniferous slash and in the branches of weakened young conifers. When in search of prey, *N. elongatum* is guided by the boring dust the bark beetles eject on the bark. The small predator is not able to catch bark beetles on the bark surface, but it fits perfectly with its elongated body in the beetle tunnels, where it can successfully grab and devour bark beetles. It usually lays its eggs on the bark around the bark beetles' entrance holes. The hatched larvae penetrate into the galleries to feed on bark beetle larvae, pupae and teneral adults. Each larva of this predator consumes 30 to 50 bark beetle larvae during its development (Dippel 1996). The beetles overwinter in the larval stage. Another species

Bark beetle predators from four different beetle families: (a) *Rhizophagus grandis* (Monotomidae), which is also used in biological control; (b) *Nemozoma elongatum* (Trogositidae), which is common on both coniferous and broadleaf trees; (c) *Nudobius lentus* (Staphylinidae), which, with its flattened, slender form, is well adapted to bark beetle tunnels; and (d) *Dromius quadrimaculatus* (Carabidae).

of bark-gnawing beetle is *Temnochila caerulea*, which is known, especially in Southern Europe, as an antagonist of the six-spined engraver beetle.

In addition, numerous other predators from 13 different beetle families predate on bark beetles. The root-eating beetles (Monotomidae), which are only a few millimetres long, include ten species of the genus *Rhizophagus* in Europe that are known to be natural enemies of bark beetles. These predatory beetles feed on the eggs or larvae of bark beetles and other insects that live subcortically. One of the most common species is *Rhizophagus depressus*, which consumed, in an experiment, 14 bark beetle larvae during their ten-week larval development (Hérard and Mercadier 1996). *Rhizophagus grandis* is a rare example of a predator specialising in just one bark beetle species. It feeds exclusively on the larvae of the great spruce bark beetle (*Dendroctonus micans*) and is used to control this bark beetle species in France.

Some of the sap beetles (Nitidulidae) are also predatory. During their larval development, they consume dozens of bark beetle larvae. The *Corticeus* species are darkling beetles (Tenebrionidae) that enter the galleries of bark beetles through their entrance or ventilation holes. They are, however, so-called facultative predators, which means that they also feed on other food, such as fungi or insect remains.

Among the numerous species of rove beetles (Staphylinidae), *Placusa depressa* and *Nudobius lentus* in particular are known to be bark beetle predators. *Nudobius lentus* is found especially frequently in pheromone traps put up for catching spruce bark beetles because it reacts to the same pheromones.

A typical community of bark feeders and their natural enemies underneath pine bark. The two teneral beetles of the six-spined engraver beetle (*Ips sexdentatus*) are still light brown in colour. The pink larva is a predatory checkered beetle. The two larvae of the steelblue jewel beetle (*Phaenops cyanea*) have a widened fore-end, and the larva of the predator *Temnochila caerulea* is cream-coloured.

Other beetle families that include predatory species are the hister beetles (Histeridae), the flat bark beetles (Silvanidae), the ironclad beetles (Zopheridae), and the ground beetles (Carabidae).

Predatory flies

More than 30 dipteran species are known as predators of bark beetles (Kenis et al. 2004). Some species from the lance fly (Lonchaeidae) and especially some from the long-legged fly (Dolichopodidae) families are among the most effective enemies of bark beetles, even though only their larvae feed predatorily on the bark beetle broods. Most adult flies are either not predatory or suck only on small, soft-shelled insects. The most important representatives of long-legged flies belong to the genus *Medetera*, of which ten predatory species are known to be antagonists of the European spruce bark beetle, in particular *Medetera signaticornis*.

The long-legged flies are among the first antagonists to arrive on a newly infested tree. They mate on the bark surface. Each female then lays up to 120 eggs in bark crevices and under bark scales near the bark beetles' entrance holes. The flies prefer standing rather than lying trees and lower stem sections rather than higher ones. After hatching, the young larvae migrate to the galleries and feed on the bark beetles' eggs and larvae by rupturing the integument of the prey with their mandibular hooks and sucking out their body fluid. To move from one bark beetle tunnel to another, the fly larvae depend on the feeding activity of the bark beetles as they cannot on their own eat their way through the phloem. During their development, they consume 5 to 20 larvae, depending on the size of the prey species (Hopping 1947). The larvae pupate

The inconspicuous adults of the long-legged fly *Medetera signaticornis* live on mites and small insects, but their larvae are important predators on bark beetle broods.

This *Medetera* fly larva (above) has scratched open a bark beetle larva of *Dendroctonus ponderosae* (below) and is slurping out its body contents.

9 Antagonists of bark beetles

The larvae of the almost four-millimetre-long lance fly *Lonchaea bruggeri* are voracious predators in bark beetle galleries.

either at the end of summer with the flies emerging before winter, or the larvae spend the winter in the brood trees.

Among the lance flies, only the genus *Lonchaea* lives under tree bark. The way of life of these flies is not yet fully known. Some feed saprophagously on waste products, while others, especially those on coniferous wood, predate on the eggs, larvae and even adults of bark beetles. They feed very wastefully and kill more than the five or six larvae needed for their development (Morge 1961). If bark beetle larvae are no longer present, lance fly larvae also live cannibalistically. New, previously unknown species are still being found in Europe.

In addition to the two families mentioned above, some robber flies (Asilidae), soldier flies (Stratiomyidae), flutter-wing flies (Pallopteridae) and house flies (Muscidae) are also among dipteran bark beetle predators.

The long-legged flies in particular are considered to be ecologically very important. They are often the most abundant antagonists found in bark beetle galleries in both deciduous and coniferous forests. The rate at which they consume their prey increases with increasing supply ('functional response'), which can lead to the larvae of the genus *Medetera* alone causing mortalities of up to 90 percent (Hopping 1947).

Other predatory insects

Some other groups of insects feed at least facultatively on bark beetles. The snakeflies (Raphidioptera), which are not related to the dipteran flies despite their name, are typical forest insects whose larvae live on bark surfaces, where they feed on insect eggs. They prefer the lower half of the tree stem where the bark is thicker, more fissured and provides better shelter. They can, however, only exploit the bark beetle larvae if the bark has been loosened by woodpeckers or by the maturation feeding of the teneral bark beetles, allowing them to access the bark beetles' breeding galleries. Their role in regulating bark beetles is therefore rather small, especially as they also eat eggs laid by other predators. The most relevant snakeflies are *Puncha ratzeburgi* and *Phaeostigma notata*, which typically occur in subalpine coniferous forests up to the tree line.

Scoloposcelis pulchella from the flower bug family (Anthocoridae) is the best known of the few true bug species to feed on bark beetles.

Mites

Predatory mites, which belong to the arachnids, are less conspicuous bark beetle predators. When examined under a magnifying glass, the rich mite fauna in a bark beetle gallery are often visible. In galleries of the European spruce bark beetle alone, which is the best investigated bark beetle species in this respect, 38 mite species have been found (Moser *et al*. 1989), and as many as 96 species are associated with the American bark beetle *Dendroctonus frontalis* (Moser and Roton 1971). The majority of these mites live on fungi, nematodes or other organisms. The tiny mites use the bark beetles merely as vectors (transport vehicles; see Section 11.1) to move from one tree to another and tap new food sources. Only a few species live predatorily on bark beetles and suck on their eggs, larvae and pupae. Important genera are *Iponemus, Pyemotes, Proctolaelaps* and *Dendrolaelaps*. The first two genera are actually parasitoids, since a single bark beetle egg is sufficient for the development of a mite larva. The adult mites suck on bark beetle larvae and pupae as well. The significance of mites

A female *Puncha ratzeburgi* with her first thoracic segment characteristically extended.

A larva of *Phaeostigma notata* feeding on a still soft teneral six-toothed spruce bark beetle (*Pityogenes chalcographus*). The larva is able to hold on to the bark surface with an adhesive organ at the end of its abdomen, which also helps it move along the bark surface.

9 Antagonists of bark beetles

A predatory mite sucking on a spruce bark beetle's egg. The tiny mites only grow to be about half a millimetre long, and are much smaller than the beetle egg. (Photo courtesy of Forest Entomology WSL.)

in regulating bark beetles has probably been greatly underestimated since death rates in bark beetle eggs of up to 90 percent have been observed (Gäbler 1947).

9.3 Parasitoid wasps

All bark beetle instars – eggs, larvae, pupae and adults – can serve as hosts for specialised parasitoids. Eggs are very rarely parasitised, probably because of their small size. Only the tiny *Trichogramma semblidis* undergoes its entire development in the egg of ash bark beetles (*Hylesinus* spp.). It is the only true egg parasitoid of bark beetles. In contrast, most parasitoids develop ectoparasitically on bark beetle larvae or pupae. For oviposition, almost all species penetrate the stem bark with their ovipositor. The length of their ovipositor and the thickness of the bark therefore determine their potential for parasitism. Once parasitoids have successfully located a host, they paralyze it by injecting it with venom and then deposit an egg on its body surface. A few species slip through the bark beetles' entrance holes and parasitize the larvae from the maternal galleries. For these species, bark thickness is not relevant. After hatching, the parasitoid larva consumes the body content of its host, leaving behind only its body shell and head capsule.

Finally, adult parasitoids also exist. They attack bark beetles when they are boring into or out of the bark, and inject an egg into them by piercing their ovipositor through their pronotum or elytra. The parasitized bark beetles enter the bark as normal and start to produce eggs. Their productivity, however, is reduced because the parasitic larvae gradually eat the body contents of the host beetles during their development and the beetle eventually dies. The larva pupates inside the beetle and the adult wasp leaves it through a hole gnawed at the end of the beetle's body (declivity). It finally emerges from the bark into the open air through one of the bark beetles' exit holes.

So-called kleptoparasitism is an interesting phenomenon whereby species that are less successful in detecting host larvae steal their host from other parasitic species (Mills 1991). It is, apparently, not uncommon in the parasitic wasps of bark beetles. Kleptoparasitoids wait until the other species has tracked down a larva and is about to insert its ovipositor into the bark. The kleptoparasitoid then pushes the firstcomer aside and starts, at the same place, to parasitize the larva.

Parasitic wasps are generally more restricted to certain bark beetle species than the predators. Egg and adult parasitoids especially have a very narrow range of hosts. The adult parasitoid *Tomicobia seitneri*, for example, attacks almost exclusively adults of the European spruce bark beetle. However, larval parasitoids, i.e., the majority of parasitic wasps, are less specific and even accept hosts from different genera (oligophagy). Adult wasps only feed on pollen, nectar and honeydew. The energy they take up increases their egg production and extends their life span.

Braconid wasps

Braconid wasps (Braconidae) are another important family of parasitoids. About 60 European species are known to parasitize bark beetles. The range of braconid species on deciduous trees differs from that on coniferous trees. Some adult parasitoids are important, but most species live ectoparasitically on fully grown larvae. One of the most common species, i.e., *Coeloides bostrichorum*, attacks bark beetles on various coniferous tree species, preferably at lower elevations. Its five-

The braconid wasp *Coeloides bostrichorum* can even parasitize larvae under thicker bark thanks to its long ovipositor.

millimetre-long ovipositor is one of the longest of all parasitic wasps of bark beetles. With it, it can reach larvae living deep inside thick bark that are not accessible to other wasps. *Dendrosoter protuberans*, another species in this family, parasitizes a wide range of bark beetles on broadleaf trees.

Pteromalids

The second important family of parasitoid wasps are the pteromalids (Pteromalidae), which are extremely diverse. It encompasses approximately 35 species of bark beetle parasitoids, most of which are larval parasitoids, as well as some adult parasitoids and hyperparasitoids (both facultative and obligatory), which attack other parasitic wasps. Some species can parasitize an extremely wide range of bark beetle hosts on conifers and broadleaves. One of the most common species is *Roptrocerus xylophagorum*. It infests bark beetles from at least ten genera, including economically relevant species such as the pine bark beetle (*Ips acuminatus*), the European spruce bark beetle, the northern bark beetle (*Ips duplicatus*) and the two pine shoot beetles (*Tomicus* spp.). *Roptrocerus xylophagorum* differs from all other parasitoids in that it slips through the bark beetles' entrance holes and parasitizes the larvae in the maternal galleries. It is especially successful when the bark beetles' breeding density is high because the larval galleries then run close to the maternal ones due to lack of space. At low densities, the larval galleries branch off almost perpendicularly from the maternal gallery, which prevents *R. xylophagorum* from accessing its hosts. This parasitoid is also successful in the stellate galleries of the six-toothed spruce bark beetle, whose larval galleries are closer

Probably very few European spruce bark beetles will emerge from these galleries because virtually all the larvae have been parasitized. The pupal chambers house the cocoons of the braconid wasp *C. bostrichorum* instead of bark beetle pupae.
⌄

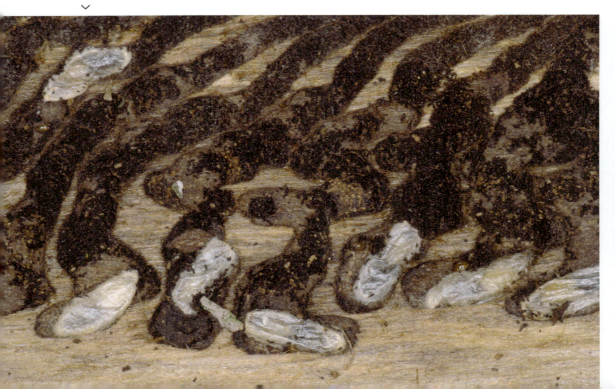

Females of the pteromalid wasp *Roptrocerus xylophagorum* access the beetles' galleries through their entrance holes to parasitize the beetle larvae.

to the maternal ones. It can, however, also parasitize through thin bark.

Some pteromalid species parasitize adult bark beetles. The most common representative is *Tomicobia seitneri*, which parasitizes beetles of the genus *Ips*. The larva develops inside the body of its host, and the fully developed wasp emerges from the dead beetle through a hole it gnaws in its body. This natural enemy has only a slight effect because parasitized beetles continue to produce eggs for some time, and because *T. seitneri* can itself

The larvae of ectoparasitic parasitoids first feed on the outside of a bark beetle larva (top). Towards the end of the parasitoid's development, only the integument and head capsule of the consumed host are left behind (bottom). (Photo courtesy of Forest Entomology WSL.)

9 Antagonists of bark beetles

The just under five-millimetre-long pteromalid wasp *Rhopalicus tutela* is one of the most common parasitoid species. It parasitizes bark beetles on both coniferous and broadleaf trees.

be parasitized by the hyperparasitoid *Mesopolobus typographi*.

In addition to the two families of parasitic wasps already mentioned, there are about 30 species of other bark beetle parasitoids (Wegensteiner *et al*. 2015). Most are small species less than half a centimetre in size, and almost all are larval parasitoids. Some, especially among the eurytomids (Eurytomidae), are facultative hyperparasitoids.

This adult parasitoid *Tomicobia seitneri* has landed on a European spruce bark beetle to inject an egg through its pronotum (above). The hatched larva feeds inside the beetle for about two weeks before it pupates. Afterwards, the adult wasp emerges through a hole from the empty beetle shell. (Photo on bottom courtesy of Forest Entomology WSL.)

9.4 Woodpeckers

The natural enemies of bark beetles include not only invertebrates, but also woodpeckers. Some other birds also sporadically catch bark beetles in flight or on the surface of bark, but woodpeckers have the most impact. They are the only birds that are able to reach beetles and their larvae hidden under the bark (see Section 7.1). Depending on the woodpecker species, they exploit bark beetles as food seasonally. In winter, other food sources such as caterpillars or ants are scarce or difficult to access. For some woodpecker species, bark beetles then make up to 99 percent of their diet (Baldwin 1968) at a time when the energy they need to maintain their body temperature is much higher.

Woodpeckers can contribute both directly and indirectly to bark beetle mortality. They peck beetles from the bark surface and dig out larvae, pupae and teneral beetles directly from the bark. But they also hack off chunks of bark containing bark beetle broods, which then fall to the ground, where the brood either desiccates, is picked up by birds or is eaten by predatory insects and small mammals. Broods remaining in the bark of a tree that has been perforated by woodpeckers dry up faster and die more quickly due to cold spells or marked temperature changes. They are also more accessible as food for other birds.

The three-toed woodpecker is a natural enemy of bark beetles in spruce forests that can have considerable impact. It loosens infested bark pieces from the stem, taking care that they do not fall and spill out the larvae. It then picks out the freshly exposed larvae. Examinations of the stomach contents of three-toed woodpeckers suggest that one individual consumes about 3200 beetle larvae per winter day (Wimmer and Zahner 2010). Infested trees attract woodpeckers from the vicinity and a prolonged, large-scale infestation allows woodpeckers to reproduce more intensely and thus to increase their population density. Woodpeckers may therefore have a strong impact on bark beetle populations, particularly at higher elevations with only one beetle generation. At lower altitudes, how-

The tiny *Entedon methion* from the family Eulophidae is only about two millimetres long. It parasitizes the eggs of bark and anobiid beetles by entering the galleries through the beetles' entrance holes.

ever, the reproductive rate of bark beetles usually remains higher than that of woodpeckers. During an outbreak of the spruce beetle *(Dendroctonus rufipennis)* in the USA, beetle mortality caused by woodpeckers – in particular three-toed woodpeckers – was around 50 percent. This mortality occurred mainly during the winter months (McCambridge and Knight 1972).

Woodpeckers in North America have been observed to behave in an interesting way: in their search for western pine beetle larvae *(Dendroctonus brevicomis)*, they stripped the bark down to a residual thickness of about half a centimetre. As a result, even parasitic wasps with short ovipositors were able to successfully parasitize the remaining larvae. This increased the local parasitism rate as much as ten times (Otvos 1979).

9.5 Pathogens

Like other insects, bark beetles may also be attacked by various fungi, viruses, protozoa or nematodes. Fungi are not only the most conspicuous but also the pathogens with the most impact. Their spores germinate on the cuticle of the body shell. The hyphae penetrate the insect's exoskeleton and spread throughout its body so that the infested beetle dies under the bark while still in its gallery. The fungal mycelium then grows through the cuticle, encasing the beetle and forming spores with which it spreads again. Numerous fungal species are associated with bark beetles. For the European spruce bark beetle, the fungus with the greatest impact is *Beauveria bassiana*, but *Metarhizium anisopliae* can also have – to a lesser extent – an effect (Keller et al. 2004).

The three-toed woodpecker (female on the left, male on the right) lives mainly in spruce forests rich in deadwood. It is a typical natural enemy of bark beetles.

A European spruce bark beetle infected with the fungus *Beauveria bassiana*.

For the beetles, infections with these fungi are fatal. Infection rates, especially towards the end of a mass outbreak, may be as high as 90 percent and more (Wegensteiner et al. 2015). The effects of fatal fungal infestations on the bark beetle larvae and beetles in their galleries should not be underestimated.

Other pathogens, such as viruses and unicellular organisms (e.g., bacteria, protozoa, microsporidia and amoebae), are ingested by feeding bark beetles and multiply in their intestinal tissue, where the toxins destroy their cells. Viruses are quite host-specific, but little is known about their distribution and effect on bark beetles. The same applies to bacteria and other microorganisms that, under laboratory conditions, cause high long-term mortality (Wegensteiner et al. 2015).

Nematodes or roundworms thrust their mouthparts – in the shape of a hollow stylet – into their host's tissue and suck it out. Roundworms, which are at most a few millimetres long, are actually parasitic, but are usually listed as pathogens. Nematodes enter their hosts' bodies through their skin, mouth or anal openings, where they then puncture cells and suck them out. Their infected hosts can, however, still complete their development. In adult bark beetles, the nematodes produce eggs and the young larvae develop in the beetle up to the last larval instar. They then migrate to the rectum and are excreted with the faeces. After a final moult, the adult nematodes mate and the females look for a new host. In other species, only certain larval instars are parasitic, while the others live freely in bark beetle galleries. Bark beetles may be infected by hundreds of nematodes, which then affect the beetles' fitness and reproductive capacity, or even lead to their death. How much nematodes contribute to regulating bark beetles is unclear, but they probably have a rather small effect.

9.6   Impact of antagonists

Although woodpeckers are the most conspicuous natural enemies of bark beetles, they are not considered to play a decisive role in the regulation of bark beetle outbreaks. There are several reasons for this: (i) the generations of bark beetles and woodpeckers are not synchronous; (ii) the reproductive rate of woodpeckers is much lower than that of bark beetles and cannot increase even when the supply of prey is abundant; (iii) the breeding and roosting places of woodpeckers in a forest are limited because they are territorial; and (iv) most woodpeckers switch to other prey according to supply and season. On the other hand, their mobility means they can quickly get to bark beetle-affected stands from adjacent forests. In infested areas in Scandinavia, for example, the woodpecker density has been found to be as much as 21 times higher than in comparable areas (Fayt et al. 2005), and in North America it increased by a factor of 50 during an infestation by the spruce beetle *(Dendroctonus rufipennis)* (Koplin 1969). However, woodpeckers have their greatest impact between outbreaks when the population densities of bark beetles are low. They extend this latency period by delaying the onset of outbreaks and accelerating the collapse of bark beetle populations.

Although the mortality of bark beetles due to predatory and parasitoid arthropods as well

This predatory bark-gnawing beetle *Temnochila caerulea* has a six-spined engraver beetle in sight as prey. The species is rare in Central Europe and is considered a relict species of primeval forests.

as to pathogens has been well studied under both laboratory and field conditions, it is not possible to generally quantify how much effect they have. However, predatory insects and mites are known to cause high mortality rates among bark beetles and are thus considered very important. Since predators are not restricted to particular prey species but also feed on other prey, a certain basic density of predatory insects is always present. They can then react swiftly when a bark beetle outbreak creates an abundant supply. Predators are always present in higher densities than parasitoids, and usually consume prey both as juveniles and adults. Similarly, the more monophagous parasitoids are able to react very quickly to a marked increase in bark beetles, as a study in mountain spruce forests showed after a storm caused extensive windthrow (Wermelinger *et al.* 2013b). The number of bark beetles and parasitoids increased very quickly and virtually synchronously, but then collapsed after three to four years. After this time, the bark of the windthrown timber became too dry for both beetles and parasitoid wasps to develop. At lower elevations, bark desiccates even faster. The mortality rate of bark beetles due to parasitoids may be as high as 100 percent in certain cases (Sachtleben 1952). Nevertheless, parasitoids are considered less important than predators.

How great the combined impact of antagonistic organisms is depends on numerous factors: the weather conditions, season, outbreak phase, interactions between antagonists (woodpeckers and predatory arthropods also feed on other predatory or parasitoid insects), local special characteristics and, last but not least, the control measures taken by humans. If there is a large supply of weakened host trees and if the bark beetle density is sufficiently high, natural enemies, including pathogens, cannot prevent bark beetle outbreaks. Depending on temperature and the susceptibility of the host trees, they do, however, play a major role during the latency phases between outbreaks and in the collapse of beetle populations during mass propagations (see Section 14.3).

9 Antagonists of bark beetles

Ecological significance of red wood ants 10

Dozens of different ant species can be found in a forest. Most are small and live in wood, litter, soil or even treetops. This chapter, however, is devoted exclusively to the large, mound-building red wood ants of the genus *Formica*, which have particularly diverse functions in forest ecosystems. Five *Formica* species commonly occur in Central European forests: *Formica rufa, F. polyctena, F. lugubris, F. paralugubris* and *F. aquilonia*. The black-backed meadow ant *(F. pratensis)*, which also belongs to the so-called *Formica-rufa* group, mainly colonizes open habitats. All species have a similar way of life, but their population sizes, number of queens and food composition may differ. In the following, most of the information refers to *F. polyctena* and *F. rufa*. Wood ants' biology, ecology and significance have been extensively studied in the past –

For red wood ants, aphids have two important functions: worker ants rely on the carbohydrate-rich honeydew of certain aphids for their operating energy, and for the queens and their broods aphids serve as a source of protein.

especially in Germany – and are summarised in the standard work of Gösswald (2012), which is the basis for much of this chapter.

10.1 Life forms and natural enemies

Ant colonies

The social behaviour of red wood ants is highly developed. They live in tightly organized colonies with different social castes that have clearly defined tasks. At the focus of each colony are one or more queens. Some so-called monogynous nests of *F. rufa* have only one queen. If the queen of a monogynous colony dies, the colony becomes extinct. Other *F. rufa* nests as well as those of other species can be polygynous with sometimes hundreds of queens, or even, in *F. polyctena*, thousands. Queens are only winged until their nuptial flight, after which they shed their wings and remain in the nest for the rest of their lives. Here, they are fed and cared for by the worker ants. The queens' main task is the production of eggs – at least 30 per day. Females develop from fertilized (diploid) eggs and males from unfertilized (haploid) eggs. Whether the eggs are fertilized or not depends, among other things, on the queen's age and the nest temperature. It is really remarkable how a queen acquires enough sperm on her single nuptial flight to supply her throughout her whole life, especially as queens can live for up to 20 years! The queen controls the development of her colony not only by producing offspring, but also by emitting pheromones. These trigger the nursing behaviour of the worker ants and probably also suppress their sexual maturation.

The other female caste consists of the non-reproductive workers. Worker ants have basically the same genetic make-up as queens, but they are smaller and usually have vestigial sexual organs. Female workers can live for up

Young queens have wings only until their nuptial flight ends. After mating, they shed their wings and spend the rest of their lives laying eggs in the nest.

A *Formica aquilonia* worker ant.

to three years. During their lifetimes they perform tasks both inside and outside the nest. Young female workers first have jobs inside, where their main task is to look after the brood in the nest. They coat the eggs with saliva to keep them moist. This also prevents them getting a fungal infection and makes it easier to transport them as they tend to stick together. They prepare the prey brought in from outside to feed to the larvae and move larvae and pupae around within the nest according to their developmental stage. The interior workers also feed the queens, which never leave the nest. Other tasks include maintaining and repairing the nest, regulating the nest's temperature, getting rid of the empty pupal exuvia, and defending the nest against invaders. The interior workers specialise in carrying out

A *Formica lugubris* male getting ready for take-off. Males are always winged, and die shortly after their nuptial flight.

10 Red wood ants

particular tasks, which are divided more finely over time.

Older workers switch from tasks inside the nest to outside duties, where they are primarily responsible for foraging for food. They hunt for insects, collect the honeydew of aphids and transport the food to the nest. The exterior workers also assemble the material for nest building and carry the nest's inmates when some of the colony moves to another nest. The timing of the transition from inside to outside duties varies greatly and does not necessarily have to be conclusive.

Male ants are always winged during their short adult lifetimes. Their sole task is to mate with the swarming queens after leaving the nest. Soon afterwards they die.

The size of a colony depends not only on the ant species but also on environmental conditions. *Formica polyctena* forms the largest populations. A large nest of this species can consist of 500 000 to five million individuals. Between November and February only the overwintering adult workers and queens live in a wood ants' nest. A few workers remain in the mound, but most of the colony members lie torpid in nest chambers belowground. The ants are virtually inactive during this period and live exclusively on the fat reserves stored in their own bodies.

Nutrition

The industrious red wood ants have a very varied diet. Roughly one-third of their food intake consists of insects and two-thirds of honeydew. The insect prey serves as a source of protein for rearing larvae and feeding the queens, while honeydew provides the energy the busy workers need. The annual food requirement of a large wood ants' nest with one

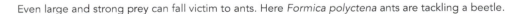

Even large and strong prey can fall victim to ants. Here *Formica polyctena* ants are tackling a beetle.

million ants is about 30 kilograms of insects (corresponding to approximately 10 million captured insects) and 500 kilograms of honeydew from aphids. In addition, they also consume some vegetable matter. Red wood ants are not specialised hunters. They collect whichever prey insects are most abundant and easiest to catch, i.e., mainly aphids, flies and moth caterpillars. Information about particularly rich hunting grounds is passed on to other workers. If the prey is large, they coordinate the hunt, and the forager ants call up recruitment by emitting volatiles. They then jointly capture the prey, secure it and transport it to the nest. Ants may also exploit larger carrion and, if food is lacking, may even consume their own brood, especially late-season larvae.

The honeydew, which aphids, especially lachnids (Lachnidae), secrete in the tree canopy, is the ants' source of carbohydrates. Red wood ants harvest the secretion and literally milk the aphids. They stroke them with their antennae, which stimulates them to secrete more honeydew.

About half of the food is transported to the nest in liquid or soft form in the ants' crop (Horstmann 1974). The crop is also called the communal stomach because its contents are regurgitated in the nest and distributed to the interior ants, which then use it for themselves and for the brood. This exchange of food is called trophallaxis. The content of one crop is passed on to about 80 other ants. Only when the crop is emptied, does the passage to the foraging worker's own stomach open, enabling it to digest the food itself. The ants exchange not only food, but also semiochemicals together with the food. These carry information about queens, food and enemies.

Given the opportunity, ants also accept carrion, such as this dead slow-worm, as food.

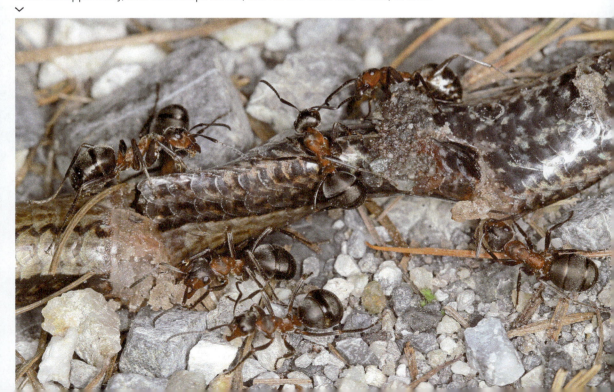

^
The members of a red wood ant colony engage in a lively exchange of food (trophallaxis), passing on at the same time important information in chemical form, for example about food type, the queen's condition, brood development or nest parasites.

Reproduction and development

Early in spring, the workers appear on the nest's surface, and shortly afterwards the queens, to sunbathe and absorb heat. Slowly the ants become active again and repair the nest where necessary. The queen starts producing the reproductive offspring, i.e., queens and males. For this purpose, she lays so-called winter eggs along the periphery of the mound. There the brood is cared for and fed by the youngest workers. The workers still live on their reserves and, at this point in time, receive hardly any food from outside the nest. They feed the hatched larvae with

A worker ant descending from a spruce with its abdomen full to bursting with honeydew it has harvested from aphids.
∨

Formica polyctena workers tending a colony of black willow aphids (*Pterocomma salicis*).

10 Red wood ants

a very nutritious secretion they produce in their glands. Without this secretion, the female larvae would become workers instead of queens and the males would die. After the fourth larval stage, the larvae moult to pupae embedded in cocoons. After a total of about five weeks of development, the winged reproductive sexes – queens and males – emerge. They swarm out and copulate in May/June under favourable weather conditions. However, mating can also occur directly in the nest.

The queens retreat inside the nest after having deposited their winter eggs. This is important because otherwise they would compete with the newly developing queens and males, and the nursing workers would give them preferential treatment. In addition, the established queens release a pheromone that would prevent the maturation of the new queens.

Inside the nest, the queen dedicates herself from now on to the production of summer eggs. These larvae are also fed and looked after by the workers, but they do not receive any gland secretions. During their development, the larvae are moved higher and higher up in the nest. Finally, the pupae are taken into the warm and dry heat centre of the mound to mature. Since the larvae hatching from the summer eggs are raised without secretions, they always develop into wingless workers. Furthermore, the pheromone released by the nearby queens prevents them from developing into additional queens. Young workers are produced until about September, when the colony starts to stock up on body reserves and prepare for the winter. From October on, the overwintering of the nest begins, and the ants seal the mound with sand and earth. They spend the winter clustered together in groups in the nest's chambers belowground.

In spring, the larvae and pupae of the sexual castes develop just below the surface of the nest.

A female worker moving a pupal cocoon (mistakenly sometimes called 'ant eggs') on the mound's periphery.

Ants' natural enemies

Although red wood ants can spray venomous formic acid from glands on their abdomen to defend themselves, they have numerous enemies. Their most important enemies are – at least among arthropods – other ants. Colonies of the same species have the same requirements and occupy the same ecological niche. This is why different ant colonies compete fiercely with each other to defend and expand their territory, and fight over productive aphid colonies.

Some insects are specialised predators on ants. They capture individual ants but do not endanger a colony as a whole. For example, the larvae of antlion lacewings (Myrmeleontidae), which are the real antlions, dig funnel-shaped pit traps in sandy soil and hide at the bottom. If an ant falls into such a pit, the antlion fires sand at it to make the ant slide into its wide-open jaws. Afterwards the antlion sucks out the prey. The ants that fall victim to antlions are mainly from smaller species.

Ant bag beetles (*Clytra* spp.) have developed a rather sophisticated predation strategy. The female drops an egg camouflaged with scales onto an ant mound, where the ants treat it as construction material and transfer it into the nest. The hatched beetle larva then feeds on the ant eggs and larvae, enclosed in a protective casing. Other natural enemies of red wood ants include mites, rove beetles (Staphylinidae), various parasitoid wasps and flies, and spiders specializing in ants.

Some vertebrate species are also important natural enemies of ants (see Section 7.1). Top of the list are green and grey-headed

10 Red wood ants

Red wood ants produce a venom containing formic acid in glands at the ends of their abdomens. They can spray it across several decimetres to defend themselves against an enemy and also use it for hunting prey.

Antlions (larvae of antlion lacewings, Myrmeleontidae) wait lurking for prey in sandy places. They hide at the bottom of the funnel-shaped pits waiting for ants to slip down. They then suck out their prey with their long sickle-like jaws (see the bottom left of the picture on the right).

woodpeckers, which feed mainly on ants. In addition, wild boars and badgers like to rummage through anthills in search of beetle larvae. They make holes, destroying the nest's structure, allowing rain to get into the nest. This can severely weaken an ant colony.

In addition to ants' real enemies, some species live in ant nests without directly harming them (myrmecophily). They benefit from the stable conditions in the nest and are relatively well protected there. However, the species of ant nest 'tenants' can range from those that are purely myrmecophilous to more antagonistic ones.

10.2 The ant nest

Ants often build their nests over old tree stumps. Each nest has an aboveground mound (or anthill), which can be up to more than one metre high, while the rest is belowground. The nest may extend as much as one to two metres belowground and be just as wide. Flatter mounds often have a deeper nest belowground, and vice versa. Ants prefer to build their nests in sunlit places along forest edges and pathways, and in clearings in conifer or broadleaf forests. Dense and uniform beech forests are unsuitable. However, a single conifer close to the nest may produce sufficient honeydew, as the tree will house aphids (especially from the *Cinara* species) all year round.

Ants use various materials to construct their anthills, such as conifer needles, bud scales, bits of branch, leaves, but also locally abundant non-vegetable matter such as small stones. If resin particles are available, they incorporate them as adhesives to stabilize the mound and to, at the same time, ward off pathogens. Nests tend to be larger in coniferous forests than in deciduous forests, where less construction material is available. Tunnels in-

A red wood ant nest with its typical, regularly shaped mound. The belowground part is about the same size. The nest needs at least a few hours of direct sunlight every day.

The centre of the ant nest is usually an old tree stump or a piece of wood.

Resin particles stabilize the nest mound and have an antiseptic effect.

side the nest connect the numerous chambers in which the brood is raised. The ants keep turning the material in the anthill around systematically. An experiment using dyed needles showed that it takes them a good month to complete the turnover of the entire mound (Kloft 1959). Sometimes a ring of excavated soil surrounds the mound, which indicates how far the belowground nest expands.

The main building materials for an ant nest are needles, pieces of wood and twigs, scales from buds and cones, and bits of leaf.

Thermoregulation

The temperature of a fully functioning ant nest remains relatively constant at 25 to 30 °C from about March to October. The ants actively maintain the temperature in this narrow range using different ways of heating and cooling for so-called 'thermoregulation'. An important heat source is solar radiation. The larger the mound, the more radiant energy it can absorb and the faster it warms up. This is why anthills in dark, cool forests are often larger than those in light, sunny forests. In spring, wood ants actively transport heat. The worker ants move out onto the surface of the mound when the first sunrays strike the nest and warm themselves in the sun. They then retreat into the still cold nest interior, where they release heat as they cool down, which warms the nest. They continue this heat transport until the target temperature is reached. In addition, the ants' metabolic heat also increases the nest temperature.

In summer, the nest must be protected from overheating. Here ventilation shafts come into play. They lead down inside the nest from the nest's surface and can be opened or closed during the day as required. On cold days and at night they are closed.

10.3 Establishing a colony

On warm or sultry days between April and July – depending on the elevation – the winged sexual castes emerge from their parental nest by the thousands. They often meet at higher points to mate. In polygynous nests, the young queens sometimes mate with the males directly in the nest. After the nuptial flight, the males die and the queens shed their wings, as they no longer need them from

In spring, red wood ants sunbathe on the surface of the mound. They transport the absorbed heat energy into the initially cool interior of the nest and increase its temperature to a relatively stable 25 to 30 °C.

Copulation of *Formica lugubris*. The queen (right) is considerably larger than the male (left).

now on. Each queen mates only once during her entire lifetime, and the sperm she takes up remains fertile for years. The further fate of a young queen varies tremendously. In general, the likelihood that she will be able to successfully establish herself as a queen in a nest is very small. In polygynous species, such as *P. polyctena*, the young queens that have the best chances are those that have mated in their nest and have thus never left it. It is much more difficult for queens that have made a swarming flight to be accepted as additional queens in an existing nest, and they are often killed. The survivors either remain in the nest as additional queens or move out with some of the workers to form daughter nests. The life span of polygynous colonies is practically unlimited because the new queens regularly rejuvenate them.

In summer, daughter nests may sometimes form spontaneously. This involves exterior workers carrying 150 000 to 200 000 ants at all developmental stages to a suitable place nearby where the workers build a new nest. They move not only the immobile eggs, larvae and pupae, but even the still inexperienced interior workers and the queens (so-called 'social carrying behaviour'). The individual nests of a colony are connected by 'ant trails', marked with scent, along which the ants transport food, the brood and adults back and forth. Sometimes the nests are even used only seasonally as summer and winter nests. Large groups of nests are called super colonies. One super colony of *F. lugubris* found in the Swiss Jura consisted of 1200 nests spread over an area of 70 hectares (Cherix and Bourne 1980).

Ant trails, on which ants exchange food and other ants, connect the individual nests of a colony to each other.

For monogynous colonies of *F. rufa*, colony foundation is more complicated and more dangerous. A monogynous colony focuses exclusively on its sole queen and no other mated queen is tolerated in the nest. Even descendants from their own nest are killed. Mated young queens therefore adopt what is known as 'temporary social parasitism'. The young *F. rufa* queen attempts to invade a nest of host ants (e. g., *F. fusca*) and to be accepted as their new queen. If the queen of the host nest is still alive, the *F. rufa* queen must kill her first. Most often, however, such takeover attempts are not successful and instead the young invading queen gets killed. If, however, she succeeds, she will be accepted as the host colony's new queen and will start to lay eggs, from which *F. rufa* larvae hatch. These are looked after and fed by the host worker ants as if they were their own sisters. The newly developing *F. rufa* workers integrate themselves into the nest and participate in all interior and exterior work. Slowly, the host workers die out, until only the continuously produced *F. rufa* workers with their queen remain. As a result, the former host ant nest is transformed into a pure *F. rufa* nest, which will, within a few years, go extinct when its queen dies.

In polygynous *F. rufa* populations, the formation of colonies proceeds along the same lines as those for *F. polyctena* described above.

When founding a daughter nest, the interior workers do not get to the new nest on their own, but are carried there by experienced exterior workers. The carrier and the carried ant interlace their mandibles, and the one to be carried bends its abdomen towards the carrier ant.

10.4 Ecological functions

Red wood ants' ecological significance has already been mentioned in earlier chapters, and some aspects are briefly described again here. The densities of ant nests in today's intensely managed forests are usually low, and the role of ants there may seem minor. Their densities in natural and semi-natural coniferous and mixed forests are, however, much higher, and there red wood ants can play an important ecological role.

The red wood ants' nest building helps to improve the soil physically, chemically and biologically. The ants loosen the soil, mix it with organic matter and enrich it with nutrients (Section 6.1). This leads to better soil respiration and fertility, which promotes the growth of trees, shrubs, berries and fungi, as well as seed production. Seeds germinate more successfully. For example, in the immediate vicinity of anthills, tree recruitment tends to be higher. Wood ants also help spread the seeds of herbaceous and woody plants (Section 2.2), and serve as food for birds, especially woodpeckers, and other vertebrates. Some birds use the formic acid that ants produce to treat their plumage and protect it against parasites (Section 7.1). Ant mounds serve as habitats for countless other invertebrates, such as beetles, springtails, wasps, flies, silverfish and mites. These subtenants do not harm their host and are called inquilines. Around 200 myrmecophilous insects are

Red wood ants also help to disperse plant seeds. If they drop them on the way to the nest, the seeds get to germinate in a new place.

This ring of ejected soil around the nest shows that the soil has been loosened and mixed while the ants were building the belowground part of their nest.

present in a single litre of nesting material (Gösswald 2012). Red wood ants tend aphid colonies like dairy cows and stimulate them to produce more honeydew by stroking them with their antennae. This also benefits honey bees and eventually, in the form of forest honey, humans.

Regulation of harmful insects

The most important role red wood ants play in the forest is in regulating other insects, especially species that are considered potential pests. Since the population size of a nest or a colony is relatively constant and does not depend on the frequency of a particular prey species, wood ants can react very quickly to mass insect propagations. In addition, they can rely more on honeydew should there be a prey shortage. *Formica polyctena* plays a particularly important role in the regulation of herbivorous insects since it forms the largest colonies and even super colonies with high nest densities. If insects, especially moth and sawfly larvae, are available in large quantities within the around 100 metre activity radius of an ant nest, the ants consume them effusively, sometimes more than they really need. The proportion of insects in red wood ants' diet can then be well over 90 percent (Gösswald 2012). In such cases, large *F. rufa* populations can harvest up to 100 000 moth caterpillars every day. During an outbreak of the European oak leafroller (*Tortrix viridana*) in an oak forest, an average *F. polyctena* nest of half a million to one million ants was estimated to collect one to two million caterpillars during the larval feeding period, which led to a significant reduction in the damage due to caterpillar feeding in the vicinity of the nest (Horstmann 1976/77). Wellenstein (1954) extensively surveyed the insects they harvested, and concluded that an average-sized ant nest could consume, on average, 3.2 million prey per year.

Ants work together to capture and exploit larger prey such as moth caterpillars.

Red wood ants can overpower even large hairy caterpillars.

In the 19th century and the early 20th century, several well-known German forest zoologists already stressed the importance of wood ants in regulating pest insects (for a summary, see Gösswald 1984 and 2012). They documented numerous cases where green oases remained around anthills in forests that had otherwise been defoliated by moth and sawfly larvae, especially in pine cultures. These green islands are estimated to cover a maximum of one hectare, which indicates the extent of the effect of a nest (Wellenstein 1954). The ants not only consume larvae, pupae and moths, but also decimate the eggs deposited by the moths, resulting in a locally marked reduction of harmful population densities. Ant colonies have also been actively and successfully relocated to infestation areas to control harmful insects. Since many wood ants need warm temperatures and sun, this tends to be particularly successful in open pine stands.

Red wood ants have similarly also been found to successfully regulate harmful populations in deciduous forests, for example the larvae of the autumnal moth *(Epirrita autumnata)* on birch trees (Laine and Niemelä 1980) or the caterpillars of the oak processionary moth *(Thaumetopoea processionea)*, which are armed with irritating hairs. In Finland, exclusion experiments were carried out with sticky bands that prevented ants *(F. aquilonia)* from getting to their foraging trees (Karhu 1998). On trees without ant access, the autumnal moth population was more than twice as large as on trees with ants. Similarly, the population of the aphid *Euceraphis punctipennis* – an aphid species that is not tended but consumed by ants – decreased by three-quarters. In contrast, populations of the shiny birch aphid (*Symydobius oblongus*), which ants tend for its honeydew, multiplied on trees visited by ants. Virtually identical results were obtained in a study in a mixed forest in England where *F. rufa* is a predator of the winter moth (*Operophtera brumata*) and the common sycamore aphid (*Drepanosiphum platanoidis*) (Skinner and Whittaker 1981). The common maple aphid (*Periphyllus testudinaceus*), which the ants tend, also became more abundant.

Despite all these striking examples of wood ants' impact on harmful organisms, their presence is no guarantee that outbreaks of herbivorous insects can be prevented. They can have a great effect during outbreaks of leaf- or needle-eating caterpillars if the caterpillar density is high and the caterpillar species is one that develops in spring, i.e., when the ants' need for food is greatest. Red wood ants – especially *F. polyctena* – can play a major role in keeping harmful herbivore populations in check and in bringing outbreaks to an end, but the type and quantity of prey available has hardly any influence on the size of ant populations and on the number of their nests (Horstmann 1976/77).

An advantage or disadvantage for a tree?

The effects of red wood ants on plants and associated organisms are manifold and their benefits are disputed. Ants are not, for example, choosy about the prey they select and also feed on some antagonists of herbivores. The way they tend aphids leads to an enormous development of aphid colonies because the tended aphids suck more actively and therefore reproduce more strongly. Moreover, the ants protect the colonies from their natural enemies. The aphid colonies are thus larger and extract more assimilates from their host plants.

Ants improve, however, the nutrient supply for plants in the immediate vicinity of their nests. This is not only beneficial for tree growth, but also for leaf-feeding insects. For example, in Finland a higher nitrogen supply to birch trees leads to a greater increase in the number of caterpillars of the autumnal moth. When, however, red wood ants (*F. aquilonia*) were excluded with sticky bands in an experiment, the large-scale positive effect of ants killing off caterpillars was found to clearly outweigh the negative effect of promoting caterpillar propagation, especially as the increase in caterpillars was limited to the immediate nest environment (Karhu and Neuvonen 1998).

Ants tend certain species of aphids to obtain honeydew, but also catch them as prey – as in this photo.

Wood ants' range of prey includes not only possible pest species, but also their natural enemies such as this parasitoid wasp.

10 Red wood ants

Transport of organisms

11

'Vector' is the scientific term for an organism that serves as a transport vehicle for other species, while the phenomenon itself is termed 'phoresy'. In some organisms, the relationship between the vector and the transported species is intense and of mutual benefit, and may thus be considered a symbiosis. Those invertebrates that typically use insects as vectors include mites, certain hymenopterans and biting lice (Mallophaga). In addition, many pathogenic viruses, bacteria, protozoans, fungi and nematodes are transported by insects and thus, for example, transferred to plants. Some species, however, feed on their hosts while being carried on or in them. This is then not really a case of phoresy, but rather of parasitism (see Sections 8.2 and 8.3).

A spruce bark beetle *(Ips typographus)* covered with numerous mites. These do not act as parasites, but use the beetle as a vector for transport to new habitats.

11.1 Vectors of invertebrates

Mites are small wingless arthropods. Their ability to actively disperse is therefore limited. In particular, species that develop in ephemeral habitats therefore tend to spread phoretically. This involves adhering themselves to a larger winged insect or using a 'stalk' they secrete to attach themselves to the vector's body. The vectors thus enable them to reach new habitats. The mites do not harm the vectors during transport as this happens when they are in an inactive stage (so-called hypope).

Phoresy is also common in mites that live in the galleries of wood insects under bark. They often attach themselves to emerging bark beetles, for example, and thus get carried to new trees. There they gain access through the entrance holes to the beetles' breeding galleries, where they feed on fungi and waste products, and reproduce. One study on the well-known European bark beetle, the spruce bark beetle *(Ips typographus)*, found that 30 percent of all beetles carried phoretic mites (Moser and Bogenschütz 1984). After the mites have reproduced, their offspring attach themselves on top or beneath the beetles' elytra or to their thorax. However, several of these mite species live parasitically on their vectors' eggs. In addition, bark beetles may transport predatory mites that feed on entomopathogenic nematodes. In this case, the beetles and the vectored predatory mites have a symbiotic relationship: the beetles transport the mites to new habitats, while the mites eliminate pathogens of the bark beetles. Interestingly, some phoretic mites of the Tarsonemidae family are vectors themselves, namely of blue stain fungi (Bridges and Moser 1986). These fungi are involved in the die-off of trees infested with bark beetles.

Burying beetles such as *Nicrophorus vespilloides* are often vectors of symbiotic mites, which use the beetles to get themselves transported to fresh carrion. In return, the mites suck out the eggs of flies whose maggots compete with the beetle larvae for food.

Females of the blister beetle *Meloe proscarabaeus* lay huge quantities of eggs in the soil. However, only a small proportion of the larvae manage to attach themselves to wild bees and get carried into a bees' nest. The next larval instars then feed predatorily on the bees' brood.

Burying beetles (Silphidae) and predatory mites (Macrochelidae) also have a symbiotic phoretic relationship. Burying beetles on fresh carcasses often carry mites on their elytra or hind legs, which detach themselves from the beetles on the carrion and feed predatorily on fly eggs. These are usually already available as flies colonize carcasses somewhat earlier than the beetles (see Section 5.1). The beetles benefit from the mites because they keep the number of competing fly maggots down. The same applies to small dung beetles (Aphodiidae) and earth-boring dung beetles (Geotrupidae), which transport the mites to animal droppings scattered in the vicinity, and likewise benefit from the mites sucking out the eggs of competing dung flies. In Austria, more than 50 phoretic mite species have been found on about 80 different vectors – most of which are beetles (Kofler and Schmölzer 2000). Other common mite vectors are bumblebees and bees.

Insects may also transport other invertebrates, such as the tiny pseudo-scorpion *Lamprochernes nodosus*. It often clings to the legs of flies, which then transfer it phoretically to new habitats. Biting lice are small, wingless insects that suck blood, especially from birds.

They use louse flies (Hippoboscidae) as vectors to move from one host to another.

The young larvae of many blister beetles (Meloidae) also reach their hosts phoretically. Females of *Meloe proscarabaeus*, for example, lay tens of thousands of eggs in the ground. Once hatched, the larvae climb up to a flower and wait for wild bees to visit it. When a bee arrives, they cling to it and let themselves be carried to the bee's nest, where the beetles' later larval instars feed on the bees' eggs, as well as on their nectar and pollen supply.

Certain parasitoid wasps of the family Scelionidae use a wide range of insects as vectors. Adult wasps attach themselves to the mature females of moths or the praying mantis *(Mantis religiosa),* which then carry them to their oviposition sites, where they parasitize their vector's eggs (Clausen 1976). This is then a more parasitic relationship than the burying beetles' symbiotic relationship with some mite species, even though it is the eggs the wasps parasitize rather than the vector itself.

11.2 Vectors of fungi

The most well-known vectors of fungi and other pathogens are bloodsucking insects that transmit human diseases. Various forest insects also transport fungi and microorganisms, but they do not affect human health. Practically all the insect species that develop in fresh wood transmit so-called ambrosia fungi, which help their larvae digest the wood components that are hard to degrade. The relationship between these insects and the fungus is also symbiotic. The fungus allows the larvae to develop in wood and, in return, the emerging adults transport the fungus to new habitats.

Nine of the ten woodwasp species (Siricidae) found in Central Europe are associated with fungi (Bachmaier 1966). The giant woodwasp *(Urocerus gigas)*, for example, colonizes various conifers (see Section 4.2). The female carries hyphae of the crust fungus *Amylostereum chailletii* in special pockets (mycangia) at the base of her ovipositor. During oviposition, the egg goes past the mycangia and is inoculated with the fungus before being inserted into the wood with the help of the strong ovipositor. The fungus then begins to grow inside the wood, and the fungal mycelium spreads. When feeding, the woodwasp larvae ingest mycelium, which enables them to break down cellulose, lignin and other wood components. Notwithstanding this symbiosis with the fungus, the development of the giant woodwasp still takes at least three years. Upon emerging from the pupa, the adult woodwasp gnaws its way out of the wood. During this process, fungal fragments find their way into the mycangia, where they become established. The emerged female once again transfers the fungus to the new tree when she lays her eggs.

Although most species of bark beetles breed in the inner bark, there are also some species that develop in sapwood. The ambrosia beetles of the genus *Trypodendron* carry fungal hyphae in their mycangia, which they transfer inside the wood when laying their eggs. The developing larvae feed exclusively on fungal mycelium. The tunnels they gnaw are therefore much shorter than those of the

Woodwasps are vectors of fungi vital for their larvae. From where they develop, the females transport the fungus in special pockets to a new tree. The photo shows a giant woodwasp *(Urocerus gigas)* in the process of driving its ovipositor (blackspine in the middle of its body) into the wood.

11 Transport of organisms

228 Ovipositor of the giant woodwasp in the middle, with a sheath above and below it. When the ovipositor penetrates the wood, the eggs, inoculated with fungal secretion, slide through it into the wood. Although the structure of the ovipositor is spiral-shaped, the wasp does not rotate on its axis when boring into the wood.

The larvae of the giant woodwasp feed primarily on the fungus *Amylostereum chailletii*, which is transmitted by the female during egg laying. (Photo courtesy of Forest Entomology WSL.)

Gallery of the striped ambrosia beetle *(Trypodendron lineatum)*. Its larvae develop in the short larval ducts branching off the horizontal maternal tunnel. In the ducts they feed exclusively on the fungus, which the female introduced into the wood when laying her eggs. She also eliminates other fungal species.

bark-feeding bark beetles as they live on the continuously regrowing fungal network and not on the wood itself. Timberworm beetles (Lymexylidae) also introduce a fungus into the wood, which serves as food for their larvae (see Section 4.2).

Certain bark-feeding bark beetles and longhorn beetles are also known to be vectors of plant pathogens, but do not feed on them. For example, the most famous bark beetle in Central Europe, the spruce bark beetle, transmits blue stain fungi, which block the trees' water-transporting vessels (xylem) and thus contribute to the die-off of trees infested with bark beetles. Further important vectors of tree diseases are elm bark beetles (*Scolytus* spp.), which transmit the Dutch elm disease, and the sawyer beetle *(Monochamus galloprovincialis)*, which is the vector of the pine wood nematode (see Section 14.4).

11 Transport of organisms

Maintaining stand vitality

12

As in human populations, in (natural) forests, there are – at any one time – weakened, sick, old and dead individuals. Such individuals, in this case trees, are part of every healthy forest and do not indicate that the population is morbid. However, trees that are weakened or under stress are less resistant to diseases or insect infestations. Insects can usually only colonize trees in sufficient numbers to kill them if the trees are already susceptible. This means that weakened trees are selectively infested, while the 'fitter' ones are spared. The selective elimination of weakened trees increases a stand's average vitality.

The vitality of a tree is not easy to define. Often the degree of foliation, which is relatively easily quantified, is taken as a measure. Correspondingly, the defoliation level, i.e., the loss of leaves or needles, is used as a proxy variable for loss of vitality. However, on extreme sites, for example, some trees may have only a few needles or leaves, and their

Insect infestation can lead to the selective death of weakened trees. This increases the average vitality of a stand.

annual growth may be minimal. However, they may have survived very adverse conditions for centuries and may be actually quite vital.

Elimination of weakened trees

Bark beetles are the most effective agents in the forest in selectively colonizing weak or injured trees. Interestingly, the trees that most frequently suffer from bark beetle attacks are mainly conifers, despite their ability to extrude resin. Resin is toxic to most insects. When subcortical bark beetles try to bore into vital coniferous trees, the trees are usually able to flush out, trap or poison the intruders with resin stored in the wood. If this is not successful, the trees react by producing additional resin and try to poison the beetle brood. The weaker a tree is, the more limited is its ability to do this, and the more likely that the beetles will colonize and ultimately kill its host (see Section 14.3). Only a few bark beetle species, however, are able to colonize living trees. The European spruce bark beetle (*Ips typographus*) is the main colonizer of Norway spruce, while the six-toothed spruce bark beetle (*Pityogenes chalcographus*) attacks young conifers. The pine bark beetle (*Ips acuminatus*), among others, can infest and kill Scots pines with reduced resistance. Among the weevils (Curculionidae), the European silver fir weevil (*Pissodes piceae*) is one example that has such selecting characteristics. It attacks mainly suppressed and weakened silver firs and eventually kills them.

Insects that can kill weakened deciduous trees include, for example, leaf-feeding moth caterpillars. The mottled umber (*Erannis defoliaria*), winter moth (*Operophtera brumata*) and gypsy moth (*Lymantria dispar*) are able to completely defoliate trees during an outbreak. The affected trees react by producing new foliage from their reserves. As a conse-

Bark beetles (here *Ips typographus*) prefer to colonize weakened or stressed conifers. The trees' resistance is reduced, and the beetles can penetrate the bark more easily.

The European silver fir weevil *(Pissodes piceae)* mainly colonizes suppressed silver fir. The feeding of the beetle larvae interrupts the sap flow in the bark, which causes the tree to die.

quence, the reserves are depleted and, especially after several consecutive years of heavy defoliation, the weakest trees die because their reserves get exhausted, while the more vital ones survive.

Dead and decomposing trees make their nutrients available to the remaining trees in the stand and provide space and light for the new growth of young, healthy trees. Over time, the young trees take the place of the dead trees and take over their functions. In the gaps left by dead trees, many more plants at first germinate and grow than will, in the end, survive. As the gap closes, the competition for light, water and nutrients increases, and suppressed and weakened trees die off, especially if they are attacked by insects. For example, if spruce adelgids (especially *Adelges* species) heavily infest suppressed young spruce trees over a long period, the growth of the trees may be greatly reduced and the plants may eventually die.

233

A healthy spruce tree can defend itself against attacking bark beetles with resin. Only if the population densities of the beetles are high, can they overcome this defence.

12 Maintaining stand vitality

Selection of tree species

During the natural development of an unmanaged forest, the tree species that prevail are those which are most competitive under the given conditions. Whether a tree species occurs locally depends not only on site factors such as climate, soil, water and nutrient availability, but also on the selection pressure of pathogens, game and insects. Trees that have germinated but are not very vital under the given conditions are preferentially attacked by insects and either die as a direct result of feeding or lose out in their competition with other tree species because of their low growth rate due, for example, to insects.

Insects can also influence the selection of tree species by transmitting diseases. One dramatic example is the elm bark beetle *(Scolytus species)*, which helped spread the introduced pathogen that causes Dutch elm disease throughout Europe. This led to a striking decline in the abundance of elm (see Section 14.4). In general, insects help to ensure that only trees that are adapted to the site and resistant to stressors can become established and reproduce.

Heavy and continuous infestations of the larch adelgid *(Adelges laricis)* mainly occur on poorly growing young spruce trees. They stunt the trees' growth even more and lead to the selection of vigorous trees. (Photo courtesy of Forest Entomology WSL.)
▼

Trees such as this Scots pine that have been weakened by drought, fungal infection or mistletoe are often attacked and killed by bark beetles. This increases the availability of light, water and nutrients for the surrounding competing trees.
▼

Shaping of ecosystems

13

All organisms have some effect on their environment. Species that physically change the availability of resources for other species are referred to as 'ecosystem engineers'. By definition, they change, maintain or create habitats and can shape entire landscapes. In general, these changes have a positive impact on the biodiversity in an ecosystem. A well-known example of an ecosystem engineer is the beaver. It fells trees, and its dam constructions can flood whole areas for a long time and thus induce changes in the local flora and fauna.

Some species of bark beetles selectively infest particular species or age classes of trees and can thus markedly regulate the composition and development of a forest. The North American mountain pine beetle *(Dendroctonus ponderosae)* only attacks pine trees, thus favouring other tree species such as fir and spruce.

This mason bee (*Osmia* sp.) has used the empty tunnel of a longhorn beetle larva for breeding. The beetle has thus created a small but valuable habitat for this wild bee species.

13.1 From microhabitats to landscapes

Forest insects can shape and change their environment in different ways and to varying degrees. Many species inconspicuously create new habitats on a small scale for other organisms. The nests of red wood ants (Chapter 10), for example, support numerous so-called 'inquilines' (subtenants), which benefit from the safe and constant environmental conditions prevailing in the ant mounds. Plant galls are often colonized by inquilines as well, which cannot produce galls themselves and therefore depend on gall producing insects. Old, abandoned oak galls often serve as breeding facilities for certain digger wasps. The caterpillars of some leaf rollers (Tortricidae) roll up leaves to form tubes for protection and as food. These tubes provide shelter for other organisms as well, such as spiders, beetles or earwigs. The tunnels and exit holes of many wood-dwelling insects (Section 4.4) create indispensable microhabitats for numerous species of wild bees to breed in.

Some insects, however, bring about large-scale changes affecting entire landscapes. If such a change happens relatively abruptly, it is called a biotic ecological disturbance, in contrast to an abiotic disturbance such as a storm, fire or flood. Biotic disturbances, especially those caused by insects, differ significantly from abiotic ones in that they are often spatially synchronized (e. g., triggered by weather conditions) and sometimes re-occur with periodic frequency. Moreover, they tend to have a selective effect, as often only one or just a few tree species are affected (Cooke et al. 2007). From a human perspective, these insects are mostly perceived as pests rather than creators of habitats. Herbivorous insects, however,

The gypsy moth *(Lymantria dispar)* is an ecosystem engineer that can influence the development of deciduous forests on a large scale. The complete defoliation by the caterpillars allows light and heat to reach the ground in the middle of summer (Photo: Ticino; 21.7.1992). This favours the development of ground vegetation, which in turn benefits many other organisms. In addition, microbial activity in the soil increases and the soil water conditions change.

generally accelerate the succession of plants. Pioneer plants invest in rapid growth and put little energy into physical and chemical defence systems against herbivores. In contrast, tree species of later successional stages invest a considerable proportion of their assimilates in such defence mechanisms (Davidson 1993). Selective herbivory on certain tree species may delay or prevent such successions by promoting non-host plants at the expense of host plants or by suppressing sensitive plants at the expense of tolerant ones.

A mass propagation of leaf-eating insects lasting one or more years during which the host trees become completely defoliated temporarily allows more light and heat to reach the ground. The ground vegetation and various other tree species benefit from the increased incidence of light and the reduced growth of the infested trees, which influences the structure and species composition of a forest. The abundant ground vegetation favours other organisms, for example by increasing the food supply for game and the availability of flower pollen and nectar for pollinating insects. In addition, the lack of a closed canopy means that more precipitation reaches the ground and the evapotranspiration of trees is reduced. This increases, at least in the short term, the water content of the soil, but also promotes the leaching of nutrients (Schowalter 2012). A large-scale outbreak in a forest has a lasting effect on its CO_2 budget and may temporarily transform it from a carbon sink into a source.

13.2 The larch budmoth in Switzerland's Engadine

The larch budmoth (*Zeiraphera griseana*) is an example of an insect that can have large-scale and persistent effects on forest development. In the valleys of the European Alps, this moth's population densities go through regular cycles of 8 to 10 years. In the Swiss Engadine, this moth was intensively studied in the second half of the 20th century, and it has become one of the most famous examples worldwide of a species with cyclic population fluctuations (Baltensweiler and Fischlin 1988).

History

The first mention in Switzerland of a 'disease' that turned extensive larch forests yellow-brown dates from 1820 in the municipality of Ardon in Valais (Coaz 1894). Yet the true cause of this observed phenomenon was only identified in 1857, when a forestry inspector brought the moths to the attention of his fellow foresters (Davall 1857). The devastation of the larch in the region around Sion, Upper Valais and the side valleys was attributed to the larvae of what was then called *Tortrix pinicolana*. In the Upper Engadine as well, the larch stands on the valley slopes were observed to turn reddish brown every few years in mid-summer. The first record of this phenomenon in the Grisons dates back to 1855, and in 1894 the cyclic outbreaks in the Upper and Lower Engadine were described for the first time (Coaz 1894). For a long time, these mass outbreaks were thought to pose a serious threat to larch forests because they often resulted in the dieback of many trees.

In the mid-20th century, when tourism in Switzerland slowly started picking up again after the Second World War, another larch budmoth outbreak was in full swing. The tourist industry in the Engadine put pressure on the authorities to apply DDT, which was, at the

The larch budmoth (*Zeiraphera griseana*) is a small, inconspicuous moth found in larch forests. In some inner-alpine valleys, the fluctuations in its populations are strikingly regular and cyclical.

time, considered a new panacea. DDT was, indeed, subsequently applied on a trial basis later. In 1948, the pressure to apply insecticides set in motion a long-term study spanning more than six decades, driven primarily by Werner Baltensweiler at the Swiss Federal Institute of Technology (ETH Zurich). In the course of this long-term study, more than 130 scientific papers were produced, which led public and scientific perceptions to change from considering the larch budmoth as a mere pest to seeing it as an ecosystem engineer and fascinating topic of study.

Ecology of the larch budmoth

The larch budmoth is a small moth with a wing span of two centimetres. It belongs to the leafroller family (Tortricidae). Its larvae reach a length of one and a half centimetres. The biology of this moth was studied in detail in the Engadine (Maksymov 1959). Its eggs overwinter in diapause under lichen or the scales of cones or bark. The young larvae hatch in mid-May, and the first two instars feed inside the base of young needle clusters. In the third and fourth larval instar, the caterpillar feeds in an open-topped fascicle, spun together out of a cluster of needles. When the needles it bites into start drying out, the caterpillar moves on to a fresh cluster. In early July, the caterpillar enters its fifth and final larval instar. It first eats away the tip of its needle fascicle and constructs a web along the branch axis. From then on, it feeds laterally on other needle clusters. This is the most destructive instar because the larva is continually moving from

(a) The young caterpillars feed inside spun together clusters of young needles; (b) later they feed on the needle fascicles from the tip; (c) in the last instar, they move along the branch axis producing webs and feeding on the needles from outside the clusters.

13 Shaping of ecosystems

one gnawed cluster of needles to another, and the bitten needles start to dry out. A single larva needs between 10 and 20 clusters of needles for its development, but it eats just half their needle mass (so-called wasteful feeding). When a mass outbreak occurs, the dried-out needles make the larch stands turn reddish brown in midsummer, though the actual extent of discolouration also depends on local precipitation. At the end of its roughly four-week development, the larvae lower themselves to the ground on a thread or free fall, and then begin their one-month pupal phase in the litter layer. The moths emerge from the end of July to September, swarming between dusk and midnight during summer and around noon under the cooler conditions prevailing in late autumn. During these flights they mate, and the females then lay up to 300 eggs over a three-week period, depending on the cycle phase.

In the 19th century, the larch budmoth's main natural enemies were thought to be birds, which is why the hunting of migratory birds in southern countries was considered deplorable (Coaz 1894). Songbirds do indeed consume large numbers of caterpillars when there is a mass outbreak of larch budmoth larvae, as does the Scottish wood ant (*Formica aquilonia*), which is common in the Engadine. These ants mostly prey on older larvae outside their needle fascicles and on pupating caterpillars on the ground. Extensive research has also identified a large number of parasitoids (Delucchi 1982) that parasitize larch budmoths at all stages of their development (eggs, caterpillars and pupae). The main parasitoids are ichneumonid wasps (Ichneumonidae) and tachinid flies (Tachinidae). In addition, sporadic outbreaks of disease such as viruses occur.

The population cycles

An intensive study of the population dynamics of the larch budmoth, focusing on the Upper Engadine, was started in 1949. It emerged that outbreaks tend to occur, on average, every 8.5 years (Baltensweiler and Fischlin 1988). Within four to five generations, the population density (abundance) fluctuates by a factor of up to 30 000!

At the peak of an outbreak, more than 20 000 larvae can be found on a single larch tree, and the sound of their faeces falling to the ground is audible. The threads spun by the larvae then hang criss-crossed over the trees, and may be caught by the wind, which helps the larvae reach other branches or trees in their quest for new sources of food. Their population builds up and collapses again within just a few generations. During a collapse, the larval mortality rate, resulting from antagonists, competition and starvation, peaks at 99.98 percent (Baltensweiler and Fischlin 1988).

The discolouration of larch stands only becomes visible at a threshold of about 100 larvae per kilogram of branches when 10 percent

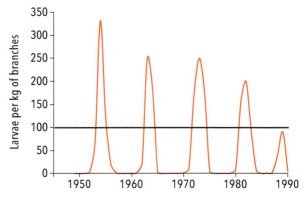

Cyclical population fluctuations of the larch budmoth in the Upper Engadine. The periodicity is on average 8.5 years, and the threshold for a visible discolouration of the larch stands is 100 caterpillars per kilogram of branches (adapted from Baltensweiler and Rubli 1999; data: A. Fischlin, ETH Zurich).

During outbreaks, the caterpillars wander restlessly along the branches just gnawing at many needles and leaving behind withering needles and webbings intermingled with excrement.

At the peak of an outbreak, the gnawed larch needles wither and turn reddish-brown, which is particularly noticeable when weather conditions are dry. The trees in the foreground are stone pines, which are not affected (Val Bever, Grisons; 1.8.1999).

of the needles are damaged (Auer 1975; see graph page 240). The regular cycles in the Engadine are limited to the optimum larch budmoth habitats, situated between 1700 and 2000 metres above sea level. Interestingly, these cycles are not limited to the Engadine and Valais, but also take place in many other inner-alpine valleys in France, Italy and Austria.

Larch can, as a tree species that sheds its needles in winter, compensate for losing needles by drawing on reserves stored in its wood to produce fresh needles later in the summer. However, their growth in years when infestations occur is severely stunted, which is reflected in narrower tree rings found in their stems. Larch-stem discs from the Engadine or larch beams from old wooden houses in the Valais often have narrow tree rings every eight to ten years, corresponding to larch budmoth cycles. In the year of maximum defoliation, the annual tree ring is often missing completely (Weber 1997). Tree-ring studies have shown that larch budmoth cycles have regularly occurred for a very long time. Wood samples taken from living larch trees and from beams in historic buildings have been used to reconstruct larch budmoth cycles over a period of 1200 years, with the outbreaks occurring every 9.3 years, on average (Esper et al. 2007). This shows that the larch and larch budmoth have co-existed for a long time.

What drives the cycles?

The astonishing regularity of the larch budmoth cycles begs the question of the mechanisms that cause them. The first detailed study of an outbreak cycle in the Engadine found that the larvae became infected with a virus as their population collapsed. This virus was deemed to be the key factor driving the population's dynamics until the next mass outbreak. If research had been stopped at that time, this explanation would probably still be considered to apply today. In subsequent outbreaks, however, viral infection barely played a role. This shows how important long-term studies are. Subsequently, several other processes were discovered that occur during mass outbreaks and shape cycles.

Negative feedback of needle quality

The interactions between larch budmoth caterpillars and their host trees have been intensively investigated (Benz 1974). The feeding of the larch budmoth was found to influence

⟨ The regularly recurring outbreaks of the larch budmoth are clearly discernible in the narrow tree rings at the face sides of stored larch logs in Val Bever in the Engadine (above) and near Münster in Upper Valais (below).

larch needles' nutritional composition, which undergoes cycles as well. At the peak of an outbreak, the larvae will consume most of the trees' needle mass, while partially gnawed needles will dry up.

As a result, the larch trees produce a smaller amount of photosynthates for their growth and reserves. If they lose more than half their needle mass, they bud again at the end of July, producing a second set of needles. However, they do so at the expense of their reserves, which cannot be fully replenished through photosynthesis of the new needles by autumn. To compensate for losing their reserves in such years, larch trees delay shedding their needles until late autumn. At the same time, they run the risk of losing the still green needles to early frosts before their nutrients and carbohydrates have been safely transferred to the trees' wood and roots, which can withstand winter conditions. For the larch budmoth, the huge numbers of caterpillars during an outbreak suffer from density stress, and their extensive feeding diminishes their food source. As a result, the mortality of the starving caterpillars increases, and the few moths that develop produce markedly fewer eggs in the autumn.

The following spring, the consequences of the larches' low reserves become apparent. The trees flush their needles later, the needles grow more slowly and remain between 30 and 70 percent shorter. They also have a higher raw fibre content, which makes them more difficult to digest, and tend to contain less protein and nitrogen than in years without a mass outbreak. As with all leaf-feeding caterpillars that overwinter at the egg stage, the timing or degree of synchrony between needle budding and the emergence of the

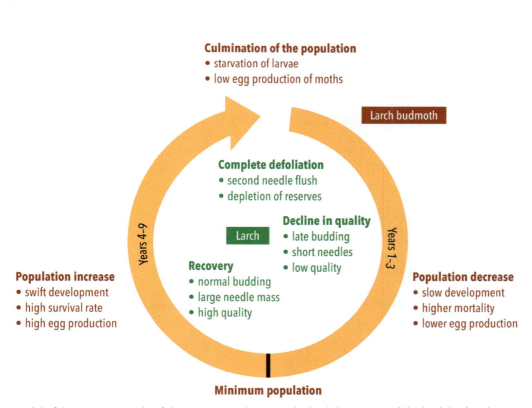

Model of the nine-year cycle of the interactions between the larch host tree and the larch budmoth.

13 Shaping of ecosystems

young larch budmoth larvae is crucial. In the years after a mass outbreak, the synchrony of these events worsens and larvae emerging at the usual temperature-triggered time fail to find fresh and tender larch needles that are readily digestible. As a result, at least the earliest larch budmoth larvae of the new population end up starving. Those larvae that do survive find needles of inferior quality that are difficult to digest and have a lower nutritional value. They therefore grow more slowly, gain less weight and have a higher mortality rate. Moreover, the moths that do develop from these larvae produce up to 90 percent fewer eggs. This delayed negative feedback triggers a drastic decline in the moth population density.

It takes about three years for larch trees to recover from an outbreak. They then produce higher-quality food, which enables the larch budmoth population to thrive and its population to increase again. These interactions between the larch budmoth and its host tree also play a key role in further drivers of the cycle, as described below.

Regulation by natural enemies

The most important natural enemies are parasitic wasps and flies, of which more than 100 species are known (Delucchi 1982). Species assemblages vary with elevation and the cycle phase. The mortality rate of larch budmoth larvae due to parasitoids is mostly less than 10 percent at the start of an outbreak. It rises to 20 percent at the culmination of the outbreak, and is as high as 80 percent when the population collapses (Baltensweiler 1968, Delucchi 1982). The cycles of the natural enemies of larch budmoth larvae lag about two years behind those of the larch budmoth itself. Newer models with time series analyses show that a simple host-parasitoid model, analogous to a predator-prey model, can explain 90 percent of larch budmoth growth rates (Turchin *et al.* 2003). The models' match with data collected in the field can be slightly improved if the impact of the variations in needle quality described above is also taken into account. The observed two-year phase shift is typical of predator-prey relationships with delayed negative feedback. This pattern demonstrates how important parasitoids are in controlling larch budmoth cycles.

⟨ If more than half of the needles fail due to budmoth feeding and withering, the larch flushes new needles in August, by when the caterpillars will have withdrawn to pupate in the ground. This reflush is, however, at the expense of the reserves stored in the wood. This leads, together with the greatly reduced assimilation due to caterpillar feeding, to the budding time and needle quality becoming unfavourable for the caterpillars in the following years.

Fitness of the two different ecotypes

The larch budmoth has two genetically distinct ecotypes (varieties): the larch form and the stone-pine form. The larch form has grey-black caterpillars that feed almost exclusively on larch needles and have a very high mortality rate on Swiss stone pine. Its eggs develop significantly faster than those of the stone-pine form, and its larval mortality on high-quality larch needles is lower (Day and Baltensweiler 1972). Its faster egg development means that the larch form is also better adapted to the timing of needle emergence (synchrony) of larch trees, which produce clusters of needles about two weeks earlier than stone pine. Furthermore, the larch form produces more eggs than the stone-pine form.

The yellowish-grey caterpillars of the stone-pine form feed mainly on new shoots of stone pine, but they also occur on larch, Scots pine and spruce. The stone-pine form develops much more slowly and produces fewer eggs than its larch counterpart, but survives better than the larch form on poor-quality larch needles. The larch and stone-pine ecotypes therefore differ in fitness, and the two forms of the moths even respond to different pheromones. They are on course to develop into two different species. Intermediate, or transitional, forms between the two ecotypes also exist that can thrive on both larch and stone pine.

The dominance relationship between the two ecotypes changes during a cycle. At the onset of a mass outbreak, the darker larch form predominates, making up 80 percent of the larvae. It develops faster on the initially high-quality larch needles than the stone-pine and intermediate forms. After complete defoliation at the culmination of an outbreak, the budburst of the larch trees is delayed and they produce needles of inferior quality. At

A larch budmoth larva with an egg of a parasitic wasp (presumably *Phytodietus griseanae*). Parasitic insects are one of the most important factors driving the larch budmoth cycles. (Photo courtesy of Forest Entomology WSL.)

this point, the stone-pine and intermediate forms, which emerge later and survive better than the larch form on poorer needles, have an advantage and their proportion rises to 80 percent. But since both these forms reproduce at a low rate, the overall density of budmoths occurring on larch trees continues to decrease. Only when the needle quality has improved does the fitter larch form prevail again and the population's reproduction rate increases once more (Baltensweiler 1993a).

In some Alpine regions, the stone-pine form of the larvae has its own cycle on stone pine, which is synchronous with its larch counterpart and has the same periodicity (Dormont et al. 2006). Since these larvae on Swiss stone pine only feed on the needles of new shoots

The stone-pine form of the larch budmoth develops mainly in this year's needle clusters, which it spins together. The light-coloured stone-pine ecotype has an orange-yellow head capsule. It reproduces at a lower rate than the larch ecotype.

and thus, unlike the larch ecotype, do not trigger new needle flushing, poor food quality cannot have a negative impact on them. This highlights how parasitoids play an important role in driving the cycle.

Moth migration and dispersal

During an outbreak, larch budmoth populations migrate locally but also disperse over a wide area (Baltensweiler and Rubli 1999). If complete defoliation occurs in ideal habitats, subsequent generations of moths move on to lower-lying areas, where the larch trees had been previously spared excessive larval feeding, to lay their eggs. Over the next few years after the trees have recovered, moths fly in the evenings against the prevailing valley winds to higher elevations, thus returning to the optimum habitats characterised by better synchrony. This is the region where their re-occurring cycles at regular intervals are most evident.

On a larger spatial scale, the windborne dispersal of larch budmoths between inner Alpine valleys is important. In areas where larch trees have been largely defoliated by an outbreak, moths leave in large numbers and are blown into neighbouring valleys by the prevailing westerly wind. This is why the cyclical fluctuations of larch budmoth populations occur not only in the Valais and Engadine, but also in many other valleys in the European Alpine arc. Their cycles are, however, staggered over time. The first outbreaks occur in the valleys of the French Maritime Alps (Briançonnais). The larch budmoth culminations are then displaced at a speed of 200–300 km per year, moving some 600 km to the East over the Alpine arc to the Aosta valley (IT), Valais, Engadine (CH), Valtellina, Dolomites (IT) and Styria (AT). The temporal shift of the outbreaks takes three to four years. Light and pheromone traps set up across the entire Alpine region have shown that countless moths are carried via Alpine passes into neighbouring eastern valleys and also onto the Swiss Plateau, where they boost local populations.

The Alpine arc has two 'epicentres', each with its own particular momentum, which superimpose their own propagation waves on the overall West-to-East movements. The epicentres are in the Briançonnais zone in France and the Engadine/Vinschgau in the eastern Alps, which are characterised by high connectivity, i.e., favourable habitats are in close proximity with only a few unfavourable habitats in between.

The significance of the larch budmoth for larch forests

The larch budmoth is described as a real pest in the older literature. However, intensive studies in the Upper Engadine have shown that fewer than one percent of individual larch trees actually die as a result of an outbreak and that most trees' growth loss is negligible (Baltensweiler and Rubli 1984). Tree mortality may, though, be higher in very dry years, which can locally jeopardize sustainable forest management. After the Second World War, discolouration of larch trees was viewed with concern because it was feared it might affect tourism (Auer 1974), but no such effects have been recorded.

At the peak of a larch budmoth outbreak, the larch forests turn reddish-brown in the middle of summer. The moths then leave the affected areas in large numbers and drift eastwards with the wind into neighbouring valleys. The discolourations thus continue eastwards across the entire Alpine arc. They begin in the Western French Alps and end about four years later in South Tyrol (Italy) and Carinthia (Austria). (a) Val Guisane, France; (b) Saastal, western Switzerland; (c) Engadine, eastern Switzerland; (d) Valle Aurina, Italy. The photos were taken between 1964 and 1979. (Photo courtesy of Forest Entomology WSL).

Indeed, the larch budmoth can be ecologically very important for inner alpine larch forests. Larch trees are highly dominant in many places today because, as a pioneer species, they have been able to benefit from previous disturbances. For instance, in the Middle Ages many spruce/stone-pine forests were cut down while during the war years fires were frequent. Moreover Swiss stone pine has been deliberately targeted for use as wood panelling. In addition, wood pasturing and mulching up until the end of the 19th century hindered the regeneration of spruce and stone pine (Coaz 1894). Such human activities enabled larch, which is a fast-growing and light-demanding pioneer tree species, to establish

The larch budmoth cycles in a nutshell

The regular cycling of larch budmoth population densities can be attributed to several factors. A cycle develops roughly as follows:

The synchrony between larch tree budding and the hatching of young larch budmoth larvae is best in habitats at higher elevations (1700 to 2000 m a. s. l.), where the moth populations start to increase. Most larvae belong to the dark larch budmoth form with high ecological fitness. At such times, the regulation of larch budmoth populations by parasitic insects cannot keep pace with the increase in larvae numbers, which can increase more than twenty times each year. At the culmination of an outbreak, the large quantities of larvae completely defoliate their host trees, which in turn causes many larvae to starve and the surviving female moths to lay fewer eggs. In the following years, the needles the larches produce are of considerably lower quality and emerge later. This favours the stone-pine and intermediate forms of the budmoth, which also feed on larch needles. However, high overall larval mortality and the moths' limited reproduction rate lead to a decline in larch budmoth populations. Furthermore, larger populations of parasitic insects exert their full devastating effect at this point, causing the larval mortality rate to rise to almost 100 percent. Many moths migrate to lower-lying areas, where the food available to them in the following year is of higher quality but where their offspring experience poorer synchrony with the budburst of their host tree. A high proportion of the moths are transported by westerly winds into adjacent Alpine valleys, prompting a wave of outbreaks that moves from West to East across the Alps. After three to four years, regional larch budmoth populations bottom out, and the quality and the timing of the emergence of the larch needles return to normal again. By this time, the populations of parasitic insects will have collapsed due to the dearth of available hosts, and the moths will then migrate back locally from lower-lying areas to their optimum habitats. The number of light-coloured stone-pine form's larvae then diminishes, and they are replaced once again by the larch form of the larvae, which proliferate more readily.

Overall, the fundamental mechanisms driving the cycle operate on a local scale, and are based mainly on regulation by natural enemies and the feedback of larch needle quality as a food source. The large-scale windborne dispersal of moths across the Alpine arc stabilises and synchronises the larch budmoth cycles. These mechanisms are explained in more detail in the text.

a firm foothold. However, a dense old larch forest barely regenerates, and shade-tolerant species such as stone pine and spruce become established and, in the absence of any new disturbances, ultimately form a climax forest.

The subalpine larch forests and the larch budmoth are highly dependent on each other in the moth's optimum range of 1700 to 2000 metres above sea level. During recurrent larch budmoth outbreaks, stone pine and spruce growing in the understorey are repeatedly damaged. As the stone-pine form of the larch budmoth only feeds on the needles of new annual shoots of stone pine, the main damage to this tree species is caused by the larvae of the intermediate larch form, which also feed on older needles. When larch trees have been completely defoliated, the larvae lower themselves to the ground and end up on the stone-pine trees in the understorey. While larch trees can compensate for being stripped of their needles by rebudding, stone pine can only do so to a very limited extent. The severest damage is suffered by stone-pine trees less than five metres tall (Baltensweiler and Rubli 1984). Studies on the mass outbreak of the larch budmoth in 1972 showed that half the pine trees defoliated by more than 90 percent were dead two years later, with further fatalities probably taking place in subsequent years (Baltensweiler 1975). In particular, young trees that are completely defoliated die immediately.

Older stone-pine trees are weakened and part of their leading shoot frequently dies. These weakened trees also often become infested by weevils such as *Pissodes pini* or bark beetles and plant lice. Larch trees can then capitalise on the death of stone-pine individuals, making use of newly available space and a greater incidence of light. These processes limit the development of stone-pine trees in the optimum larch budmoth habitats and thus delay the transformation of larch forests to mixed larch and pine climax forests.

Naturally, the complete loss of needles at the culmination of an outbreak, although temporary, also affects other needle-eating insects, such as caterpillars or sawfly larvae, which almost completely disappear in the

At the peak of an outbreak, the larch budmoth caterpillars lower themselves from the defoliated larch trees and feed on the young stone pines and spruces in the understorey. While the larch, as a deciduous tree species, rebuds after an infestation, the weakened stone pines cannot compensate for the needle loss. They often die off directly or as a result of a secondary infestation by insects. This impedes the development of larch forests into pine forests.

13 Shaping of ecosystems

peak years of a larch budmoth outbreak (Lovis 1975). Accordingly, the larch budmoth significantly influences the insect fauna in affected larch forests.

Climate change and larch budmoth cycles

The maximum population densities during the last three cycles (1989, 1999, 2009) did not reach even half the previous levels in the Engadine, which is why in most places the larch forests were spared widespread discolouration. This is also reflected in the annual tree ring densities in Valais, which remained unaffected during this period (Esper *et al.* 2007). Nonetheless, the roughly nine-year periodicity of outbreaks was not disrupted. Why lower maxima were reached in recent cycles is unclear, but is probably related to climate change. Warmer autumns and milder winters increase the respiration of the overwintering eggs, which could lead to their energy reserves becoming exhausted (Baltensweiler 1993b). In addition, the crucial synchrony between larval hatching and the emergence of needles may have worsened in the spring. Already in earlier centuries, periods with below-average temperatures were found to result in lower growth losses during outbreaks of the larch budmoth (Weber 1997).

Those stone pines affected by the larch budmoth that do not die immediately are often attacked by the banded pine weevil *(Pissodes pini)*.

13.3 Bark beetles create new habitats

Some bark beetle species are also ecosystem engineers, although they are mainly known as pests (see Section 14.3). By killing large numbers of living trees, they also change entire landscapes and create habitats for other organisms. In European spruce forests, the European spruce bark beetle *(Ips typographus)* is the best-known example of this phenomenon. This beetle usually colonizes weakened or newly dead trees. It therefore not only initiates the decomposition and recycling of wood (Section 4.2), but also creates small-scale habitats for subsequent wood-dwelling organisms such as numerous fungi and insects. Under certain circumstances, however, mass outbreaks of these beetles can occur. They then attack apparently healthy trees across a large area and kill them. Although this behaviour makes the beetle a pest for humans, a large number of bark and wood-dwelling (saproxylic) organisms nevertheless benefit from this important ecosystem engineer.

Creating deadwood

Trees colonized by the spruce bark beetle also serve as habitats for many of its predatory and parasitoid natural enemies (see Chapter 9). Spiders, mites, fungi and microorganisms can establish under the bark that bark beetles have perforated and partially detached. Even after the bark has fallen off, the still standing stems serve as breeding substrate for many insects – especially beetles – and woodpeckers. The empty tunnels of longhorn and other beetles, for example, may subsequently be used by wild bees as nesting sites. Woodpecker cavities in dead trees may subsequently be used by vertebrates that cannot make their own cavities, such as tits, nuthatches, owls, pigeons and starlings, as well as bats, dormice and other mammals. Both standing and lying stems are often colonized by conspicuously large bracket fungi, such as the red belt conk. Many amphibians hibernate under and in lying deadwood, and tree stumps protruding above the ground vegetation are ideal for reptiles sunbathing. Deadwood, which takes decades to decompose, is used as a habitat by a wide variety of beetles, ants, bees, wasps, flies and mosquitoes,

While in 1999 a clear discolouration of the larch trees was observed in the Engadine at least in Val Bever (top, 1.8.1999), in 2009 the infestations remained limited to smaller groups of larch, such as at Lake Silvaplana (bottom, 14.7.2009).

Infestations by the European spruce bark beetle *(Ips typographus)* changes the local forest structure and creates new habitats.

depending on its degree of decomposition (see Chapter 4). In a study in the Bavarian Forest National Park, the stand edges created during bark beetle infestations proved to be hotspots for insect biodiversity (Müller et al. 2008). In particular, the diversity of wild bees and wasps was much greater along the edges of former infestation spots than in the intact forest.

Open habitats

An infestation of previously dense spruce stands by the spruce bark beetle leads the trees to shed needles and twigs, which creates open sunny habitats. Sanitation felling of the infested trees may also create such clearings, although the important deadwood is removed. This triggers a vigorous growth of herbaceous plants, such as raspberry, blackberry, wild strawberry, rosebay willowherb (or fireweed) and fern, before pioneer trees, such as willow, birch, rowan and finally again spruce and other climax tree species, become dominant. This process can take decades, depending on the local climatic conditions. During this period the former 'infestation area' remains very different from the surrounding forest. It not only provides food for herbivorous and flower-visiting insects, but it is also a habitat for specific small mammal and bird fauna. Such areas provide, moreover, good grazing for game.

Deadwood produced by bark beetles provides not only a basis for many fungi, insects and birds to live on, but also an important structural element. A sand lizard and a grass snake bask in the sun on a tree stump sticking out from the ground vegetation.

253

Sixteen years after a large-scale infestation by the spruce bark beetle, the dead trees have collapsed and a rich vegetation of herbaceous plants and pioneer trees has developed. The new habitat provides a good food supply and varied cover for birds, small mammals and game for a few decades until a closed spruce forest develops again.

Economic significance

Economic damage

14

Insects not only provide important ecosystem services, as described in the previous chapters, but may also, if they propagate excessively, cause economic damage. Classifying an infestation as 'damage' is always anthropocentric. From an ecological point of view, however, insect infestations are a normal event in forest dynamics. For humans, even the aesthetic impairment of a single ornamental plant, such as feeding marks, discolouration or web covers, may be considered damaging. In the forest, economic damage involves mainly reduced tree growth and seed production (see Section 2.4), as well as the die-back of crown parts, entire trees or even stands. In some cases the protection service of an entire forest may be impaired. The mass propagation of insects is usually a reaction to an excessive supply of host plants, e.g., in monocultures, or to a loss – even temporary – of tree vigour. Thus, so-called 'pests' have a regulatory role, which is not, however, desirable in commercially managed forests.

The European spruce bark beetle *(Ips typographus)* is the forest insect that causes the greatest economic damage in Europe. Spruce trees that are infested with these bark beetles usually die.

When moth caterpillars completely defoliate coniferous trees, the consequences can be fatal because, unlike deciduous trees, they cannot flush new foliage. In this photo, a caterpillar of the pine hawk moth *(Sphinx pinastri)* is feeding on a pine needle.

Potentially harmful species can be inconspicuous or even rare over a long period of time, only to 'explode' under certain environmental conditions. Such population fluctuations can be episodic or – more rarely – cyclical (as with the larch budmoth, cf. Section 13.2).

Animal pests – mainly in the form of insects – destroy 18 percent of the total production of agricultural crops worldwide (Oerke 2006). Added to this are the losses arising from pests that damage stored product. For forests, which are mostly less intensively managed production systems, quantitative information on damage by pest insects is only available for some individual species. Global losses in forests due to insect infestations are, however, likely to be much lower than in the agricultural sector and subject to strong fluctuations.

Insect infestations can manifest themselves directly in the loss of plant biomass, assimilation area, photosynthates, and entire organs. Depending on the tree species, age and season, plants are able – in various ways – to more-or-less compensate such losses. Seedlings and young plants are usually damaged more readily than large, fully grown trees, which have more reserves and are therefore better able to compensate. They can compensate insect feeding in spring during the active growth period more easily than in summer. In general, deciduous trees flush new leaves in the same year after a loss of more than 50 percent of their foliage (Hodkinson and Hughes 1982).

Insect infestations can also have indirect consequences, such as facilitating secondary infestations by other organisms or impairing the carbohydrate supply for symbionts such as mycorrhizal root fungi. Large-scale infestations can also lead to higher nitrogen concentrations in the run-off water of entire catchments, both through leaching from leaves, bark and faeces and the increased turnover of soil organic matter, triggered by higher insolation due to loss of foliage. Finally, insects can have an economic impact as vectors of diseases.

The literature on the countless species of insects that feed or suck on forest trees is extensive. However, the majority of these forest insects are hardly ever economically relevant. The following sections focus on some important species that can cause forest owners in Europe, as well as the general public, considerable economic loss.

The food of the large and characteristically coloured caterpillars of the gypsy moth *(Lymantria dispar)* ranges broadly. They prefer, however, oak, beech, and sweet chestnut. Each caterpillar devours about one square metre of leaf surface in its lifetime.

14.1 Leaf- and needle-feeding insects

Defoliators are the largest group of potential forest pests. Broadleaf trees can survive defoliation by insects fairly well as they can reflush new foliage and at least partially replace the consumed leaf area. Nevertheless, they are weakened by such infestations. Some parts of the crown may die off, especially if the trees are repeatedly defoliated in successive years. This then makes them more susceptible to colonisation by other insects and fungi. Coniferous trees, apart from the deciduous larch, do not normally survive a complete defoliation.

Moth caterpillars

The most important defoliators of broadleaf trees are moth caterpillars. These include some of the most 'notorious' forest pests in Europe. For example, the gypsy moth *(Lymantria dispar)* is a polyphagous caterpillar on oak, beech, sweet chestnut, stone fruit and pip fruit as well as many other tree species. After hatching in spring, the larvae develop by summer into caterpillars up to eight centimetres long with characteristic red and blue raised spots. At the peak of an outbreak, the infestation may amount to two to four million caterpillars per hectare (Duvigneaud 1974). During its development, each caterpillar consumes about one square metre of leaf surface, in addition to biting off leaf pieces, which then fall to the ground (Doane and McManus

Male (left) and female (right) of the gypsy moth. The behaviour of the morphologically distinct sexes also differs: while the female is largely flightless, the male flies restlessly through the forest during daytime in search of females.

1981). After pupation, the flightless females produce an egg mass of up to over a thousand eggs coated in abdominal hairs. While in Central Europe outbreaks of gypsy moths occur at irregular intervals, they are more regular and frequent in southeastern Europe with up to hundreds of thousands of hectares of infested forests. In extensively managed forests without any commercial function, these caterpillars are of little importance. In the extensive oak forests of Germany and southeastern Europe, however, mass outbreaks markedly reduce wood growth and acorn production. Subsequent secondary infestation by, e.g.,

The females of the gypsy moth lay clutches of eggs embedded in abdominal hair. After hatching in spring, the neonate caterpillars remain close to the clutches for several days.

jewel beetles or oak powdery mildew, can lead to widespread tree mortality. Moreover, in the vicinity of residential areas, the caterpillars may annoy humans. During outbreaks, the hyperactive caterpillars prowl restlessly in search of new food sources, climbing all kinds of objects and even entering houses through open windows. The gypsy moth was introduced from Europe to North America in 1869, where it quickly became the pest with the most impact on broadleaf trees. The control measures against this moth cost more than 7.5 billion US dollars in the three years from 1993 to 1995 alone (Mayo et al. 2003).

The nun moth *(Lymantria monacha)*, a sibling species of the gypsy moth, can also cause extensive damage. In the last century, mass propagations of this species, especially in spruce and pine forests in Eastern Europe and Russia, repeatedly killed trees across large areas and caused severe growth losses. The pine moth *(Dendrolimus pini)* also used to be a typical forest pest in East Germany, damaging millions of hectares of pine forests (Wellenstein 1978). Today, silvicultural measures or insecticides keep the caterpillars in check.

Various loopers (Geometridae) also sporadically defoliate large areas of forest. The winter moth *(Operophtera brumata)* and the mottled umber *(Erannis defoliaria)* are notorious defoliators of various broadleaf trees. In most cases, the 'damage' remains largely aesthetic, and the trees usually recover well even after they have been completely defoliated. They subsequently rebud, which means the growth losses remain negligible. The winter moth's name has to do with the fact that, in Central Europe, the males fly at a very unusual time of year for moths, namely from October up to early winter. Only the males swarm, whereas the females are flightless. Among the owlet moths (Noctuidae), the pine beauty moth *(Panolis flammea)* is an especially dreaded pest on pine. It defoliated 170 000 hectares of pine forest in eastern Germany and Poland at the beginning of the 20th century (Schwenke 1978).

Leafrollers (Tortricidae) include some typical defoliators as well. The caterpillars of the European oak leafroller *(Tortrix viridana)* feed on oak leaves, preferably in the upper part of the canopy. Long-term infestations reduce growth, weaken the trees and predispose them to infestation by other insects. Infestations by these caterpillars have been one

After an outbreak of the gypsy moth, this sweet chestnut forest in Ticino, Switzerland, was completely defoliated in mid-July. Two weeks later, the trees rebudded again and produced new foliage from their reserves. The weakened trees often suffer secondary infestation by other insects or fungi. If the trees are repeatedly infested or their water and nutrient supply are unfavourable, they can die as a result.

14 Economic damage

of the many factors contributing to the oak decline in Europe.

Sawflies

Sawfly larvae are more relevant economically for coniferous than for broadleaf trees, which react much less sensitively to feeding. In particular, the larvae of some conifer sawflies (Diprionidae) have repeatedly caused severe damage in pine stands throughout Europe. The outbreaks are usually rather short, lasting one to four years, but can affect tens of thousands of hectares, especially in the pine forests of Eastern Europe. The European pine sawfly *(Neodiprion sertifer)* attacks rather young trees in well-sunlit places, as well as ornamental pines in gardens. However, the mortality of the infested trees generally remains low, at a maximum of 10 percent (Pschorn-Walcher 1982). The pine web-spinning sawfly *(Acantholyda posticalis)* has appeared in Northern and Eastern Europe with long-lasting propagations, particularly in the last century. During World War II, 250 000 hectares of pine forests in Poland became infested at the peak of an outbreak (Pschorn-Walcher 1982). The pine forests affected consisted of large-scale plantations of pine monocultures, which for the larvae represented an unnaturally large supply of probably not very vital host plants. Such extensive pine plantations no longer exist in this form today.

In Central Europe, the spruce web-spinning sawfly *(Cephalcia abietis)* feeding in old stands and the lesser spruce sawfly *(Pris-*

No sooner have the broadleaf trees budded in spring than they are temporarily defoliated again at the end of May by caterpillars of the winter moth.

The mottled umber *(Erannis defoliaria*, above) and the winter moth *(Operophtera brumata*, below) occur sporadically en masse. Their caterpillars may then completely defoliate stands of broadleaf trees, particularly in warmer locations. The upper photo depicts the horseshoe-like form typical for loopers when they are moving.

14 Economic damage

˄
This infestation by the spindle ermine *(Yponomeuta cagnagella)* looks spectacular, as the caterpillars can defoliate whole trees and cover them with webs. However, the 'damage' is mostly aesthetic, as the shrubs rebud again in summer.

A male of the European pine sawfly *(Neodiprion sertifer)* with its long pectinate antennae typical of the entire family of conifer sawflies (Diprionidae).
˅

The pine false webworm (*Acantholyda erythrocephala*) has often infested hundreds to thousands of hectares of pine plantations.

tiphora abietina) in young stands of spruce can permanently weaken or deform their host trees.

Beetles

Besides the larvae of moths and sawflies, some beetle species are also well-known leaf- and needle-eaters. Adult northern cockchafers (*Melolontha hippocastani*) feeding on the foliage of oak, maple, beech and other broadleaf trees can weaken their host trees, but with mostly negligible effect. However, the feeding of their larvae ('grubs') on the roots of various young trees – in the case of the common cockchafer (*M. melolontha*), also on the roots of agricultural crops – occasionally leads to severe damage. According to anecdote, in 1473, the Ecclesiastical Court of Lausanne issued an ultimatum, on behalf of

A colony of European pine sawfly larvae. The larvae only spare the most recent needles from the current year.

The well-camouflaged green larvae of the lesser spruce sawfly *(Pristiphora abietina)* feed on new needles. The young shoots then look as if they have been scorched by fire. If young spruce trees are repeatedly infested heavily, they can become bushy. (Photo courtesy of Forest Entomology WSL).

'all clerical and divine authorities', to the cockchafers raiding Bernese territory 'to leave all places where food for people and livestock is growing' or they would be summoned before the Bishop of Lausanne. However, the 'foolish and unreasonable creatures' paid no attention to this threat and were excommunicated and cursed in God's name (Zürn 1901).

In some years, the beech leaf-mining weevil *(Orchestes fagi)* makes a conspicuous appearance in spring. While feeding, the larva burrows a gallery (mine) across the leaf from its midrib to the tip of the leaf, where it pupates, leaving a striking brown blotch mine on the tip of the leaf. However, the damage to the beech trees is usually short-term and not serious, even though it is visually very evident.

14.2 Sucking insects

Plant-sap suckers pierce the plant tissue with their proboscises and suck up the liquid contents. Spider mites suck out leaf cells, thus reducing the photosynthetically active leaf area. They are particularly important in agriculture. Other groups such as plant lice suck on photosynthates in the conducting cells of the phloem (the innermost part of the bark that transports photosynthates). Aphids, scale insects and adelgids play a major role in forests.

Sucking insects do not have the same economic impact on forests as leaf feeders. Often an infestation is small-scale and only a limited number of trees are affected. This is especially the case for trees suffering from moderate

A newly hatched beetle (left) of the beech leaf-mining weevil *(Orchestes fagi)*. Its larvae mine and pupate in beech leaves. In a heavy infestation, the beetles' light brown mines give the beech forest a brownish appearance (right). However, the infestation usually has no other negative effects on the trees.

drought stress. In order to be able to extract water from the soil, the plant increases the osmotic pressure in the tissue by enriching the cells with sugar as well as nitrogenous and osmotically active substances. The sucking insects benefit from the increased concentrations of energy sources and nutrients, but their sucking activity weakens the plant and often leads to yellowing and wilting. This can occur in, for example, spruce when in dry years the spruce bud scale *(Physokermes piceae)* heavily propagates. In large trees, the scales usually just reduce tree growth. However, the yellowed needles die off and must be replaced by new ones the following year. Spruce trees – especially blue spruce – may be damaged by the green spruce aphid *(Elatobium abietinum)*. It sucks on the older needles, which die off after a severe infestation, and often at the end only the last needle class is left. If this occurs repeatedly over several years, it weakens even large trees and makes them susceptible to secondary pest insects such as bark beetles.

In some years, beech aphids *(Phyllaphis fagi)* are particularly abundant on beech trees. Again, infestations several years in succession cause growth losses or even the death of young plants.

The silver fir woolly aphid *(Dreyfusia nordmannianae)*, which belongs to the spruce adelgids, was introduced to Europe more than 100 years ago. Here, it undergoes only partial cycles on silver fir since this heteroecious species also requires Oriental spruce for a complete cycle. The aphids suck on the needles and can cause significant damage to young trees in silver fir plantations and even their death.

14.3 Bark beetles and other bark colonizers

For a tree, insects developing in the bark are more important than insects feeding on the foliage. If the sap-flow in the phloem is interrupted around the whole stem by bark feed-

Sucking damage by aphids and scale insects makes plants susceptible to attack by other insects. Left: green spruce aphid *(Elatobium abietinum)*; right: brown globules of the large spruce bud scale *(Physokermes piceae)*, both on spruce. The scale insects secrete honeydew, which is quickly colonized by black sooty mould fungi. (Photo on left courtesy of Swiss Forest Protection WSL.)

Aphids such as the elder aphid *(Aphis sambuci)* have great reproductive potential. Their evolutionary success is due to: their parthenogenic reproduction (no need to find a mate), viviparous reproduction (on the right in the photo), host alternating (optimisation of nutrition), formation of winged individuals as required, and symbiosis with ants.

Heavy infestation by the silver fir woolly aphid *(Dreyfusia nordmannianae)* can kill young silver firs.

ers, the tree is bound to die. While insects feeding in the sapwood do destroy parts of the water-conducting vessels, this usually only weakens the structural stability of a tree unless the wood feeders are associated with pathogens (see Section 14.4). In Central Europe, bark beetles cause most of the significant economic damage.

The spruce bark beetle – the most destructive forest insect in Central Europe

All bark beetle species able to kill vigorous trees colonize coniferous trees. Most of these species are monophagous, i.e., specialised in one or a few tree species. Since the use of spruce for timber production is so widespread, the spruce bark beetle *(Ips typographus)* is the species with the most detrimental impact in Europe – not only among bark beetles, but among forest insects in general. Bark beetle 'calamities' were already seen as significant in the early days of forest entomology in the 18th century: 'observation teaches us that among the multitudinous insects which feed on the different tree taxa according to their characters nary a one is as harmful and horrible as this very bark beetle' (Jäger 1784).

The pioneer bark beetle males search for suitable host trees to colonize, which are very often weakened spruce trees. The beetles rely primarily on visual cues to find them, as well as on 'tree-borne' volatiles. If they succeed in overcoming the exuding resin with which the tree defends itself against the attackers,

European spruce bark beetles usually attack groups of spruce trees, thereby producing typical infestation spots.

they penetrate the bark and each male creates a 'nuptial chamber'. It emits aggregation pheromones to attract more males to better overcome the tree's defence system, as well as two to three females to mate in the nuptial chamber. Each mated female constructs a longitudinal maternal gallery in which she deposits eggs in small niches excavated alternately on the left and right side. The beetle transports the boring dust it produces while feeding backwards to the entrance hole using its declivity, i.e., the rear end of its elytra (forewings). The hatched larvae feed in larval galleries, which diverge more-or-less at right angles from the maternal gallery. They then pupate in pupal chambers at the end of their larval galleries. After the teneral beetles have emerged from the pupae, they carry out 'maturation feeding' in the brood system before they leave their brood tree. Alternatively, they overwinter in the brood systems under the bark. After producing the first offspring, a fraction of the parental females take flight again and create a second, so-called 'sister brood'. At lower elevations, two generations are usually produced per year.

The actual damage to the tree is caused by the larval galleries, which run across the phloem vessels, thus interrupting the vertical sap flow from the tree crown to the roots. In addition, the beetles carry a blue stain fungus, which blocks the water-conducting vessels in the sapwood and thus interrupts the water and nutrient transport from the roots to the

Despite being only five millimetres in size, the spruce bark beetle is the forest insect with the greatest potential for damage.

One male and two females in a newly initiated gallery system. In the centre is the nuptial chamber where the sexes copulate. Each female has started excavating a maternal gallery. Some eggs are visible in the egg niches along both galleries. (Photo on bottom courtesy of Forest Entomology WSL.)

14 Economic damage

Developing breeding galleries on a lying stem. The larval galleries diverge laterally from the longitudinal maternal galleries, which run vertically in a standing tree. The larvae have different ages and the lengths of their galleries therefore vary according to the order in which the eggs were laid.

crown. This manifests itself in a red discoloration of the tree crown, and the interrupted sap flows eventually lead to the death of the infested tree.

The European spruce bark beetle follows two different strategies. At low population densities it is very dependent on newly dead or severely weakened trees. Their low resistance enables the beetle to colonize the trees and establish a brood. It cannot infest healthy spruce during this phase as the trees' defence system will be intact and trap the beetles, which attack individually when their populations are low, in resin. However, if the beetles are able to build up their populations in wind-thrown stems after, for example, a storm, they will be abundant enough to jointly colonize

When the larvae are fully grown (top), they pupate in a pupal chamber. The newly emerged spruce bark beetles (bottom) are still light and soft. They harden during their maturation feeding in the bark and become dark brown in colour. (Photo on bottom courtesy of Forest Entomology WSL.)

The European spruce bark beetle also introduces a blue stain fungus into the wood, which clogs the water-conducting vessels in the sapwood and leads to the death of the tree. Although the physical properties of the wood remain unchanged, the sales price for blue-stained wood is lower.

even vigorous trees with an intact resin defence. The increased risk of getting trapped in the resin is more than balanced by the nutritional benefit of the trees' high-quality phloem. If the beetles' density remains high, large-scale infestations of healthy spruce will occur. The more vital the spruce tree is, the more beetles will be needed to attack it simultaneously and successfully colonize it. The threshold for successful colonisation of a healthy spruce tree is estimated to be about 200 beetles (Fahse and Heurich 2011).

Ironically, the spruce bark beetle 'abuses' and benefits from exactly the same substances (monoterpenes) that the tree produces to defend itself against infestation. The toxic resin compounds attract beetles to potential host trees, and the beetles use similar compounds as pheromones to attract more conspecifics to better overcome the host.

Mass outbreaks

Bark beetle outbreaks usually develop as follows: a major storm provides ample supply of downed spruce stems with still nutritious bark, but with an already reduced resin defence system. This allows the spruce bark beetles, which are always present in low densities, to multiply and increase their populations. Depending on the elevation and slope aspect, the trees' bark becomes too dry for breeding after one or two years, and the increased beetle population then infests living trees along the windthrow edges, where the trees have been weakened by the storm and the unusual insolation reaching the newly exposed stems. Local beetle populations build up in scattered windthrows and on individual overthrown trees inside the stand as well. Depending on the weather conditions, the individual

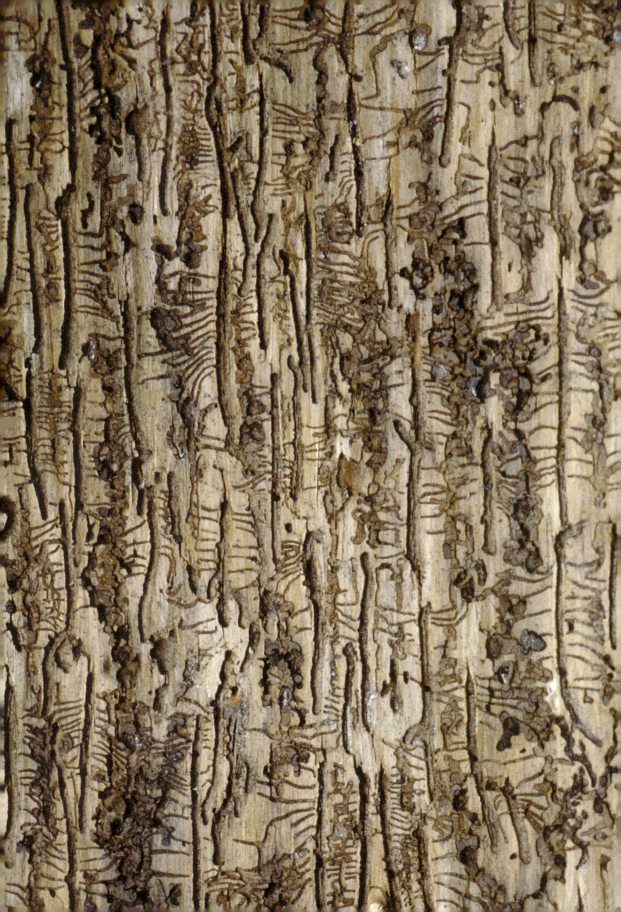

infestation spots may coalesce to form a large infestation area. After a few years, outbreaks collapse for one or more reasons: cooler weather conditions during beetle development, sufficient precipitation for the host trees to recover, increase in natural enemies (see Chapter 9) or, in managed forests, appropriate control measures. These measures mainly involve timely sanitation felling of the infested trees across a large area and removing them from the forest before the beetles emerge.

In the recent past, large-scale infestation events in Central Europe occurred after the hurricanes 'Vivian' (1990), 'Lothar' (1999), 'Gudrun' (2005) and 'Kyrill' (2007). The abundant supply of downed spruce trees led to high beetle populations, which subsequently infested large numbers of living trees. As a result, tens of millions of cubic metres of wood became infested (Grégoire and Evans 2004). In Switzerland alone, eight million cubic metres of spruce were killed after 'Lothar'. This outbreak, though, was greatly reinforced by the heatwave of 2003 shortly after the storm. This corresponds to more than one and a half times the annual cut in Switzerland. After such major events, huge amounts of windthrown timber flood the market and the timber price falls. As a result, salvaging windthrows and beetle-infested trees is financially bad business, especially in mountain forests.

In addition to the loss of timber, the loss of protection may be critical for mountain forests. Trees that have been killed by beetles remain standing for some time, but eventually they break down. This jeopardizes the protection they provide for the settlements and traffic routes beneath them against rockfall, mudflows and avalanches, and confronts forest owners with a difficult decision: does it make more sense to harvest the dead trees, which is usually not profitable, and install artificial barriers? Or is it better to leave the dead trees standing as they will continue to provide protection for several years, and rely on the natural regeneration taking over the protective function in due time?

The local water runoff and composition can also change during a spruce bark beetle outbreak. Investigations in a large infestation area

When just a few bark beetles attack a vigorous tree, individual beetles get stuck in the resin (on the right above the drop of liquid).

◁ Piece of detached bark from a densely colonized spruce. The horizontal larval galleries and the subsequent maturation feeding of the teneral beetles interrupt the sap flow in the phloem and the bark becomes detached from the tree.

14 Economic damage

If spruce stands are weakened and the weather conditions are favourable for the propagation of the beetles, the individual infestation spots can coalesce to form extensive infestation areas.

have shown that, after the bark beetles had killed a large proportion of the spruce trees, the water flow into groundwater and runoff into streams increased markedly and the nitrate content of the groundwater was higher for seven years (Kennel 2002, Huber 2005).

In addition to the economic and ecological (Section 13.3) effects of bark beetle outbreaks, the large-scale die-off of spruce trees also means a non-material loss for humans. A gigantic bark beetle outbreak in the Bavarian Forest National Park with an infested area of around 60 square kilometres of spruce forest turned the shady and relaxing mountain spruce forests into an open landscape with thousands and thousands of dead tree skeletons. Knowing that new life is being created in this dead wood and that the area as a whole

Outbreaks of the spruce bark beetle are almost always triggered by disturbances such as windthrow (top), drought or clear cutting (bottom). The stand edges are attacked first. (Photo on bottom by Anton Bürgi WSL.)

Spruce bark beetle infestations also jeopardize the effect of protection forests. Ideally, the dead, standing or fallen trees continue to provide protection against avalanches and rockfall until the natural regeneration can take over their protective function.

is slowly developing into pleasant woodland again is often little comfort. The largest contiguous deadwood area in Switzerland was created by a spruce bark beetle infestation after the storm 'Vivian' in Canton Glarus. There, most spruce trees within an area of about one hundred hectares were killed in the space of two years. A decade later, however, a young pioneer forest had already re-established.

Between 1995 and 2013, the growing stock of spruce on the Swiss Plateau has decreased by almost one-third. This decrease is due to the two severe storms that occurred at the end of the last century, as well as to bark beetle infestations and drought (Camin et al. 2015). The subsequent natural regeneration has led to a significantly higher proportion of broadleaves. Towards the end of this century, the higher temperatures associated with climate change will make possible an additional annual generation of European spruce bark beetles in many places in Europe (Jakoby et al. 2019). As a result, spruce will fall victim to bark beetles more often, fostered further by more frequent droughts.

Other bark beetles

What the spruce bark beetle is for spruce, the silver fir bark beetle *(Pityokteines curvidens)* is for silver fir, and the pine bark beetle *(Ips acuminatus)* and the pine shoot beetles *(Tomicus* spp.) for Scots pine. They are all, however, less aggressive and have less impact than the spruce bark beetle. Other bark beetles that can lead to mortality in weakened stands are the six-toothed spruce bark beetle *(Pityogenes chalcographus)* on the young growth of spruce, the great spruce bark beetle

14 Economic damage

Extensive infestations also affect how people perceive a forest emotionally. Instead of the former dense and shady forest in the Bavarian Forest National Park, a grassland landscape dotted with tree skeletons has temporarily evolved at higher elevations after the long-lasting outbreak of spruce bark beetles.

(*Dendroctonus micans*) on older spruce trees, and the large larch bark beetle (*Ips cembrae*) on larch. Some species also transmit diseases (see Section 14.4).

Bark beetles are not only able to kill living trees, but some species also devalue stored timber by excavating tunnels in the sapwood. When the mother beetles lay their eggs in the wood, they also introduce an 'ambrosia' fungus, on which the larvae then feed. Other economically relevant species are the striped ambrosia beetle (*Trypodendron lineatum*) and the introduced black timber bark beetle (*Xylosandrus germanus*). The large timberworm (*Hylecoetus dermestoides*) is not a bark bee-

With the warmer temperatures expected in the future, the European spruce bark beetle will take flight two to three weeks earlier in spring. Because the generation time will become shorter towards the end of this century, one more beetle generation, on average, per year is likely to occur.

14 Economic damage

tle, but it has a similar lifestyle and impact. Timber yards are therefore sometimes irrigated, covered with foil or treated with insecticides.

The mountain pine beetle in North America

It is worthwhile to briefly expand the Central European focus of this book to have a look at the world's largest unprecedented infestation by a forest insect. The mountain pine beetle *(Dendroctonus ponderosae*; a bark beetle) has been undergoing a gigantic mass outbreak in the pine forests of western North America since the beginning of this century. The infested area now extends from the Canadian provinces of British Columbia and Alberta along the Rocky Mountains to Arizona in the south of the United States. By 2010, the total infested area extended over 250 000 square kilometres (Bentz *et al.* 2010). In Alberta, the beetle has expanded its host range from lodgepole pine *(Pinus contorta)* to Jack pine *(P. banksiana)*. The factors leading to this historically unique infestation are forests weakened by drought, pine stands that are overly mature and uniform due to many years of firefighting and suppression, and higher temperatures related to climate change. Higher temperatures shorten the generation time of the bark beetle – particularly at higher altitudes – and increase the survival rate of the overwintering larvae (Logan and Powell 2001).

The six-toothed spruce bark beetle (*Pityogenes chalcographus*, lower galleries) is occasionally associated with the European spruce bark beetle (galleries on the top right). However, it mainly colonizes thinner branches in the crown or younger plants.

The death of trees in this order of magnitude has also had consequences for the carbon balance of the forests. The dead stands have developed from being a carbon sink to becoming a carbon source that was estimated to have emitted about 270 megatons of carbon by 2020 (Kurz et al. 2008). Over time, however, the ground vegetation, the understorey and the newly emerging regeneration will compensate for the carbon emissions of the rotting trees, and the growing forests will once again become carbon sinks.

The approximately five-millimetre-long mountain pine beetle *(Dendroctonus ponderosae)* is the cause of the largest mass outbreak of a forest insect ever recorded. In North America, pine trees died at the beginning of this century across an area covering millions of hectares.

Other bark and wood boring beetles

In addition to the bark beetles described above, several other groups within the wee-

The newly infested, red-coloured pine trees are part of the front of the spreading infestation of the mountain pine beetle (British Columbia, Canada; 2009). The upper green bands indicate where wildfire occurred earlier and the trees are still too young for an infestation.

vil family (Curculionidae) can cause the death of trees – although to a much lesser degree. Apart from some *Pissodes* species on pine trees, the large pine weevil *(Hylobius abietis)* in particular has affected conifers in northern and eastern Europe. Its larvae develop in the old stumps of coniferous trees, and are therefore economically irrelevant. The adult beetle, however, feeds on the bark of coniferous trees, preferably at the stem base of young plants. This causes the young trees to die and creates problems in large-scale plantations or afforested clear cuttings. Among the jewel beetles (Buprestidae), the steelblue jewel beetle *(Phaenops cyanea)* can cause some mortality in pine trees as can the oak splendour beetle *(Agrilus biguttatus)* in oak trees. In these cases, the stands that are affected will have been weakened by, for example, severe drought stress. Longhorn beetles (Cerambycidae) play a negligible role as pests.

14.4 Transmission of plant diseases

As mentioned earlier, some insects, especially beetles, inoculate the wood with a symbiotic fungus during oviposition. The fungus then serves the hatched larvae directly as food or assists them in decomposing the wood. Examples include ambrosia beetles and woodwasps (Sections 4.2 and 11.2).

Other insects may transmit plant-pathogenic fungi, viruses or nematodes without the transmitting insect (vector) directly benefiting. At best, the infection makes it easier for later

The higher temperatures in recent decades allow the mountain pine beetle to complete a full generation per year even in the pine forests of the Yellowstone National Park that grow up to 3000 metres above sea level. This has allowed, for the first time, extensive infestations of white-bark pines.

In Scandinavian and Eastern European countries, the maturation feeding of the large pine weevil (*Hylobius abietis*) can cause significant economic damage in large-scale plantations of young conifers. (Photo courtesy of Forest Entomology WSL.)

The steelblue jewel beetle (*Phaenops cyanea*) colonizes, almost exclusively, weakened pines, which it can quickly kill.

generations, which are dependent on weakened trees for their larval development, to colonize the tree. The best-known example is the transmission of the introduced sac fungus *Ophiostoma novo-ulmi*, which causes Dutch elm disease, by the elm bark beetles (*Scolytus* spp.). When the beetle larvae develop in elms weakened by Dutch elm disease, the emerging teneral beetles transport the sticky fungal spores to healthy trees. There, the beetles carry out a maturation feeding in the bark at branch bifurcations, thereby transmitting the pathogen. The maturation feeding of the beetles itself has basically little direct effect on the elm trees. However, the introduction of *Ophiostoma* fungi is fatal for the trees, as the infection kills them over time. In return, the ailing trees provide the elm bark beetles with suitable breeding places, where their offspring become infected with fungal spores again before they leave the trees. The elm has therefore been pushed to the edge of extinction in Europe and North America. In Switzerland, a pronounced wave of Dutch elm disease became apparent from around 1975 onwards (Nierhaus-Wunderwald and Engesser 2003). As a result, the number of elm trees decreased by 25 percent between 1985 and 2013 (Abegg et al. 2014). However, the tree species as such is hardly endangered, as the beetles prefer larger trees for their maturation feeding and the younger elms can reproduce in time before becoming affected by Dutch elm disease. As with previous infections, resistant elm genotypes have also been able to establish. Moreover, the decline in elm trees has probably also decimated the populations of elm bark beetles.

Another example of beetles acting as vectors of a plant pathogen is the sawyer beetle (*Monochamus galloprovincialis*). It transmits the introduced pine wood nematode (*Bursaphelenchus xylophilus*). After the beetle larvae have developed on infected dying pine trees, the nematodes settle in the spiracles of the emerging beetles and are transported to healthy pine trees, where the beetles then carry out their maturation feeding and lay their eggs. The pine wood nematode was first discovered in Europe in Portugal in 1999 and has since led to the death of hundreds of thousands of trees in this region. So far, its spread to the rest of Europe has been prevented.

Breeding galleries of the large elm bark beetle (*Scolytus scolytus*), a vector of the Dutch elm disease.

280 Should the sawyer beetle *(Monochamus galloprovincialis)* emerge from wood infested with the pine wood nematode, it transmits the nematodes to healthy pine trees during its maturation feeding.

Insects and human health 15

Insects and mites play an important role in human health worldwide, especially as vectors of major diseases such as malaria, dengue-, West Nile- and yellow fever, sleeping sickness, river blindness, plague and borreliosis. In most cases, stinging insects transmit the pathogens, such as viruses, bacteria, protozoa and nematodes, to healthy people when sucking blood. The pathogens undergo an obligatory part of their development cycle in the insect. They are often dependent on a specific insect species to complete their cycle successfully. Ticks, lice, true bugs, fleas, flies and, above all, the notorious mosquitoes can serve as vectors (Aspöck 2002). Among the forest insects, only a few species are of medical significance for humans. However, mosquitoes and their pathogens may also develop in pockets of still water in European floodplain forests.

Other insects can harm people by injecting venom, which may be life-threatening, especially for people who are particularly sensitive

Castor bean tick *(Ixodes ricinus)* attached to its host's skin for a blood meal. These ticks can transmit various diseases.

or allergic. In contrast to those species that can harm human health, some other insects have products that are used in medicine.

15.1 Disease-transmitting ticks

In addition to the Asian tiger mosquito (*Aedes albopictus*), which was introduced in Central Europe at the turn of the century, it is mainly ticks, as carriers of disease, that are relevant in human medicine in Europe. The castor bean tick *(Ixodes ricinus)* is the most important disease vector. It belongs to the mites, and lives in forests particularly along forest edges and the sides of paths. If the weather is warm enough, it can be active at any time of the year. In winter, however, ticks enter a state of torpor when the temperature falls below about 6 °C. All instars suck blood and can transmit pathogens. However, the larva (the first, six-legged instar) usually cannot penetrate human skin. Therefore, mostly the eight-legged nymph and adult instars are relevant for human health. The ticks wait on blades of grass or low shrub branches for mammals to pass. They rarely climb higher than one metre above the ground, and retreat down to the ground again under dry conditions as they are sensitive to drought. The questing tick lies in wait ready to react to sudor, carbon dioxide and the body heat of a passing host animal. On contact with a potential host, it attaches itself to its fur or skin. If the host is acceptable, the tick looks for an appropriate spot on the host's body where the skin is thin and moist, and starts sucking blood. It first bites the skin with its chelicerae (jaws) to make a small opening, and then inserts its so-called hypostome into the tissue. During the process it exudes a secretion that has anticoagulant and anti-inflammatory effects, and also numbs the area so that the host does not notice the process. The barbed hypostome is anchored in the skin, which is why it takes some pulling

This adult female tick is 'questing' with raised forelegs for a passing animal. Her proboscis is located under the two palps pointing forward on her head.
⌄

to remove a tick. The sucking act lasts two to three days for the larvae, and about one week for the older instars. Larvae and nymphs drop to the ground after their blood meal, where they digest the blood and molt to the next instar. Afterwards they wait for a new host. An adult female increases her weight up to 200 times when feeding on blood. She mates with a male during her blood meal – if a male is present on the same host at the same time – and then drops to the ground to lay up to several thousand eggs in the litter. Each tick instar prefers different hosts: the larvae mainly attach themselves to small mammals such as mice and hedgehogs, while the nymphs and adults go for hares, foxes, roe and red deer, and, of course, also humans. It takes the ticks several years to complete their development, depending on the availability of hosts, and the individual instars can survive for months to years without food.

The two most serious tick-borne diseases transmitted are tick-borne encephalitis (TBE, or meningoencephalitis) and Lyme disease (borreliosis). Tick-borne encephalitis is caused by a virus that, in Switzerland, is present in 0.5 to 3.0 percent of ticks at elevations below 1000 meters above sea level (BAG 2015). There is a vaccine against this virus, but the disease cannot be treated with antibiotics.

The bacterium *Borrelia burgdorferi* is the pathogen that causes Lyme disease or borreliosis. Here antibiotics are an effective treatment, but there is no vaccine against it. Regardless of the geographical location, about half of all ticks are vectors of these bacteria in Central Europe. The two diseases manifest themselves in flu-like symptoms and neurological disorders that can become life-threatening.

Interestingly, the transmission pathways of the two diseases are quite different. The viruses of tick-borne encephalitis are partly passed on by the maternal tick directly to her eggs and thus to the offspring. Non-infected ticks have to suck on the host's skin in the

After a blood meal, a fully saturated tick weighs up to 200 times more than before. Note the small dark spot on the right behind the tick's head. This is the scutum that covered half of its body before its meal.

immediate vicinity of an already infected tick in order to acquire the virus. Since the virus is located in the tick's saliva, it is immediately transmitted to a new host when the tick sucks on it.

The *Borrelia* bacterium, on the other hand, is hardly ever passed on to the offspring during oviposition. The ticks can only acquire the bacteria when sucking on an infected host, and they transmit them to a new host at their next blood meal. Since the bacteria first have to migrate from the gut via the body cavity into the tick's salivary gland, it takes about one day after a tick bite for the *Borrelia* bacteria to be transmitted to the new host.

15.2 Caterpillars with urticating hairs

A few caterpillars in Europe have poisonous urticating hairs. They feed on the foliage of woody plants and are often found on single trees or along hedges and sun-exposed forest edges. The brown-tail moth *(Euproctis chrysorrhoea)* is present all over Europe. Its caterpillars exploit a wide range of food, but prefer to feed on the foliage of oak, fruit trees, hawthorn, blackthorn and dog rose. The gregariously living caterpillars spend the winter in silk nests containing up to a hundred larvae, and resume their feeding in spring. It is only the last instar that lives solitarily. They pupate at the end of June in the branches of their host plant, and the moths emerge in mid-summer. The name 'brown-tail moth'

Female of the brown-tail moth *(Euproctis chrysorrhoea)*. When depositing her eggs, she covers them with the golden hairs of her tail tuft. It is not, however, the moth's hairs that are venomous, but those of the caterpillar.

The caterpillars of the brown-tail moth spend the winter clustered together in their silk nest. They resume feeding when the leaves flush in spring.

285

The caterpillars of the brown-tail moth live solitarily during the last instar. They typically have two orange-red spots on their abdomens, which are clearly visible in the photo.

refers to the fact that the female moths, in particular, have a shiny reddish-brown tuft of hair at the end of their abdomen with which they cover their eggs.

The caterpillars of the brown-tail moth, as well as of the species described below, have tiny urticating hairs. These remain active even on old exuviae (moulting remains) and in old nests, retaining their urticating effect for months or even years. The symptoms after contact with the hair of these species are similar: the affected body parts become inflamed and itchy, and the conjunctiva and respiratory tract are irritated. Allergy sufferers may also experience hypersensitivity reactions. Animals can also be affected. If, for example, a dog's mouth touches such caterpillars, the dog's tongue can turn necrotic and die back (Grundmann et al. 2000). If such caterpillar nests pose a hazard to people in residential areas and need to be removed, protective equipment must be worn.

The oak processionary moth (Thaumetopoea processionea) is found in warmer regions of Southern and Central Europe. The female moths lay their eggs on the branches of oak trees in autumn. When the leaves flush the following spring, the young caterpillars hatch and begin to feed on the leaves in the tree crown. They are nocturnal and rest during daytime on the tree's stem or branches. Initially they form clusters while resting, and then towards the end of their development rest in nests up to one metre long. At night, the caterpillars march in processions of several rows' width to their feeding places. These processions, which may be up to ten metres in length, are what gave them their name. The caterpillars only develop urticating hairs from the third larval instar onwards. They pupate in their silk nests in July and the moths emerge in August. With climate change, this species' range seems to be expanding.

Another important processionary is the pine processionary moth (Thaumetopoea pityocampa). It also occurs in Southern and Central Europe, where it colonizes conifers, especially pines. The moths fly in July and lay their eggs in cylindrical egg masses around pine needles. After hatching, the caterpillars feed gregariously on the needles at night, but do not form processions at this stage. During the day and cool weather, they remain in their nests. Unlike the species described above, the caterpillars overwinter as adolescent caterpillars in their white winter nests, which are visible from quite far away. In spring, they resume feeding on the needles. From March onwards, they crawl down the stem in a single-row procession to the ground to look for a suitable place for pupation in the litter. Their urticating hairs, which the caterpillars have from the third caterpillar instar on, have been studied

‹ Caterpillars of the oak processionary moth (Thaumetopoea processionea). It is not their long white hairs that are urticating, but rather the microscopically small setae.

The nocturnal caterpillars of the pine processionary moth *(Thaumetopoea pityocampa)* rest in their silk nest during the day and in winter.

extensively in this species. It is not their long and conspicuous hairs that urticate, but tiny little setae just a few tenths of a millimetre in length. They are arranged in so-called 'mirrors', with densities of 60 000 setae per square millimetre (Petrucco *et al.* 2014). These can be ejected when the caterpillars are disturbed, and the setae release their toxin like cannulas into the attacker's skin. The urticating hairs of the pine processionary moth can remain active for many years.

The caterpillars of some other moth species also produce silk nests, but are harmless. Examples are the small Eggar moth *(Eriogaster lanestris)*, which feeds on birch and other tree and shrub species, and the black-veined white *(Aporia crataegi)* on hawthorn and fruit trees.

Moth of the pine processionary moth. (Photo courtesy of Forest Entomology WSL.)

15 Human health

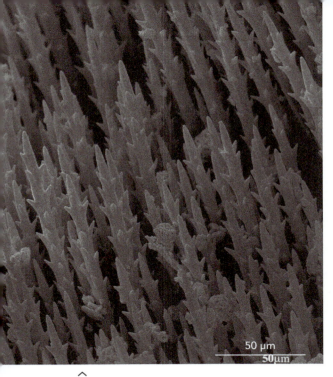

Image of the approximately 0.1-millimetre-long, venomous urticating hairs produced with a scanning electron microscope. (Photo by Elisabeth Schraner UZH.)

In spring the caterpillars migrate to the ground in single rows to pupate in the litter.

Pine tree with 'winter nests' of the pine processionary moth. The traces of caterpillar feeding are clearly visible near the nests.

15.3 Stinging insects

In contrast to stinging insects that transmit pathogens, some stinging insects have a sting that is itself painful for recipients. These include sucking insects, such as mosquitoes or horseflies, as well as stinging wasps and bees, which are equipped with a stinger and venom sac. In the temperate zone of Central Europe, only a few species are common or intrusive enough to be medically relevant. They use their stings to ward off enemies and, in some cases, also to attack prey (see Section 8.1). The injected venom contains enzymes, acids and amines, such as histamine, which cause itching, redness and swelling of the tissue and can lead to sepsis and circulatory disturbances. For most people, a sting is only a temporary albeit painful annoyance. However, if the sting is around the neck or mouth, for example, or in people with hypersensitivity reactions, its consequences may be fatal.

15.4 Medically useful insects

In medicine, insects and mites are known not only for the harm they do, but some also for the curing substances they produce. Insect extracts have been more frequently used in the past, but some forms are still in use today and may well become more important again in the future. Most of these beneficial insects are not typical forest species, but some may also occur in open forests or along forest edges. Spanish flies *(Lytta vesicatoria)*, from the blister beetle family (Meloidae), feed on leaves from ash and other trees and shrubs. They produce a toxin called 'cantharidin', which they can squeeze out of their knee joints to ward off enemies. During mating, the poison is transferred from male to female and eventually passed on to the eggs, which are thus also protected against predators. However, some insects and frogs are immune to the poison. They consume these beetles and use

This common horsefly *(Haematopota pluvialis)* is sucking on human skin. When the weather is sultry and skin sweat-covered, these flies may be a real nuisance.

the ingested poison for their own defence. In contact with human skin, cantharidin leads to severe blistering. Ingesting the substance even in smallest amounts has a lethal effect. This poison has been used for a long time not only for murdering people, but also, in a highly diluted form, for medical purposes. It is applied to boost blood circulation and to treat rheumatism, kidney issues and remove warts. In addition, men have sometimes used it as an aphrodisiac, often with fatal consequences (Ghoneim 2013).

Products from bees, wasps or scale insects have also been used for various purposes in homeopathy and traditional medicine. For example, propolis, a resinous substance that honeybees excrete to line their hives, is known to have an antibiotic effect.

It is not only extracts from insects that are used in medicine. Some species are used medically – similar to leeches for bloodletting – as living organisms. The South American Mayas and indigenous Australians traditionally used blowfly maggots (Calliphoridae) for treating wounds, and they were also used during the Second World War. When inserted into a festering wound, the maggots feed on the decaying and necrotic tissue and, with their antiseptic saliva, support the healing process (Schowalter 2013). Since the resistance of pathogens to synthetic antibiotics is becoming more and more widespread, this biological treatment is being viewed more seriously again. For example, the larvae of the common green bottle fly *(Lucilia sericata)* are now commercially bred under sterile conditions in laboratories, and they can be ordered on the Internet. In the wild, this common fly species occurs in all habitats and develops in carrion.

Substances obtained from the Spanish fly (*Lytta vesicatoria*; a blister beetle) were in the past used not only to treat kidney problems and warts, but also as an aphrodisiac.

Today the maggots of the common green bottle fly *(Lucilia sericata)* are being used once again to clean and disinfect wounds.

16 Usable insect products

Some insects provide valuable natural products that humans use. Others can be eaten directly as food. Many of these 'beneficial insects' live in forests, or at least woodland, but only a few of them are European species. For this reason, the focus of this chapter extends geographically somewhat beyond Europe.

16.1 Edible products

Honey

Honey is certainly the best-known edible insect product. People all over the world consume the honey that the honeybee (*Apis mellifera*) produces. They have used it for millennia as a sweetener and food, and also as a health product and in medicine because it has an antimicrobial effect. Honey is a high-quality substrate, containing various sugars such as glucose and fructose, fatty acids, proteins, vitamins and minerals. Honeybees originally lived in forests and colonized tree hollows.

Silkworms *(Bombyx mori)* spin themselves a cocoon for pupation with a valuable silk thread. After killing the pupa, the thread can be unwound from the cocoon and used commercially. The pupae are also consumed as food in Asia.

Honeybees *(Apis mellifera)* have been very important for humans for thousands of years. From the pollen they collect from flowering plants, they produce the familiar bee honey.

Initially, people simply raided the bees' nests in a very unsustainable way. Later, tree beekeepers (in German 'Zeidler') managed the forest bees actively and selectively and were respected as skilled workers. They made artificial tree hollows in living trees for bee colonies to settle in and then over the following years exploited their honey and wax. In Russia and Eastern Europe, the know-how for this traditional form of beekeeping has been maintained and is today more actively used. Hardly any wild honeybee colonies can, however, still be found living in forests in Central Europe today. Wild honeybees should not be confused with wild bees: these are solitary and do not produce honeycombs.

Domesticated bee colonies are bred and managed in artificial beehives to ensure their honey production is constant and high. Honey production in the European Union in 2018 amounted to 259 000 tonnes, which corresponds to 14 percent of the world's honey production and is the second highest honey yield after China (EC 2020).

Honeybees live in strictly organized colonies, each with a queen bee belonging to one female caste, and tens of thousands of workers making up the other female caste, and a few hundred drone bees, who make up the male caste. The workers use the honeycombs made of wax to stock their honey and pollen, which they feed to the brood that hatches

When the bee colony becomes too large for the brood chamber, part of the colony forms a swarm of ten thousand or so bees with their old queen. They hang in a cluster on a convenient object nearby and wait for their scout bees to find a suitable new nesting chamber.

16 Insect products

Honeybees have been kept as domestic animals for thousands of years and bred specifically to increase yield and reduce aggression. In artificial beehives, which are widely used worldwide, several colonies live side-by-side with a separate entrance for each colony.

Bees store their honey in capped cells. The honeycombs provide us with two valuable products: honey and wax.

from the eggs the queen produces. Field-workers perform a sophisticated so-called 'waggle dance' on the surface of the honeycomb to convey information to the other worker bees about where to find flowers providing nectar and pollen or aphids producing honeydew. Their dance includes information about direction, distance, and yield (Seeley 2010). The colony's population peaks in early summer, and the queen moves out with some of the colony to look for a new nesting site. In the old nest, a new queen, reared by the worker bees and mated during her nuptial flight, takes over the task of producing offspring. Beekeepers today have various ways of preventing the bees from swarming or of intercepting the flying bees, as swarming colonies produce less honey.

Other edible products

Another insect product used in some countries is the so-called 'royal jelly', which is also produced by honeybees. This is a very nutritious substance produced by the workers and fed exclusively to the developing queens.

The 'manna' known from the Bible most likely consisted of the sugary honeydew of scale insects living on tamarisks (Schimitschek 1980). This excrement quickly crystallizes in the dry air of Sinai.

Tree beekeeping is an old craft. To breed and exploit bees commercially, the beekeeper makes tree cavities for the colonies. In some places in Central Europe, this almost extinct craft is experiencing a revival today. The cavities are hollowed out in large, living trees at a height of several metres. The opening for working and maintaining the cavity is otherwise kept closed. The bees enter the cavity through the extra entrance hole on the left of the 'maintenance opening'. (Picture on left by Adam Gottlob Schirachs.)

16.2 Commodities

Silk

The silk thread of the domestic silkmoth *(Bombyx mori)* caterpillars has been used for more than 5000 years in China to produce a valuable fabric and a surgical thread (Anelli and Prischmann-Voldseth 2009). For a long time, silk was an important commodity over which China had the monopoly, exporting it to Europe along the Silk Road. In the 6th century A.D., the silkmoth and its host tree, the mulberry tree, were smuggled from China to the Byzantine Empire. As a consequence, silk production became established in Europe. Silkmoths were, for example, farmed in Switzerland, from the 16th century onwards, especially in Ticino, where numerous mulberry trees still bear witness to this today. The silk threads were processed by the silk industry in Zurich, which prospered particularly in the 18th and 19th centuries. At the end of the 19th century, Zurich was the world's second largest producer of silk fabrics (Schmid 2000). Silk is light and resistant, and was used for luxury clothing, ladies' stockings and later also for fishing lines and parachutes. Although silk has now largely been replaced by cheaper synthetic fibres, natural silk is once again increasingly in demand as a raw material for valuable fabric.

The silkmoth became, like the honeybee, domesticated. Its caterpillars are bred on leaves of the mulberry tree. To pupate, each caterpillar spins a cocoon from a silk thread that is 10 to 30 thousandths of a millimetre thin but more than three kilometres long (Schmid 2000). After killing the pupa and treating the cocoon in hot water, up to a thousand metres of silk can be unwound from the cocoon and spun to make a yarn. The cultivated form of the silkmoth cannot fly and does not survive in the wild, but the ailanthus silkmoth *(Samia cynthia)*, which was also introduced for silk production, has established in several European countries as an integral part of the lepidopteran fauna. Its host plant – the tree of heaven – has also spread and has become a problematic invasive plant in many places.

The silk thread of a silkmoth's cocoon would extend, if unwound, about three kilometres. Of this, up to a thousand metres can be used for silk production.

Varnishes, dyes and tanning agents

Scale insects have long been used as suppliers of dyes, varnishes and waxes – and in some cases still are. An important product is the lac of the scale insect *Kerria lacca*, which lives on various tree species in India, China and Southeast Asia. Its lac-containing scale covers can completely cover whole branches. The lac was not only used to produce the early shellac records, but also in shoe soles and shoe polish, artificial fruit and flowers, ink, electrical insulation, dentures, pyrotechnical products, leather and wood-care products, sealing wax, adhesives, varnish and food colourants (Clausen 1954).

Scale insects were already used in prehistoric times to produce dyes. In the Mediter-

The domestic silkmoth *(Bombyx mori)* is the moth species most frequently used in silk production. Bred over thousands of years, the moth can no longer fly. Its caterpillars are reared on branches of the mulberry tree.

After killing off the silkmoth pupae with hot water, the cocoons are placed in warm water to dissolve the adhesive that glues the threads together so that the silk thread can be removed. The threads from several cocoons are unwound at the same time and then spun to make a yarn. The raw silk thread is washed with soapy hot water to get rid of the sticky adhesive.

ranean region, the females and larvae of the kermes scales (*Kermes vermilio*, *K. ilicis*), which colonize evergreen oaks, provided the pigment red crimson (also known as cochineal), one of the oldest organic pigments. In the Middle Ages, this valuable dye even served as a currency. The scale insect *K. vermilio* has been recently introduced to, among other places, Switzerland and England, together with holm oaks (Wermelinger and Forster 2015). Other valuable and durable dyes were also produced from scale insects in other continents and exported to Europe. For example, some scale insects that live on prickly pear cacti were, for a long time, the most important export article in Latin America, along with silver (Anelli and Prischmann-Voldseth 2009).

The dyes are still used today for dyeing cloth, as paints, in cosmetics and as food colourants. Scale insects were still being used as recently as 2006, for example, to produce the red colour of the famous Campari aperitif.

Galls are plant tissue growths that are triggered by other organisms, mostly insects. Plant-hormone-like substances from the gall producer induce a genetically defined transformation of the plant tissue, which is specific to each gall maker. Thus it is usually possible to identify the galling species simply and reliably from the gall.

Until recently, various oak galls, produced by gall wasps (Cynipidae), were used commercially, especially in Eastern and South-Eastern Europe. They served as a valuable raw mate-

16 Insect products

Bubble-shaped brood chambers of the kermes scale insect *(Kermes vermilio)*. The eggs develop in these remains of the dead female. After hatching, the so-called 'crawlers' spread over the branches – visible here as tiny red dots on the branches and leaves.

Cross-section through a brood chamber of a kermes scale insect. From the adult females and larvae, a precious 'red crimson' dye has been extracted since time immemorial.

rial for producing ink, dyes, pharmaceutical products and, due to their high tannin content, tanning agents. In Central Europe as well, collecting and selling oak galls provided foresters in former times with a welcome additional source of income.

In Turkey and neighbouring regions, the galls of *Andricus gallaetinctoriae* – also called Aleppo or Levante galls – supplied the light-resistant 'iron gall ink'. Some official documents have had to be written since antiquity and right up to the 20th century in the permanent ink made from these galls. The galls were also used to dye leather and for tanning, as up to 60 percent of their contents consist of tanning agents (Gauss 1982). In the 19th century, tens of thousands of tons of galls were

16 Insect products

still being imported annually from the Middle East to Central Europe (Hellrigl 2010). Today, however, this trade has stopped.

The galls of the knopper gall wasp (*Andricus quercuscalicis*) also have a high tannin content. They were even specifically cultivated in oak plantations in Eastern Europe and the Balkans for tanning purposes. For a complete cycle with asexual and bisexual generations, the gall wasp needs two hosts: both the pedunculate and the Turkey oak. In Central Europe, where the Turkey oak does not occur naturally, an incomplete cycle with only asexual generations may develop.

Wax

In addition to honey, honeybees also supply wax, which used to be at least as valuable as honey. To this day, this coveted commodity is used primarily in cosmetics and pharmaceuticals as well as for the production of candles,

The galls of the knopper gall wasp (*Andricus quercuscalicis*) develop mainly on pedunculate oaks (see also the photos on page 35). The galls used to be used in tanneries, as they have a high tannin content.

Towards the autumn, an opening forms at the top of the maturing knopper galls. The gall wasp pupae overwinter in the galls, which fall to the ground. In spring, the adult wasps then emerge through the prepared opening.

furniture polish, sculptured figures, casting moulds and seals. In addition, treating surfaces of wood, stone, pottery and leather with wax gives them a good finish and seals them. Fruit is waxed to make it shinier and to preserve it better. In Madame Tussaud's famous wax museum, the heads are also made of a mixture of beeswax and plant-based Japan wax. In 2005, more than 4000 tonnes of beeswax were produced as a commodity in the European Union alone (CBI 2009).

16.3 Insects as food for human consumption

Unlike in Asia, Africa, Australia and America, insects are not traditionally consumed as food in Europe. Worldwide, however, more than 2000 insect species, most of which are forest insects, are considered edible and eaten (Ramos-Elorduy 2009). These mainly include beetle larvae (especially those of scarab beetles, weevils and longhorn beetles [Scarabaeidae, Curculionidae, Cerambycidae]), hymenopterans (ants; larvae and pupae of wasps and bees), grasshoppers, caterpillars, true bugs and cicadas (Johnson 2010). Insect tissue has a high fat and protein content and is therefore not only very rich in energy, but also in essential amino acids, minerals and vitamins. One of the most important species used as food is the palm weevil (*Rhynchophorus* spp.). Its fat larvae are known as 'sago worms' in East Asia, Latin America and Africa and consumed in raw, smoked, roasted or steamed form as food and luxury foodstuffs. The sago palm trees (*Metroxylon* species)

Insects are a valuable food source, but are not traditionally used as food in Europe, unlike in other continents, where insects have been known as food for a long time.

are even intentionally felled so that the weevils can lay their eggs on the stem. Only one month after felling, the first grub-like larvae can be excavated out of the wood and subsequently consumed (Johnson 2010). The palm weevil has also been recently introduced in the Mediterranean region, where it is harmful for palms of any kind (see Section 17.2).

In Asia, people eat the pupae of the silkmoth (described above). In North America, the caterpillars of the pandora moth *(Coloradia pandora)* are a traditional food. These caterpillars, which feed on pine needles, are still valued as a delicacy by the Paiute indigenous people in the Southwest of the USA (Weaver and Basgall 1986).

Since insects have never been of any importance as a food in Europe, selling them for human consumption has long been prohibited in the European Union. However, efforts are underway to have this high-quality protein source approved as food. For example, in 2017 three non-forest insect species, namely migratory locusts, house crickets and mealworms, were registered for consumption in Switzerland. Such efforts also make sense from an ecological point of view. Insects convert plant biomass into animal biomass about ten times more efficiently than warm-blooded animals. In addition, insect breeding produces significantly lower greenhouse gas emissions, requires much less space and generates less waste (Durst and Shono 2010). Overall, producing insects pollutes the environment much less than traditional meat farming. However, regulations are also needed to ensure insects are bred sustainably, hygienically and in an environmentally friendly way.

Insects are also produced as pet food. For example, until a few years ago the pupae of wood ants (sometimes also called 'ant eggs') were sold as food for birds and fish, in addition to the locusts and mealworms mentioned above.

Introduced species 17

Since the beginning of global trade and human travel, organisms have been moved around between continents. Animal species that reached new continents after the discovery of America in 1492 are called 'neozoa.' Most of them were, and still are, conveyed accidentally as stowaways during the transport of commodities, in luggage, souvenirs and vehicles, or in packaging. By 2008, 1590 species of invertebrates – mainly insects – had arrived and become established in Europe (Roques 2010). Introduction rates increased sharply, particularly after the Second World War. Today, about 20 new species of insects enter Europe every year, of which roughly a third are introduced via imported woody plants. The number of introductions often correlates with the volume of traded goods (Wermelinger 2014).

How alien species arrive in new regions varies. While several insect species have been deliberately introduced for the biological control of pest insects, some Mediterra-

The Asian longhorned beetle (*Anoplophora glabripennis*) has already arrived on several continents. This beetle can infest almost all broadleaf tree species. When it emerges from the wood, it leaves behind a large circular hole.

nean species have extended their distribution range further north to take advantage of temperatures becoming higher and winters milder with global warming. The main reason, however, for alien insect species occurring on native trees and shrubs is that they have been accidentally transported with imported ornamental plants and woody products. Foreign wood insects usually first establish in residential areas, where exotic tree species are more likely to be available as possible hosts, the local climate is usually milder and street trees permanently suffer from latent stress. Once an alien insect species has become established in an urban environment, the risk that it will spread into forest areas is substantial.

Most of the introduced species are not pests in their areas of origin, where a dynamic balance has co-evolved between the herbivore's reproductive rate, its natural enemies, and the defence mechanisms of its host plant. When a new species enters another ecosystem that has not yet adapted to it, such regulatory interactions are often lacking. Species with high reproductive capacities may then exploit empty ecological niches and sometimes become pests.

17.1 Invasive species in forests

Not every alien species necessarily becomes invasive, i.e., has an economic or ecological impact. Most remain completely inconspicuous. However, some species have become – or can potentially become – invasive in for-

Infestations by the chestnut gall wasp *(Dryocosmus kuriphilus)*, which is only about three millimetres long, can lead to chestnut fruit production failing completely.

ests. These include the long-established black timber bark beetle *(Xylosandrus germanus)*, the silver fir woolly aphid *(Dreyfusia nordmannianae)* and the Douglas fir woolly aphid *(Gilletteella cooleyi)*, as well as some species introduced as recently as this century.

Chestnut gall wasp

The chestnut gall wasp *(Dryocosmus kuriphilus)*, which originates from Southern China, has caused major yield losses in sweet chestnut fruit production areas since its introduction to Europe in 2002. During summer, the tiny females – no males are known of the species – lay their eggs in the buds for the following year's shoots. When the leaves flush in the subsequent spring, the larvae begin to feed and trigger the formation of irregular galls on leaves and shoots. From June onwards, the wasps emerge from the multi-chamber galls. The gall formation distorts the leaves, and can drastically reduce a tree's leaf area and impede the production of chestnut fruits. With six galls per branch, the loss may amount to as much as 80 percent (Battisti et al. 2014). The wasp is usually transported with plant material that includes infested buds. In Italy, a Chinese parasitoid wasp *(Torymus sinensis)* was released to control the gall wasp. It is currently controlling gall wasp infestations very effectively. Chestnut production has therefore returned to a normal level in most places. The future will show whether this success is permanent.

Asian longhorned beetle

The Asian longhorned beetle (Anoplophora glabripennis; 'ALB') was introduced from China to North America and later, at the be-

A gall of the chestnut gall wasp can house five to ten larvae, each of which develops in its own chamber. The galling distorts leaves and can lead to the death of shoots.

ginning of this century, to Europe as well. It can grow to be over three centimetres long and has a distinctive colouring. It can colonize virtually all deciduous trees, but clearly has a preference for maple, horse chestnut, willow, birch and poplar. The female beetle lays its eggs one by one in the funnels she gnaws in the tree's bark. The young larvae first feed on the phloem under the outer bark and then bore into the wood. The larvae take two years to develop. A few weeks after they pupate, the adult beetles emerge.

Infestations with the beetle in Europe have, until now, been mainly limited to trees in residential areas in parks and gardens and along roadsides, as well as in small patches of woodland. The beetle has, however, the potential to infest and kill trees in forests on a large scale. In order to prevent the beetles spreading and to reduce the risk of infested branches breaking off and causing damage, both the infested trees and, prophylactically, nearby potential host trees must be felled and eliminated. This can become quite expensive for the local authorities involved. In the USA, for example, 373 million dollars were spent on controlling, monitoring and replanting in the first ten years after the 'ALB' was introduced (Haack *et al.* 2010).

The beetles are usually introduced with the wood used for the packaging of goods such as granite stones, which come mainly from China. They may then become distributed throughout a particular region when newly infested wood is transported inland. Such infestations have been observed in recent years across almost all of Europe.

A very similar-looking sibling species of the Asian longhorned beetle, the citrus longhorned beetle (A. *chinensis*; 'CLB'), has become established in northern Italy in an area of more than 400 square kilometres (Schröder *et al.* 2012). Its larvae have been mainly transported with ornamental trees and bonsais. Over time, the beetle is likely to spread throughout Europe either through new introductions or through the inland transport of infested plant material.

Box tree moth

The caterpillars of the box tree moth *(Cydalima perspectalis)*, which also originates from East Asia, feed exclusively on box trees. While they are mainly a problem in gardens and

The larvae of the Asian longhorned beetle tunnel deep into the wood. After two years of development, the adult beetles leave the wood through large circular holes.

The Asian longhorned beetle is a quarantine pest throughout Europe and must be controlled by law.

parks, they have also attacked natural box trees occurring in the shrub layer of forests, causing high losses (Kenis *et al.* 2013). However, the box tree is able to resprout even after complete defoliation as long as the caterpillars do not completely destroy the green bark of the branches through feeding. Another major problem for box trees is the fungus *Cylindrocladium buxicola*, which has also been recently introduced.

The emerald ash borer on its way to Europe

The emerald ash borer (*Agrilus planipennis*) is native to East Asia. The larvae of this buprestid beetle feed in the bark of ash trees, which leads to the rapid death of the affected trees. The beetle was first introduced to North America, where it has already killed millions of ash trees in green urban areas and in forests. The cost of the resulting damage runs into billions. Since 2003 the beetle has also been detected in the Moscow region and is now slowly spreading westwards. It is likely to arrive in Europe sooner or later – either through introduction or natural dispersal. When it does, it will further decimate the ash stands that have already been badly hit by the ash dieback pathogen (*Hymenoscyphus fraxineus*).

17.2 Other alien species on woody plants

In addition to the species described above, many other alien wood insects can be found which have had either hardly any impact as pests or are more relevant on woody plants in the ornamental plant and agricultural sectors. In agriculture, for example, the walnut husk fly (*Rhagoletis completa*) and, in particular, the spotted wing Drosophila (*Drosophila suzukii*; a fruit fly) are well-known pests. The walnut husk fly makes fruit husks slimy, while the Drosophila makes berries, grapes and other soft fruits inedible. The brown marmorated stink bug (*Halyomorpha halys*), which originates from East Asia, has already become a major problem in the USA and has also caused some damage to European crops. In certain years, conspicuous mass outbreaks of the sycamore lace bug (*Corythucha ciliata*),

The box tree moth (*Cydalima perspectalis*) is a notorious pest particularly for garden owners. It has, however, also been known to attack natural box trees in forests.

17 Introduced species

the horse chestnut scale *(Pulvinaria regalis)* and particularly the horse chestnut leaf miner *(Cameraria ohridella)* have been noticeable on trees in urban areas. Such infestations weaken the trees and reduce their aesthetic value. The western conifer seed bug *(Leptoglossus occidentalis)*, which can often be seen on window-panes in autumn when searching for overwintering sites, has hardly any effect on its host plants. In summer, the bugs suck on the seeds of conifer cones.

The harlequin ladybird *(Harmonia axyridis)* appeared in Central Europe at the beginning of this century and has become really invasive in gardens, green urban areas, fields and meadows, and along forest edges. The ladybird escaped from greenhouses, where it had been deliberately released for aphid control, and has since spread extremely fast all over Europe. This had considerable ecological consequences because the larvae of the harlequin ladybird feed not only on aphids, but also on other aphidophagous ladybird larvae. Today, this alien species has become one of the most common ladybird species in many European countries and has severely suppressed several native ladybird species (Roy *et al.* 2012).

Four examples of insects on woody ornamental plants that have been introduced in Central Europe in the last two decades: (a) horse chestnut leaf miner *(Cameraria ohridella)*, (b) oak lace bug *(Corythucha arcuata)*, (c) brown marmorated stink bug *(Halyomorpha halys)*, (d) western conifer seed bug *(Leptoglossus occidentalis)*.

The red palm weevil *(Rhynchophorus ferrugineus)* was introduced from Asia to the Mediterranean area and has infested all species of palms. Its larvae eat their way through the plant tissue to the vegetative growing point, thus causing the plant to die. The red palm weevil is currently spreading northwards and is likely to damage palms planted for ornamental purposes in many places.

The red palm weevil *(Rhynchophorus ferrugineus)* has been introduced in Spain and is currently spreading throughout the Mediterranean area, as well as northwards – like the palms themselves.

Endangered forest insects 18

Although the extinction of species is a natural evolutionary process, many more species have recently become extinct than in previous centuries (Smith et al. 1993). In many cases, the extinction of a species can be attributed to direct or indirect human influences. Whether humans can be considered part of the biosphere and their impact also a natural process of evolution remains a philosophical question.

In Central Europe, the loss of species has varied according to habitat type. It tends to be highest in intensively managed agricultural areas, while forest habitats are usually less affected (Seibold et al. 2019). But many factors in forests have also had a negative impact on insect diversity. From a historical perspective, the forested area is significantly smaller today (see Section 1.2). Moreover, some forest types such as alluvial forests have become rarer, forest management has markedly changed most forests' composition and structure, and the

Many endangered insect species live in deadwood. The colourful jewel beetle *Anthaxia candens* is an endangered species in most countries in Central Europe. Its larvae develop under the bark of dying branches and trunks of various cherry tree species.

The woodland brown *(Lopinga achine)* is a species protected throughout Europe. It prefers open forests rich in shrubs and particular grass species as food for its caterpillars. Increasingly dense and dark forests are therefore a threat to this species.

structural richness of most forest edges has become poorer. However, forest management does not always have a negative impact on biodiversity. For example, so-called 'coppice forests with standards' – a forest type created by exploiting wood selectively and multifunctionally – contain valuable habitat trees for saproxylic species. They also provide a habitat for species that need sunlit and warm forests.

Unlike in the rest of the world, in Europe the proportion of forested area has actually increased in recent times. In Switzerland, for example, it has been steadily increasing since about 1850. Today forests cover about one-third of the country's total area (Scheidegger *et al.* 2010). The artificial monocultures of, in particular, spruce and pine established in Central Europe in the last century for timber production are increasingly being transformed into more natural forests that are better adapted to the site conditions and to future climates. This transformation can be brought about by promoting natural regeneration and planting tree species potentially adapted to climate change. The critical factors affecting the conservation of forest biodiversity today are mainly: dense forests becoming darker, the lack of old habitat trees, the lack of deadwood large in size and in advanced decay stages, and the monotony of many forest edges. A forest edge is an ecologically important interface (ecotone) between the forest and open landscape. It often consists of a very narrow belt of shrubs or even an abrupt transition from the tree stands to fields, meadows or paths. In Switzerland, the total length of forest edges is estimated to be over 110 000 kilometres (almost three times the circumference of the earth!) (Abegg *et al.* 2014).

What must be known to assess whether a species is at risk of extinction is at least its abundance and distribution and, if possible, population trends. Among forest insects, such information is available mainly for beetles and the few butterflies occurring in forests. This is why Red Lists of endangered species have been produced for at least some of these groups. In contrast, little is known about how endangered the species-rich flies, mosquitoes or Hymenoptera (except bees), for example, are. The current Red Lists are based on the criteria of the IUCN (International Union for Conservation of Nature). The four national categories of endangerment are RE (Regionally Extinct), CR (Critically Endangered), EN (Endangered), and VU (Vulnerable). These classifications increasingly form the basis for legislating on species conservation.

18.1 Endangered forest butterflies

The intensive management of forests in the last century led to shrubs and softwoods such as willows and poplars, which are valuable for many insects, becoming largely eliminated. In addition, the transformation of formerly open stands into denser forests resulted in many forests becoming darker. In Switzerland, for example, the average standing volume of timber increased between 1985 and 2013 from 335 cubic metres to 374 cubic metres per hectare (Abegg et al. 2014). This has led to the herbaceous vegetation on the forest floor becoming impoverished and microclimates changing, which has affected, for example, the development of butterflies living in the forest.

So-called 'flagship species' are a good means to implement measures to conserve or promote certain habitat types. Flagship species are animals or plants whose popularity and aesthetic value make it easier to explain and justify protective measures to the public. Many other species with similar habitat requirements can subsequently benefit from the measures in favour of these prominent species. When promoting open forest species, for example, such flagship species may include certain orchids and, above all, some butterflies living in the forest. They rely on sunlit forests, forest edges and clearings, as their caterpillars feed either on grasses and herbs or on the foliage of bushes and broadleaf trees standing alone or growing along forest edges. A typical example is the woodland brown *(Lopinga achine)*, whose caterpillars feed on various grasses. It occurs in warm, open broadleaf and mixed forests with ground vegetation and is considered vulnerable in Europe (category VU). The butterfly needs sunlit perches on low bush branches. In recent years, several measures have therefore been successfully implemented to promote

The lesser purple emperor *(Apatura ilia)* flies along paths and forest edges and in clearings of broadleaf forests where poplars and willows grow as food for its caterpillars.

The rare *Pericallia matronula* is the largest and one of the most beautiful tiger moths. Its caterpillars feed on leaves of broadleaf trees as well as on herbaceous ground vegetation. As it takes two years for the larvae to develop, the adult moths normally appear only every second year.

this butterfly by thinning dense forests. Such measures benefit not only other caterpillars that feed on the ground vegetation, such as those of the pearl-bordered fritillary (*Boloria euphrosyne*) and some ringlets (*Erebia ligea, E. aethiops*), but also rare species whose caterpillars feed on the leaves of various light-demanding softwoods or shrubs. These include the purple emperors (*Apatura* spp.), the admirals (*Limenitis* spp.), the Camberwell beauty (*Nymphalis antiopa*), the large tortoiseshell (*Nymphalis polychloros*) and some hairstreaks (*Satyrium* spp.). Few Red Lists for moths, which represent the overwhelming majority of the order Lepidoptera, are, however, available for European countries.

The caterpillars of the Camberwell beauty (*Nymphalis antiopa*) live gregariously on birch, elm, or here on willow. The adult moths fly throughout almost the entire vegetation season. This species has become very rare, especially in the lowlands.

The poplar lappet *(Gastropacha populifolia)* has always been a rare species. It is on the Red List throughout Europe.

18.2 Endangered deadwood dwellers

When agriculture started to spread several thousand years ago, the area of the primeval forests in Europe began to decrease. As a result, some deadwood-dwelling (saproxylic) insects also became regionally extinct (Siitonen 2012). Up until the mid-20th century, wood was used intensively as a construction material and fuel. This led to the destruction of many old stands of oak, especially in the last century. Oak is a tree species that often develops cavities filled with wood mould in old age, which makes it extremely valuable for saproxylic insects. Trees with a great variety of structures (microhabitats), such as most old oaks, are called habitat trees.

Since the Second World War, the volume of deadwood has increased significantly in many European countries, especially in the last 30 years. The main reasons for this increase are: forest management has become less intensive, the use of firewood has declined, several severe storms occurred at the turn of the century, and the ecological awareness of forest managers and the general public has grown. The threshold value for the conservation of most saproxylic beetles is currently considered to be between 20 and 80 cubic metres of deadwood per hectare, depending on the forest type (Wermelinger *et al*. 2013a). However, the populations of numerous deadwood insects are still declining. The factors contributing to this decline include:
– Trees being harvested before they reach senescence, which prevents the emergence of old habitat trees;
– Ancient trees in semi-open wood pastures disappearing;

- Wood 'damaged' by storms or forest fires often still being systematically removed;
- Poor quality and small-diameter timber increasingly being used as energy wood;
- The planting of exotic tree species in some situations.

For certain species, old orchards can be a substitute for open forests with old habitat trees. A mould-filled hollow in this apple tree served as a habitat for generations of a population of the highly endangered hermit beetle (*Osmoderma eremita*). Once the cavity had become rotten down to the ground, the population became extinct. The tree, however, is still alive and bears fruit!

Almost 11 percent of all saproxylic beetles occurring in Europe have been classified as endangered (Nieto and Alexander 2010). The beetle families that provide the most solid basis for this extinction risk classification are those with large and beautiful species such as the longhorn beetles (Cerambycidae), jewel beetles (Buprestidae), flower chafers (Cetoniidae) and stag beetles (Lucanidae).

Among the flower chafers, 10 of the 18 species occurring in Switzerland are classified as endangered (Monnerat *et al.* 2016). A prime example of a threatened species is the hermit beetle *(Osmoderma eremita)* (category EN). The grub-like larvae of this grand flower chafer develop over a period of three years in large hollows in old trees, for example in cavity-rich oak trees. However, the role of the tree species is minor compared to the amount of rotten wood mould present in the cavities. Hermit beetles may inhabit suitable cavities for generations and decades. The beetles tend to be very attached to their habitats and range at most some 200 metres from their breeding trees (Ranius 2006). For a population to survive, suitable habitat trees must be available and well connected.

In Switzerland, the jewel beetle *Chalcophora mariana* is a very rare species and is found at only one location in an inner-alpine valley. Apart from those species that have always been found only locally, such as *Anthaxia hungarica*, some other jewel beetles also used to be more common but are now in sharp decline, such as *Ovalisia rutilans*. Several species have disappeared from the Swiss Plateau, but they are able to survive in warm alpine valleys and south of the Alps. Of the 89 jewel beetles present in Switzerland, 40 percent are listed on the Red List.

The marbled rose chafer (*Protaetia lugubris*) exploits very similar habitats to the hermit beetle. Its larvae live not only in hollows, but also in other decaying deadwood.

18 Endangered forest insects

The larvae of the jewel beetle *Anthaxia manca* live in thin, dying branches of elm trees along forest edges. It is considered highly endangered.

The painted jewel beetle *(Buprestis novemmaculata)* colonizes dead larch, spruce and pines trees and is restricted to warm areas.

The longhorn beetles species are in a similar situation, as 38 percent are considered endangered in Switzerland and two species even thought to be extinct (Monnerat *et al.* 2016). Many large species are classified as endangered, such as the huge *Ergates faber*, the great capricorn beetle *(Cerambyx cerdo)* and the splendid Rosalia longicorn *(Rosalia alpina)*. They all develop in large deadwood from tree species specific to the beetles. The Rosalia longicorn has become a flagship species and has adorned several European stamps. Its larvae take on average three years to develop in fungus-infected beech wood. The populations of the Rosalia longicorn have been able to recover somewhat since the mid-20th century as a result of the general increase in deadwood and also through targeted sup-

port measures. Like the great capricorn beetle, it is regarded as one of the 168 European primeval forest relict beetle species (Eckelt *et al.* 2018). *Morimus asper*, another endangered species, develops in tree stumps and lying stems. The strikingly beautiful *Purpuricenus kaehleri* lives in warm forests. Its larvae develop in thin branches of various broadleaf trees.

The stag beetle family includes only seven species in Central Europe, two of which are very rare: the little-known *Ceruchus chrysomelinus* and the proper stag beetle *(Lucanus cervus)*. This stag beetle is well known, as it is depicted in many drawings and paintings and is protected in most countries. In southern European areas it is still quite common. Its larvae develop in the ground on the thick roots of

The Rosalia longicorn *(Rosalia alpina)* is a flagship species not only among the endangered longhorn beetles, but also among many other deadwood inhabitants. It requires old, sunlit beech wood for its development.

The longhorn beetle *Purpuricenus kaehleri* is rare in several European countries. Its distribution is limited to warm regions.

Morimus asper occurs mainly in southern regions and is very rare in Central Europe. The flightless species can spread only to a limited extent.

An endangered species with positive population trends is the longhorn beetle *Leptura annularis*. It occurs along the edges of humid alder forests.

dead trees, preferably oaks. The larval development takes up to eight years. Adult beetles like seeking out old oak trees to lick the sap the trees exude.

Rare saproxylic species include some other beetle families such as the click beetles (Elateridae), as well as members of many other insect groups, particularly flies, mosquitoes and hymenopterans. For most groups, however, the data basis for setting up Red Lists is too limited. Only for wild bees is sufficient information available to assess how endangered they are. One conspicuous rare bee species that develops in old wood is, for example, the violet carpenter bee (*Xylocopa violacea*).

Chlorophorus herbstii is threatened in many European countries. The larvae of this longhorn beetle develop in dry, thin broadleaf branches. The adult beetles may be found on flowers.

18 Endangered forest insects

The flattened beetle *Ostoma ferruginea* occurs in old forests, where it lives under the bark of rotten wood.

The primeval stag beetle *(Lucanus cervus)* is one of the best known beetles, although it has become very rare in many regions and is protected in most countries.

The forest caterpillar hunter *(Calosoma sycophanta)* has become endangered in Western and Central Europe. It likes to hide in rotten deadwood and lives predatorily on large moth caterpillars. This large ground beetle is most likely to be observed during mass outbreaks of one of its prey species.

326 Not only beetles, but other wood-dwelling organisms are also endangered. The violet carpenter bee *(Xylocopa violacea)* gnaws tunnels in old wood for its offspring to develop in.

Bibliography

Abegg M., Brändli U.-B., Cioldi F., Fischer C., Herold-Bonardi A., Huber M., Keller M., Meile R., Rösler E., Speich S., Traub B., Vidondo B., 2014. Viertes Schweizerisches Landesforstinventar – Ergebnistabellen und Karten im Internet zum LFI 2009–2013 (LFI4b). Eidg. Forschungsanstalt WSL, Birmensdorf (www.lfi.ch/resultate; online publiziert am 06.11.2014).

Alfaro R.I., Shepherd R.F., 1991. Tree-ring growth of interior Douglas-fir after one year's defoliation by Douglas-fir tussock moth. For. Sci. 37: 959–964.

Allan J.D., Wipfli M.S., Caouette J.P., Prussian A., Rodgers J., 2003. Influence of streamside vegetation on inputs of terrestrial invertebrates to salmonid food webs. Can. J. Fish Aquat. Sci. 60: 309–320.

Anelli C.M., Prischmann-Voldseth D.A., 2009. Using beeswax and cochineal dye: An interdisciplinary approach to teaching entomology. Amer. Entomol. 55: 95–105.

Askew R.R., 1971. Parasitic insects. Heinemann Educ. Books, London. 316 pp.

Aspöck H., 2002. Zecken, Insekten und andere Gliederfüsser als Erreger und Überträger von Krankheiten. Denisia 184: 397–445.

Asshoff R., Köhler G., Schweingruber F.H., 1999. Dendroökologische Untersuchungen an Linden (Tilia sp.) in einem Gradationsgebiet der Tessiner Gebirgsheuschrecke Miramella formosanta (Fruhstorfer, 1921) (Acrididae, Catantopinae). Mitt. Schweiz. Entomol. Ges. 72: 329–339.

Auer C., 1974. Ein Feldversuch zur gezielten Veränderung zyklischer Insektenpopulationsbewegungen – Quantitative Ergebnisse von Grossversuchen mit DDT und Phosphamidon gegen den grauen Lärchenwickler (Zeiraphera diniana Gn.) im Goms, Kanton Wallis, 1963–1972. Schweiz. Z. Forstwes. 125: 333–358.

Auer C., 1975. Ziel und Stand der Forschungen über den grauen Lärchenwickler (LW) 1949–1974. Bündner Wald 1/1975: 7–32.

Bachmaier F., 1966. Übersicht und Bestimmungstabelle der europäischen nadelholzbewohnenden Siriciden (Hymenoptera, Symphyta). Anz. Schädl.kde. 39: 129–132.

BAG, 2015. Frühsommer-Meningoenzephalitis (FSME)/Zeckenenzephalitis. Bundesamt für Gesundheit BAG, Bern (www.bag.admin.ch/themen/ medizin/00682/00684/01069).

Baldwin P.H., 1968. Predator-prey relationships of birds and spruce beetles. Proc. North Central Branch E.S.A. 23: 90–99.

Baltensweiler W., 1968. Ein Modellobjekt tierökologischer Forschung: der Graue Lärchenwickler, Zeiraphera griseana (= Semasia diniana). Biol. Rundschau 6: 160–167.

Baltensweiler W., 1975. Zur Bedeutung des Grauen Lärchenwicklers (Zeiraphera diniana Gn.) für die Lebensgemeinschaft des Lärchen-Arvenwaldes. Mitt. Schweiz. Entomol. Ges. 48: 5–12.

Baltensweiler W., 1993a. A contribution to the explanation of the larch bud moth cycle, the polymorphic fitness hypothesis. Oecologia 93: 251–255.

Baltensweiler W., 1993b. Why the larch bud-moth cycle collapsed in the subalpine larch-cembran pine forests in the year 1990 for the first time since 1850. Oecologia 94: 62–66.

Baltensweiler W., Fischlin A., 1988. The larch bud moth in the Alps. In: Berryman A.A. (Ed.), Dynamics of forest insect populations. Plenum Press, New York. 331–351.

Baltensweiler W., Rubli D., 1984. Forstliche Aspekte der Lärchenwickler-Massenvermehrungen im Oberengadin. Mitt. Schweiz. Anst. Forstl. Vers. wes. 60: 5–148.

Baltensweiler W., Rubli D., 1999. Dispersal: an important driving force of the cyclic population dynamics of the larch bud moth, Zeiraphera diniana Gn. For. Snow Landsc. Res. 74: 3–153.

Barber J.R., Conner W.E., 2007. Acoustic mimicry in a predator–prey interaction. PNAS 104: 9331–9334.

Battisti A., Benvegnu I., Colombari F., Haack R.A., 2014. Invasion by the chestnut gall wasp in Italy causes significant yield loss in *Castanea sativa* nut production. Agric. For. Entomol. 16: 75–79.

Bentz B.J., Régnière J., Fettig C.J., Hansen E.M., Hayes J.L., Hicke J.A., Kelsey R.G., Negrón J.F., Seybold S.J., 2010. Climate change and bark beetles of the western United States and Canada: direct and indirect effects. BioScience 60: 602–613.

Benz G., 1974. Negative Rückkoppelungen durch Raum- und Nahrungskonkurrenz sowie zyklische Veränderung der Nahrungsgrundlage als Regelprinzip in der Populationsdynamik des Grauen Lärchenwicklers, *Zeiraphera diniana* (Guenée) (Lep., Tortricidae). Z. Ang. Entomol. 76: 196–228.

Bogenschütz H., Kammerer M., 1995. Untersuchungen zum Massenwechsel des Schwammspinners, *Lymantria dispar* L. (Lepidoptera, Lymantriidae), in Baden-Württemberg. Mitt. Dtsch. Ges. Allg. Angew. Entomol. 10: 113–118.

Bollmann K., Bergamini A., Senn-Irlet B., Nobis M., Duelli P., Scheidegger C., 2009. Konzepte, Instrumente und Herausforderungen bei der Förderung der Biodiversität im Wald. Schweiz. Z. Forstwes. 160: 53–67.

Boxall R.A., 2001. Post-harvest losses to insects – a world overview. Int. Biodeterior. Biodegrad. 48: 137–152.

Brändli U.B., Bollmann K., 2015. Artenvielfalt. In: Rigling A., Schaffer H.P. (Eds), Waldbericht 2015. Zustand und Nutzung des Schweizer Waldes. Bundesamt für Umwelt, Bern; Eidg. Forschungsanstalt WSL, Birmensdorf. 70–73.

Bridges J.R., Moser J.C., 1986. Relationships of phoretic mites (Acari: Tarsonemidae) to the bluestaining fungus, *Ceratocystis minor*, in trees infested by southern pine beetle (Coleoptera: Scolytidae). Environ. Entomol. 15: 951–953.

Brockhaus, 1811. Brockhaus Conversations-Lexikon, Leipzig. pp. 237 (online unter www.zeno.org/nid/20000801550).

Burgess A.F., 1911. *Calosoma sycophanta*: Its life history, behavior, and successful colonization in New England. USDA Bureau of Entomology Bull. 101: 94 pp.

BUWAL, WSL, 2005. Waldbericht 2005 – Zahlen und Fakten zum Zustand des Schweizer Waldes, Bern. 151 pp.

Cambefort Y., 1984. Étude écologique des coléoptères Scarabaeidae de Côte d'Ivoire. Université d'Abidjan, Station d'écologie tropicale de Lamto, N'douci, Côte d'Ivoire. 294 pp.

Cambefort Y., Hanski I., 1991. Dung beetle population biology. In: Hanski I., Cambefort Y. (Eds), Dung beetle ecology. Princeton University Press, Princeton, New Jersey. 36–50.

Camin P., Cioldi F., Röösli B., 2015. Holzvorrat. In: Rigling A., Schaffer H.P. (Eds), Waldbericht 2015. Zustand und Nutzung des Schweizer Waldes. Bundesamt für Umwelt, Bern; Eidg. Forschungsanstalt WSL, Birmensdorf. 32–33.

CBI, 2009. The honey and other bee products market in the EU. CBI Market Information Database. 32 pp.

Chapman A.D., 2009. Numbers of living species in Australia and the world (2nd edition). Australian Biological Resources Study, Canberra. 80 pp.

Cherix D., Bourne J.D., 1980. A field study on a super-colony of the red wood ant *Formica lugubris* Zett. in relation to other predatory arthropodes (spiders, harvestmen and ants). Rev. Suisse Zool. 87: 955–973.

Ciesla W.M., 2011. Forest entomology – a global perspective. Wiley-Blackwell, Chichester. 400 pp.

Clausen C.P., 1976. Phoresy among entomophagous insects. Annu. Rev. Entomol. 21: 343–368.

Clausen L.W., 1954. Insect fact and folklore. Collier Books/Macmillan Co. 222 pp.

Coaz J., 1894. Über das Auftreten des grauen Lärchenwicklers (*Steganoptycha pinicolana* Zell.) als Schädling in der Schweiz und den angrenzenden Staaten. Stämpfli, Bern. 21 pp.

Coleman D.C., Crossley D.A. Jr., Hendrix P.F., 2004. Fundamentals of Soil Ecology. Academic Press, Burlington. 386 pp.

Cooke B.J., Nealis V.G., Régnière J., 2007. Insect defoliators as periodic disturbances in northern forest ecosystems. In: Johnson E.A., Miyanishi K. (Eds), Plant disturbance ecology. The process and the response. Elsevier, Amsterdam. 487–525.

Cordillot F., Klaus G., 2011. Gefährdete Arten in der Schweiz. Synthese Rote Listen, Stand 2010. Umwelt-Zustand Nr. 1120, Bundesamt für Umwelt, Bern. 111 pp.

Dajoz R., 1998. Les insectes et la forêt. Lavoisier Tec Doc, Paris. 594 pp.

Davall A., 1857. *Tortrix pinicolana* Zeller – Eine neue Phaläne (Blattwikler) auf der Lärche. Schweiz. Forst-Journal 8: 197–210.

Davidson D.W., 1993. The effects of herbivory and granivory on terrestrial plant succession. Oikos 68: 23–35.

Day K.R., Baltensweiler W., 1972. Change in proportion of larval colourtypes of the larchform *Zeiraphera diniana* when reared on two media. Entomol. Exp. Appl. 15: 287–298.

De Jong Y., Verbeek M., Michelsen V., de Place Bjørn P., Los W., Steeman F., Bailly N., Basire C., Chylarecki P., Stloukal E., Hagedorn G., Wetzel F.T. *et al.*, 2014. Fauna Europaea – all European animal species on the web. Biodiv. Data J. 2: e4034 (online-Datenbank www.fauna-eu.org).

Delucchi V., 1982. Parasitoids and hyperparasitoids of *Zeiraphera diniana* [Lep., Tortricidae] and their role in population control in outbreak areas. Entomophaga 27: 77–92.

Dickson J.G., Conner R.N., Fleet R.R., Kroll J.C., Jackson J.A. (Eds), 1979. The role of insectivorous birds in forest ecosystems. Academic Press, New York. 381 pp.

Dippel C., 1996. Investigations on the life history of *Nemosoma elongatum* L. (Col., Ostomidae), a bark beetle predator. J. Appl. Entomol. 120: 391–395.

Doane C.C., McManus M.L. (Eds), 1981. The gypsy moth: Research toward integrated pest management. U.S. Dept. Agric., Washington D.C. 757 pp.

Dormont L., Baltensweiler W., Choquet R., Roques A., 2006. Larch- and pine-feeding host races of the larch bud moth *(Zeiraphera diniana)* have cyclic and synchronous population fluctuations. Oikos 115: 299–307.

Durst P.B., Shono K., 2010. Edible forest insects: exploring new horizons and traditional practices. In: Durst P.B., Johnson D.V., Leslie R.N., Shono K. (Eds), Forest insects as food: humans bite back. FAO regional office for Asia and the Pacific, Bangkok. 1–4.

Duvigneaud P., 1974. La synthèse écologique. Doin, Paris. 296 pp.

EC, 2020. Honey market presentation. European Commission, Agriculture and Rural Development. 25 pp. (download from https://ec.europa.eu/info/food-farming-fisheries/animals-and-animal-products/animal-products/honey_en)

Eckelt A., Müller J., Bense U., Brustel H., Bussler H., Chittaro Y., Cizek L., Frei A., Holzer E., Kadej M., Kahlen M., Köhler F., Möller G., Mühle H., Sanchez A., Schaffrath U., Schmidl J., Smolis A., Szallies A., Németh T., Wurst C., Thorn S., Christensen R.H.B., Seibold S., 2018. 'Primeval forest relict beetles' of Central Europe: a set of 168 umbrella species for the protection of primeval forest remnants. J. Insect Conserv. 22: 15–28.

Esper J., Büntgen U., Frank D.C., Nievergelt D., Liebhold A., 2007. 1200 years of regular outbreaks in alpine insects. Proc. R. Soc. B 274: 671–679.

Fahse L., Heurich M., 2011. Simulation and analysis of outbreaks of bark beetle infestations and their management at the stand level. Ecol. Model. 222: 1833–1846.

FAO, 2015. Food and Agriculture Organization of the United Nations – Statistics Division. (faostat3.fao.org/download/q/ql/e).

Fayt P., Machmer M.M., Steeger C., 2005. Regulation of spruce bark beetles by woodpeckers – a literature review. For. Ecol. Manage. 206: 1–14.

Gäbler H., 1947. Milbe als Eiparasit des Buchdruckers. Nachrichtenbl. Deut. Pflanzenschutzd. 1: 113–115.

Gauss R., 1954. Der Ameisenbuntkäfer *Thanasimus (Clerus) formicarius* Latr. als Borkenkäferfeind. In: Wellenstein G. (Ed.), Die grosse Borkenkäferkalamität in Südwestdeutschland 1944–1951. Forstschutzstelle Südwest, Ringingen. 417–429.

Gauss R., 1982. Familienreihe Cynipoidea. In: Schwenke W. (Ed.), Die Forstschädlinge Europas, 4. Band: Hautflügler und Zweiflügler. Paul Parey, Hamburg. 234–254.

Ghoneim K., 2013. Cantharidin toxicosis to animal and human in the world: a review. Stand. Res. J. Toxicol. Environ. Health Sci. 1: 1–16.

Bibliography

Glutz von Blotzheim U.N., Bauer K.M., 1993. Handbuch der Vögel Mitteleuropas. Band 13/I und 13/II, Passeriformes. Aula Verlag, Wiesbaden.

Gösswald K., 1984. Schutz vor Insektenfrass durch Waldameisen (Teil I). Waldhygiene 15: 129–204.

Gösswald K., 2012. Die Waldameise – Biologie, Ökologie und forstliche Nutzung. AULA-Verlag, Wiebelsheim. 630 pp.

Grégoire J.C., Evans H.F., 2004. Damage and control of BAWBILT organisms – an overview. In: Lieutier F., Day K.R., Battisti A., Grégoire J.C., Evans H.F. (Eds), Bark and wood boring insects in living trees in Europe – a synthesis. Kluwer Academic Publishers, Dordrecht. 19–37.

Grundmann S., Arnold P., Montavon P., Schraner E.M., Wermelinger B., Hauser B., 2000. Toxische Zungennekrose nach Kontakt mit Raupen des Pinienprozessionsspinners (Thaumetopoea pityocampa Schiff.). Kleintierpraxis 45: 45–50.

Haack R.A., Hérard F., Sun J.H., Turgeon J.J., 2010. Managing invasive populations of Asian Longhorned Beetle and Citrus Longhorned Beetle: a worldwide perspective. Annu. Rev. Entomol. 55: 521–546.

Hanski I., 1987. Nutritional ecology of dung- and carrion-feeding insects. In: Slansky F.J., Rodriguez J.G. (Eds), Nutritional ecology of insects, mites, and spiders. John Wiley & Sons, New York. 837–884.

Hawkins B.A., Cornell H.V., Hochberg M.E., 1997. Predators, parasitoids, and pathogens as mortality agents in phytophagous insect populations. Ecology 78: 2145–2152.

Hebert P.D.N., Ratnasingham S., Zakharov E.V., Telfer A.C., Levesque-Beaudin V., Milton M.A., Pedersen S., Jannetta P., deWaard J.R., 2016. Counting animal species with DNA barcodes: Canadian insects. Phil. Trans. R. Soc. Lond. B 371: 20150333.

Hellrigl K., 2010. Pflanzengallen und Gallenkunde – Plant galls and cecidology. For. Observ. 5: 207–328.

Hérard F., Mercadier G., 1996. Natural enemies of Tomicus piniperda and Ips acuminatus (Col., Scolytidae) on Pinus sylvestris near Orléans, France: temporal occurrence and relative abundance, and notes on eight predatory species. Entomophaga 41: 183–210.

Hoch G., Zubrik M., Novotny J., Schopf A., 2001. The natural enemy complex of the gypsy moth, Lymantria dispar (Lep., Lymantriidae) in different phases of its population dynamics in eastern Austria and Slovakia – a comparative study. J. Appl. Entomol. 125: 217–227.

Hodkinson I.D., Hughes M.K., 1982. Outline in ecological studies: Insect herbivory. Chapman & Hall, London. 77 pp.

Hollinger D.Y., 1986. Herbivory and the cycling of nitrogen and phosphorus in isolated California oak trees. Oecologia 70: 291–297.

Hopping G.R., 1947. Notes on the seasonal development of Medetera aldrichii Wheeler (Diptera, Dolichopodidae) as a predator of the Douglas fir bark-beetle, Dendroctonus pseudotsugae Hopkins. Can. Entomol. 79: 150–153.

Horstmann K., 1974. Untersuchungen über den Nahrungserwerb der Waldameisen (Formica polyctena Foerster) im Eichwald III. Jahresbilanz. Oecologia 15: 187–204.

Horstmann K., 1976/77. Waldameisen (Formica polyctena Foerster) als Abundanzfaktoren für den Massenwechsel des Eichenwicklers Tortrix viridana L. Z. Ang. Entomol. 82: 421–435.

Huber C., 2005. Long lasting nitrate leaching after bark beetle attack in the highlands of the Bavarian Forest National Park. J. Environ. Qual. 34: 1772–1779.

Jäger J.H., 1784. Beyträge zur Kanntniß und Tilgung des Borkenkäfers der Fichte oder der sogenannten Wurmtrockniß fichtener Waldungen. Mauke, Jena. 52 pp.

Jakoby O., Lischke H., Wermelinger B., 2019. Climate change alters elevational phenology patterns of the European spruce bark beetle (Ips typographus). Glob. Change Biol. 25: 4048–4063.

Jansson C., von Brömssen A., 1981. Winter decline of spiders and insects in spruce Picea abies and its relation to predation by birds. Holarct. Ecol. 4: 82–93.

Jiao Z.B., Wan T., Wen J.B., Hu J.F., Luo Y.Q., Zhang L.S., Fu L.J., 2008. Functional response and numerical response of great spotted woodpecker Picoides major on Asian longhorned beetle Anoplophora glabripennis larvae. Acta Zool. Sin. 54: 1106–1111.

Bibliography

Johnson D.M., Bjørnstad O.N., Liebhold A.M., 2004. Landscape geometry and travelling waves in the larch budmoth. Ecol. Letters 7: 967–974.

Johnson D.V., 2010. The contribution of edible forest insects to human nutrition and to forest management. In: Durst P.B., Johnson D.V., Leslie R.N., Shono K. (Eds), Forest insects as food: humans bite back. FAO regional office for Asia and the Pacific, Bangkok, Thailand. 5–22.

Karhu K.J., 1998. Effects of ant exclusion during outbreaks of a defoliator and a sap-sucker on birch. Ecol. Entomol. 23: 185–194.

Karhu K.J., Neuvonen S., 1998. Wood ants and a geometrid defoliator of birch: predation outweighs beneficial effects through the host plant. Oecologia 113: 509–516.

Karpachevski L.O., Perel T.S., Bartsevich V.V., 1968. The role of Bibionidae larvae in decomposition of forest litter. Pedobiologia 8: 146–149.

Keller S., Epper C., Wermelinger B., 2004. *Metarhizium anisopliae* as a new pathogen of the spruce bark beetle *Ips typographus*. Mitt. Schweiz. Entomol. Ges. 77: 121–123.

Kenis M., Wermelinger B., Grégoire J.C., 2004. Research on parasitoids and predators of Scolytidae – a review. In: Lieutier F., Day K.R., Battisti A., Grégoire J.C., Evans H.F. (Eds), Bark and wood boring insects in living trees in Europe – a synthesis. Kluwer Academic Publishers, Dordrecht. 237–290.

Kenis M., Nacambo S., Leuthardt F.L.G., Di Domenico F., Haye T., 2013. The box tree moth, *Cydalima perspectalis*, in Europe: horticultural pest or environmental disaster? Aliens 33: 38–41.

Kennedy C.E.J., Southwood T.R.E., 1984. The number of species of insects associated with British trees: a re-analysis. J. Anim. Ecol. 53: 455–478.

Kennel M., 2002. Wie wirkt sich grossflächiger Borkenkäferbefall auf Abfluss und Wasserqualität aus? LWF-aktuell 34/2002: 26–29.

Klasing K.C., 1998. Comparative avian nutrition. CAB International, Oxon. 350 pp.

Kloft W., 1959. Zur Nestbautätigkeit der Roten Waldameise. Waldhygiene 3: 94–98.

Kofler A., Schmölzer K., 2000. Zur Kenntnis phoretischer Milben und ihrer Tragwirte in Österreich. Ber. nat.-med. Verein Innsbruck 87: 133–157.

Koplin J.R., 1969. The numerical response of woodpeckers to insect prey in a subalpine forest in Colorado. Condor 71: 436–438.

Kurz W.A., Dymond C.C., Stinson G., Rampley G.J., Neilson E.T., Carroll A.L., Ebata T., Safranyik L., 2008. Mountain pine beetle and forest carbon feedback to climate change. Nature 452: 987–990.

Laine K.J., Niemelä P., 1980. The influence of ants on the survival of mountain birches during an *Oporinia autumnata* (Lep., Geometridae) outbreak. Oecologia 47: 39–42.

Liebhold A., Elkinton J., Williams D., Muzika R.M., 2000. What causes outbreaks of the gypsy moth in North America? Popul. Ecol. 42: 257–266.

Llewellyn M., 1972. The effects of the lime aphid, *Eucallipterus tiliae* L. (Aphididae) on the growth of the lime *Tilia x vulgaris* Hayne. J. Appl. Ecol. 9: 261–282.

Logan J.A., Powell J.A., 2001. Ghost forests, global warming, and the mountain pine beetle (Coleoptera: Scolytidae). Amer. Entomol. 47: 160–172.

Lovis C., 1975. Contribution à l'étude des tenthrèdes du mélèze (Hymenoptera: Symphyta) en relations avec l'evolution dynamique des populations de *Zeiraphera diniana* Guinée (Lepidoptera: Tortricidae) en Haute-Engadine. Mitt. Schweiz. Entomol. Ges. 48: 181–192.

Maksymov J.K., 1959. Beitrag zur Biologie und Ökologie des Grauen Lärchenwicklers *Zeiraphera griseana* (Hb.) (Lepidoptera, Tortricidae) im Engadin. Mitt. Schweiz. Anst. Forstl. Versuchswes. 35: 277–315.

Mantel K., 1990. Wald und Forst in der Geschichte – Ein Lehr- und Handbuch. M.&H. Schaper, Alfeld-Hannover. 518 pp.

Matsuura K., Yashiro T., 2006. Aphid egg protection by ants: a novel aspect of the mutualism between the tree-feeding aphid *Stomaphis hirukawai* and its attendant ant *Lasius productus*. Naturwiss. 93: 506–510.

Bibliography

Mattson W.J., Addy N.D., 1975. Phytophagous insects as regulators of forest primary production. Science 190: 515–522.

Mattson W.J. Jr., 1980. Herbivory in relation to plant nitrogen content. Ann. Rev. Ecol. Syst. 11: 119–161.

May R.M., 1988. How many species are there on earth? Science 241: 1441–1449.

Mayo J.H., Straka T.J., Leonard D.S., 2003. The cost of slowing the spread of the gypsy moth (Lepidoptera: Lymantriidae). J. Econ. Entomol. 96: 1448–1454.

McCambridge W.F., Knight F.B., 1972. Factors affecting spruce beetles during a small outbreak. Ecology 53: 830–839.

Mills N.J., 1985. Some observations on the role of predation in the natural regulation of Ips typographus populations. Z. Ang. Entomol. 99: 209–215.

Mills N.J., 1991. Searching strategies and attack rates of parasitoids of the ash bark beetle (Leperisinus varius) and its relevance to biological control. Ecol. Entomol. 16: 461–470.

Misof B., Liu S., Meusemann K., Peters R.S., Donath A., Mayer C., Frandsen P.B., Ware J., Flouri T., Beutel R.G., Niehuis O., Petersen M., Izquierdo-Carrasco F. et al., 2014. Phylogenomics resolves the timing and pattern of insect evolution. Science 346: 763–767.

Mitchell B., Rowe J.J., Ratcliffe P., Hinge M., 1985. Defecation frequency in roe deer (Capreolus capreolus) in relation to the accumulation rates of faecal deposits. J. Zool. 207: 1–7.

Möller G., 2009. Struktur- und Substratbindung holzbewohnender Insekten, Schwerpunkt Coleoptera – Käfer. Dissertation Fachbereich Biologie, Chemie, Pharmazie, Freie Universität Berlin. 293 pp.

Monnerat C., Barbalat S., Lachat T., Gonseth Y., 2016. Rote Liste der Prachtkäfer, Bockkäfer, Rosenkäfer und Schröter. Gefährdete Arten der Schweiz. Umwelt-Vollzug, Nr. 1622, Bundesamt für Umwelt, Bern; Info Fauna – CSCF, Neuenburg; Eidg. Forschungsanstalt WSL, Birmensdorf. 118 pp.

Morge G., 1961. Die Bedeutung der Dipteren im Kampf gegen die Borkenkäfer. Arch. Forstwes. 10: 505–511.

Moser J.C., Bogenschütz H., 1984. A key to the mites associated with flying Ips typographus in South Germany. Z. Ang. Entomol. 97: 437–450.

Moser J.C., Roton L.M., 1971. Mites associated with southern pine bark beetles in Allen Parish, Louisiana. Can. Entomol. 103: 1775–1798.

Moser J.C., Eidmann H.H., Regnander J.R., 1989. The mites associated with Ips typographus in Sweden. Ann. Entomol. Fenn. 55: 23–27.

Müller J., Bussler H., Gossner M., Rettelbach T., Duelli P., 2008. The European spruce bark beetle Ips typographus in a national park: from pest to keystone species. Biodivers. Conserv. 17: 2979–3001.

Müller O., 1957. Biologische Studien über den frühen Kastanienwickler Pammene juliana (Stephens) (Lep. Tortricidae) und seine wirtschaftliche Bedeutung für den Kanton Tessin. Z. Ang. Entomol. 41: 73–111.

Nentwig W., 1985. Prey analysis of four species of tropical orb-weaving spiders (Araneae: Araneidae) and a comparison with araneids of the temperate zone. Oecologia 66: 580–594.

Nierhaus-Wunderwald D., Engesser R., 2003. Ulmenwelke – Biologie, Vorbeugung und Gegenmassnahmen. Merkbl. Prax. WSL 20: 6 pp.

Nieto A., Alexander K.N.A., 2010. European red list of saproxylic beetles. Publications office of the European Union, Luxembourg. 56 pp.

Nieto A., Roberts S.P.M., Kemp J., Rasmont P., Kuhlmann M., García Criado M., Biesmeijer J.C., Bogusch P., Dathe H.H., De la Rúa P., De Meulemeester T., Dehon M., Dewulf A., Ortiz-Sánchez F.J., Lhomme P., Pauly A., Potts S.G., Praz C., Quaranta M., Radchenko V.G., Scheuchl E., Smit J., Straka J., Terzo M., Tomozii B., Window J., Michez D., 2014. European red list of bees. Publications office of the European Union, Luxembourg. 86 pp.

Oerke E.C., 2006. Crop losses to pests. J. Agric. Sci. 144: 31–43.

Ollerton J.O., Coulthard E., 2009. Evolution of animal pollination. Science 326: 808–809.

Otvos I.S., 1979. The effects of insectivorous bird activities in forest ecosystems: an evaluation. In: Dickson J.G., Connor R.N., Fleet R.R., Kroll J.C., Jackson J.A. (Eds), The role of insectivorous birds in forest ecosystems. Academic Press, London. 341–374.

Bibliography

Owen F.D., 1980. How plants may benefit from the animals that eat them. Oikos 35: 230–235.

Payne J.A., 1965. A summer carrion study of the baby pig *Sus scrofa* Linnaeus. Ecology 46: 592–602.

Perrins C.M., 1991. Tits and their caterpillar food supply. Ibis 133 suppl. 1: 49–54.

Petrucco Toffolo E., Zovi D., Perin C., Paolucci P., Roques A., Battisti A., Horvath H., 2014. Size and dispersion of urticating setae in three species of processionary moths. Integr. Zool. 9: 320–327.

Pimentel D., 1975. Introduction. In: Pimentel D. (Ed.), Insects, science and society. Academic Press, New York. 1–10.

Piñol J., Espadaler X., Canellas N., 2012. Eight years of ant-exclusion from citrus canopies: effects on the arthropod assemblage and on fruit yield. Agric. For. Entomol. 14: 49–57.

Polet D., 2011. The biggest bugs: An investigation into the factors controlling the maximum size of insects. Eureka 2: 43–46.

Pschorn-Walcher H., 1982. Unterordnung Symphyta, Pflanzenwespen. In: Schwenke W. (Ed.), Die Forstschädlinge Europas, 4. Band: Hautflügler und Zweiflügler. Paul Parey, Hamburg. 4–234.

Rader R., Bartomeus I., Garibaldi L.A., Garratt M.P.D., Howlett B.G., Winfree R., Cunningham S.A., Mayfield M.M., Arthur A.D., Andersson G.K.S., Bommarco R., Brittain C. et al., 2016. Non-bee insects are important contributors to global crop pollination. PNAS 113: 146–151.

Ramos-Elorduy J., 2009. Anthropo-entomophagy: Cultures, evolution and sustainability. Entomol. Res. 39: 271–288.

Ranius R., 2006. Measuring the dispersal of saproxylic insects: a key characteristic for their conservation. Popul. Ecol. 48: 177–188.

Ratzeburg J.T.C., 1844. Die Ichneumonen der Forstinsecten in forstlicher und entomologischer Beziehung. Nicolaische Buchhandlung, Berlin. 224 pp.

Rogers L.L., 1987. Seasonal changes in defecation rates of free-ranging white-tailed deer. J. Wildl. Manage. 51: 330–333.

Roques A., 2010. Taxonomy, time and geographic patterns – Chapter 2. BioRisk 4: 11–26.

Roques A., Raimbault J.P., Delplanque A., 1984. Les Diptères Anthomyiidae du genre Lasiomma Stein. ravageurs des cônes et graines de Mélèze d'Europe (*Larix decidua* Mill.) en France. II. Cycles biologiques et dégâts. Z. Ang. Entomol. 98: 350–367.

Rörig G., 1903. Studien über die wirtschaftliche Bedeutung der insektenfressenden Vögel. Untersuchungen über die Nahrung unserer Vögel, mit besonderer Berücksichtigung der Tag- und Nachtraubvögel. Verlagsbuchhandlung Paul Parey, Berlin. 122 pp.

Roy H.E., Adriaens T., Isaac N.J.B., Kenis M., Onkelinx T., San Martin G., Brown P.M.J., Hautier L., Poland R., Roy D.B., Comont R., Eschen R. et al., 2012. Invasive alien predator causes rapid declines of native European ladybirds. Diversity Distrib. 18: 717–725.

Sachtleben H., 1952. Die parasitischen Hymenopteren des Fichtenborkenkäfers *Ips typographus* L. Beitr. Entomol. 2: 137–189.

Scheidegger C., Bergamini A., Bürgi M., Holderegger R., Lachat T., Schnyder N., Senn-Irlet B., Wermelinger B., Bollmann K., 2010. Waldwirtschaft. In: Lachat T., Pauli D., Gonseth Y., Klaus G., Scheidegger C., Vittoz P., Walter T. (Eds), Wandel der Biodiversität in der Schweiz seit 1900. Ist die Talsohle erreicht? Bristol Stiftung, Zürich; Haupt, Bern. 124–160.

Scherney F., 1959. Unsere Laufkäfer. Neue Brehm-Bücherei, Ziemsen Verlag, Wittenberg. 79 pp.

Schimitschek E., 1980. Manna. Anz. Schädl.kd. Pflanzenschutz Umweltschutz 53: 113–121.

Schmid J., 2000. Seide. In: Pro Natura – Schweizerischer Bund für Naturschutz (Ed.), Schmetterlinge und ihre Lebensräume – Arten, Gefährdung, Schutz. Fotorotar, Egg. 42–44.

Schmid U., 1996. Auf gläsernen Schwingen: Schwebfliegen. Staatl. Museum für Naturkunde, Stuttgart. 81 pp.

Schmidt M., Kriebitzsch W.U., Ewald J., 2011. Waldartenlisten der Farn- und Blütenpflanzen, Moose und Flechten Deutschlands. BfN-Skripten 299, Bundesamt für Naturschutz, Bonn. 111 pp.

Schmitz H., Bleckmann H., 1998. The photomechanic infrared receptor for the detection of forest fires in the beetle *Melanophila acuminata* (Coleoptera: Buprestidae). J. Comp. Physiol. A 182: 647–657.

Schowalter T.D., 1992. Heterogeneity of decomposition and nutrient dynamics of oak *(Quercus)* logs during the first 2 years of decomposition. Can. J. For. Res. 22: 161–166.

Schowalter T.D., 2012. Outbreaks and ecosystem services. In: Barbosa P., Letourneau D.K., Agrawal A.A. (Eds), Insect outbreaks revisited. Wiley-Blackwell, West Sussex. 246–265.

Schowalter T.D., 2013. Insects and sustainability of ecosystem services. CRC Press, Boca Raton. 346 pp.

Schröder T., Pfellstetter E., Kaminski K., 2012. Zum Sachstand des Citrus-Bockkäfers, *Anoplophora chinensis,* in der EU und den in der Kommissionsentscheidung 2008/840/EG festgelegten Bekämpfungsstrategien unter besonderer Berücksichtigung des Monitorings. J. Kulturpflanzen 64: 86–90.

Schwenke W., 1978. *Panolis* Hbn. In: Schwenke W. (Ed.), Die Forstschädlinge Europas, 3. Band: Schmetterlinge. Paul Parey, Hamburg. 305–313.

Scutareanu P., Roques A., 1993. L'entomofaune nuisible aux structures reproductrices mâles et femelle des chênes en Roumanie. J. Appl. Entomol. 115: 321–328.

Seeley T.D., 2010. Honeybee democracy. Princeton University Press, Princeton. 280 pp.

Seibold S., Gossner M.M., Simons N.K., Blüthgen N., Müller J., Ambarlı D., Ammer C., Bauhus J., Fischer M., Habel J.C., Linsenmair K.E., Nauss T., Penone C., Prati D., Schall P., Schulze E.D., Vogt J., Wöllauer S., Weisser W.W., 2019. Arthropod decline in grasslands and forests is associated with landscape-level drivers. Nature 574: 671–674.

Setälä H., Huhta V., 1991. Soil fauna increase *Betula pendula* growth: Laboratory experiments with coniferous forest floor. Ecology 72: 665–671.

Siitonen J., 2012. Threatened saproxylic species. In: Stokland J.N., Siitonen J., Jonsson B.G. (Eds), Biodiversity in dead wood. Cambridge University Press, Cambridge. 356–379.

Skinner G.J., Whittaker J.B., 1981. An experimental investigation of inter-relationships between the wood-ant *(Formica rufa)* and some tree-canopy herbivores. J. Anim. Ecol. 50: 313–326.

Smith F.D.M., May R.M., Pellew R., Johnson T.H., Walter K.R., 1993. How much do we know about the current extinction rate? TREE 8: 375–378.

Speight M.C.D., 1989. Saproxylic invertebrates and their conservation. Council of Europe, Strasbourg. 82 pp.

Spradbery J.P., 1977. The oviposition biology of siricid woodwasps in Europe. Ecol. Entomol. 2: 225–230.

Spradbery J.P., 1990. Predation of larval siricid woodwasps (Hymenoptera: Siricidae) by woodpeckers in Europe. Entomol. 109: 67–71.

Stokland J.N., Siitonen J., Jonsson B.G., 2012. Biodiversity in dead wood. Cambridge University Press, Cambridge. 509 pp.

Stork N.E., 2018. How many species of insects and other terrestrial arthropods are there on earth? Annu. Rev. Entomol. 63: 31-45.

Strong D.R., Lawton J.H., Southwood R., 1984. Insects on plants. Community patterns and mechanisms. Blackwell, Oxford. 313 pp.

Surlykke A., Miller L.A., 1985. The influence of arctiid moth clicks on bat echolocation; jamming or warning? J. Comp. Physiol. 156: 831–843.

Swift M.J., Heal O.W., Anderson J.M., 1979. Decomposition in terrestrial ecosystems. Blackwell Scient. Publications, Oxford. 372 pp.

Szujecki A., 1987. Ecology of Forest Insects. Polish Scientific Publishers, Warszawa. 601 pp.

Turchin P., Wood S.N., Ellner S.P., Kendall B.E., Murdoch W.W., Fischlin A., Casas J., McCauley E., Briggs C.J., 2003. Dynamical effects of plant quality and parasitism on population cycles of larch budmoth. Ecology 84: 1207–1214.

Ulyshen M.D., 2015. Insect-mediated nitrogen dynamics in decomposing wood. Ecol. Entomol. 40: 97–112.

van Emden H.F., Rothschild M. (Eds), 2004. Insect and bird interactions. Intercept Limited, Andover. 301 pp.

van Noordwijk A.J., McCleery R.H., Perrins C.M., 1995. Selection for the timing of great tit breeding in relation to caterpillar growth and temperature. J. Anim. Ecol. 64: 451–458.

Vinson S.B., 1990. How parasitoids deal with the immune system of their host: an overview. Arch. Insect Biochem. Physiol. 13: 3–27.

Wachmann E., Saure C., 1997. Netzflügler, Schlamm- und Kamelhalsfliegen – Beobachtung, Lebensweise. Weltbild Verlag, Augsburg. 159 pp.

Watson E.B., 1922. The food habits of wasps. Bull. Chambers Hortic. Soc. London 1: 26–31.

Watson E.J., Carlton C.E., 2003. Spring succession of necrophilous insects on wildlife carcasses in Louisiana. J. Med. Entomol. 40: 338–347.

Weaver R.A., Basgall M.E., 1986. Aboriginal exploitation of *Pandora* moth larvae in East-Central California. J. Calif. Great Basin Anthropol. 8: 161–179.

Weber U.M., 1997. Dendroecological reconstruction and interpretation of larch budmoth (*Zeiraphera diniana*) outbreaks in two central alpine valleys of Switzerland from 1470–1990. Trees 11: 277–290.

Wegensteiner R., Wermelinger B., Herrmann M., 2015. Natural enemies of bark beetles: Predators, parasitoids, pathogens and nematodes. In: Vega F.E., Hofstetter R.W. (Eds), Bark beetles: Biology and ecology of native and invasive species. Academic Press, London. 247–304.

Wellenstein G., 1954. Die Insektenjagd der Roten Waldameise (*Formica rufa* L.). Z. Ang. Entomol. 36: 185–217.

Wellenstein G., 1978. *Dendrolimus* Germar. In: Schwenke W. (Ed.), Die Forstschädlinge Europas, 3. Band: Schmetterlinge. Paul Parey, Hamburg. 435–445.

Wermelinger B., 2014. Invasive Gehölzinsekten: Bedrohung für den Schweizer Wald? Schweiz. Z. Forstwes. 165: 166–172.

Wermelinger B., Forster B., 2015. First record of the scale insect *Kermes vermilio* (Planchon, 1864) (Hemiptera, Coccoidea) in Switzerland. Mitt. Schweiz. Entomol. Ges. 88: 361–365.

Wermelinger B., Lachat T., Müller J., 2013a. Forest insects and their habitat requirements. In: Kraus D., Krumm F. (Eds), Integrative approaches as an opportunity for the conservation of forest biodiversity. European Forest Institute, 152–157.

Wermelinger B., Obrist M.K., Baur H., Jakoby O., Duelli P., 2013b. Synchronous rise and fall of bark beetle and parasitoid populations in windthrow areas. Agric. For. Entomol. 15: 301–309.

Werner M.R., Dindal D.L., 1987. Nutritional ecology of soil arthropods. In: Slansky F.J., Rodriguez J.G. (Eds), Nutritional ecology of insects, mites, spiders, and related invertebrates. John Wiley & Sons, New York. 815–836.

Weseloh R.M., 1985. Changes in population size, dispersal behavior, and reproduction of *Calosoma sycophanta* (Coleoptera: Carabidae), associated with changes in gypsy moth, *Lymantria dispar* (Lepidoptera: Lymantriidae), abundance. Environ. Entomol. 14: 370–377.

Williams I.H., 1994. The dependence of crop production within the European Union on pollination by honey bees. Agric. Zool. Rev. 6: 229–257.

Wimmer N., Zahner V., 2010. Spechte – Leben in der Vertikalen. G. Braun Buchverlag, Leinfelden-Echterdingen. 112 pp.

Wise D.H., Schaefer M., 1994. Decomposition of leaf litter in a mull beech forest: comparison between canopy and herbaceous species. Pedobiologia 38: 269–288.

Zettel J., 2007. Massenvorkommen von Springschwänzen im Schnee: die sonderbare Biologie von *Ceratophysella sigillata*. Pest Control News 37: 18–20.

Zhong H., Schowalter T.D., 1989. Conifer bole utilization by wood-boring beetles in western Oregon. Can. J. For. Res. 19: 943–947.

Zürn E.S., 1901. Maikäfer und Engerlinge, ihre Lebens- und Schädigungsweise, sowie ihre erfolgreiche Vertilgung. H. Seemann Nachfolger, Leipzig. 36 pp.

Bibliography

Photo credits

All photos by the author (248) apart from[1]:

Forest Entomology, WSL (26): pp. 57c, 57b, 69b, 73tr, 88tl, 88b, 124b, 139br, 181b, 192bl, 202, 205b, 205c, 206b, 240b, 246l, 257, 259, 275, 279b, 280b, 290t, 299b

Swiss Forest Protection, WSL: p. 277tl

Anton Bürgi, WSL: p. 284b

Doris Hölling, WSL: p. 136

Adam Gottlob Schirachs (from 'Wald-Bienenzucht', 1774): p. 309l

Elisabeth Schraner, University of Zurich: p. 300tl

[1] b= bottom, c= centre, t= top, l= left, r= right

Glossary

abdomen	rear body part
aggregation pheromone	volatiles attracting conspecifics
ambrosia fungus	fungus associated with insects and serving them as nutrition
anemophily	flower pollination by wind
antagonist	natural enemy
anther	pollen-producing organ of flowers
aphidophagous	feeding on aphids
arthropods	animal phylum; invertebrates with segmented body, jointed appendages and exoskeleton
assimilate	product (essentially sugars) produced by photosynthesis
brown rot	fungal decay degrading primarily cellulose; infected wood becomes brown and fractures cubically
calyx	outermost flower parts (sepals)
cellulase	enzyme breaking down cellulose into sugars
chelicerae	jaws of arachnids
chitin	soft and elastic component of the insect exoskeleton
coevolution	mutual adaption of two species during evolution
consumer	organism living on a lower trophic level
cuticle	solid insect shell (exoskeleton)
declivity	downward sloping rear end of beetle elytra
decomposer	organism breaking down dead organic matter
dendrotelm	water-filled tree holes
detritivorous	living on dead organic matter
detritus	dead organic matter
diapause	interruption in development triggered by external factors to avoid adverse environmental conditions
diploid	cell (organism) with two copies of genetic material
ecotone	transition area between two different ecosystems
ecotype	genetically differing race within a species
ectoparasite	parasite living on the body surface of its host
elaiosome	nutritious appendage of a plant seed
elytra	tough fore wings
endemic	occurring permanently in a particular region

endoparasite	parasite living inside the host's body
epidemic	widely prevalent, or at outbreak levels
extraintestinal digestion	predigestion outside the body
exuviae	moulting remains (integument)
flagship species	attractive species facilitating protective measures for biodiversity
folivorous	feeding on leaves or needles
fungivorous	feeding on fungi
habitat	living space of a species
habitat tree	usually old tree with many microhabitats
haploid	cell (organism) with one copy of genetic material
herbivorous	feeding on plant material
heteroecious	with alternating hosts
hyperparasitism	parasitism of a parasitic larva by another parasitoid
hyphae	filaments forming the fungal mycelium
hypope	modified, inactive nymphal mite stage
hypostome	tick mouthpart that sucks blood
idiobiont	parasitoid that permanently immobilizes its host after oviposition
inquiline	species using nests, galls, holes, etc. of other species without affecting them
integument	outermost body layer
invertebrates	animals without a spinal column
kairomone	volatile that has a negative effect on its emitter and a positive effect on the receptor
koinobiont	parasitoid that does not permanently immobilize its host after oviposition; the host continues to develop
macrofauna	soil organisms 10 to 20 mm in size (after Swift *et al.* 1979)
mandible	pair of insect appendages, often forming jaws
maturation feeding	feeding of an adult insect to reach sexual maturity
mesofauna	soil organisms 0.2 to 10 mm in size (after Swift *et al.* 1979)
metabolite	product of metabolic reactions
microfauna	soil organisms smaller than 0.2 mm (after Swift *et al.* 1979)
microhabitat	distinct structure on living trees serving as an essential substrate for organisms
migration	directed movement of a population to a new habitat
mine	insect gallery in the leaf interior

Glossary

mineralisation	transformation of an element from organic to inorganic form
monogynous	ant colony with a single (mated) queen
mortality	death rate
multiparasitism	multiple parasitism of a host by different parasitoids
mutualism	mutually beneficial relationship between two species
mycangium	structure to transport symbiotic fungi
mycelium	fungal network consisting of hyphae
mycorrhizal fungus	symbiotic fungus living on plant roots
myrmecochory	spreading of seeds by ants
myrmecophily	positive association between ants and plants
necrophage	scavenger
nectary	nectar-producing gland in flowering plants
nematode	roundworm
oligolectic	specialised preference for pollen of a few closely related flowers
oligophagous	feeding on only a few plant or animal hosts
oviposition	process of laying eggs
ovipositor	organ for depositing eggs
palps	sensing appendages near mouth
parasite	organism living parasitically in all its developmental stages
parasitoid	organism living parasitically only in its larval stage and killing its host
parental care	parental strategy to enhance offspring fitness
parthenogenesis	asexual reproduction without fertilisation
pathogen	infectious agent causing disease
pheromone	volatile chemical emitted to elicit a behavioural reaction of conspecifics
phloem	living soft inner bark transporting assimilates
phloeophagous	living on phloem tissue
phoresy	transportation of an organism by another species
photosynthate	product (sugars) produced via photosynthesis
phytophagous	see herbivorous
polygynous	ant colony with several (mated) queens
polylectic	collecting pollen from a wide range of unrelated flowers, depending on supply
polyphagous	living on a wide range of plant or animal hosts

Glossary

population	individuals of the same species that are demographically, genetically, or spatially distinct from others
primary consumer	first order consumer = herbivore
producer	species producing its biomass from inorganic compounds; mostly green plants
pronotum	dorsal cover of the thorax
s.l.	sensu lato (lat.): in a broad sense
saprobiontic	living on dead organic matter (mainly for fungi and plants)
saprophagous	see detritivorous
saproxylic	dependent on living or dead wood
sapwood	young woody part of a tree stem that conducts water
secondary plant metabolite	chemical produced by plants that is not directly needed for growth
sensory receptor	cell receiving and transducing signals
spiracle	opening in the exoskeleton where a tracheal tube ends (stigma)
stylet	hard piercing mouthpart
subcortical	under the bark
superparasitism	multiple parasitism of a host by parasitoids belonging to the same species
symbiosis	close positive interaction between two different organisms
synanthropic	wild species associated with humans
territoriality	defending an individual's territory
tibia	lower leg of insects
tracheae	respiratory network of tubes used for gas exchange in arthropods
trophallaxis	transfer of liquid food to other individuals
trophic level	ecological position in a food web
trophobiosis	food-based symbiosis
ubiquist	organism that occurs in several different ecosystems
vector	organism that transports another species
white rot	fungal decay degrading primarily lignin; the wood becomes white and fibrous
wood pasture	woodland managed through grazing
xylophagous	feeding on wood and bark
zoophagous	feeding on live animals
zoophily	flower pollination by animals

Glossary

Species and subject index
(Bold numbers refer to photos, 'f' means 'and following')

Abax sp. 139
Acanthocinus aedilis **51**, **59**
Acantholyda erythrocephala **262**
Acantholyda posticalis 260
Aceria fraxinivora 29, **30**
Acherontia atropos 127, **128**
Adalia bipunctata **136**
Adelges laricis **234**
Adelges sp. 233
adelgid
    balsam woolly 152
    larch **234**
admiral 316
Aedes albopictus 282
Agathomyia wankowiczii 82, **84**
Aglia tau **7**
Agrilus biguttatus **53**, 54, 277
Agrilus planipennis 310
Agrilus viridis 54
Amara sp. 139
amber 1f
ambrosia 55f, 226f, 274
Ampedus sanguineus **72**
Ampedus sp. 84
Anastatus japonicus 170
Anastrangalia sanguinolenta 64
Anatis ocellata **137**
Ancistrocerus sp. **148**
Andrena bicolor **14**
Andrena vaga **22**
Andricus gallaetinctoriae 300
Andricus quercuscalicis **35**, 301
anemophily 18
Anoplophora chinensis 309
Anoplophora glabripennis 118, **305**, 307, **308**
Anoplotrupes stercorosus 98, **99**
ant
    black-backed meadow 201
    carpenter 73, **75**, 94, 118, **131**
    jet **75**
    moisture 75, 94, 118, 120
    red wood **28**, 94, 107, **108f**, 118, 120, **201**f,
    240, 303
ant lion 156, 209, **210**
antagonist 133f, 181f, 244
Anthaxia candens **313**
Anthaxia hungarica **53**, 318

Anthaxia manca **320**
Anthaxia quadripunctata 57, **58**
Anthocoris nemorum 149, **151**
Anthrenus pimpinellae **101**
Apatura ilia **315**
Apatura sp. 316
aphid
    ash leaf-nest **48**
    beech 264
    black willow **206**
    common sycamore 221
    Douglas fir woolly 307
    elder **129**, **265**
    gree spruce 264, **265**
    linden 48, **49**, **153**
    shiny birch 221
    silver fir woolly 264, **266**, 307
    walnut **131**
    woolly honeysuckle **48**
Aphis sambuci 129, **265**
Aphodius fimetarius **100**
Aphodius sp. 98
Aphomia sociella 102, 157, **159**
Apis mellifera 22, **24**, **128**, 293, **294**
Aporia crataegi 287
Aradus conspicuus **80**
Araneus diadematus **143**, 160, **161**
Araniella cucurbitina **163**
Arctia caja **123**
Argynnis paphia **27**
Arma custos 148
Aromia moschata **54**
Atanycolus genalis **170**
Austrolimnophila ochracea **77**
bark beetle
    ash **56**, 190
    beech 185
    birch **56**
    black timber **55**, 274, 307
    elm **14**, 229, 234, **279**
    European spruce **15**, 54, **181f**, **192f**, **197**,
    223f, **232**, 241, 251f
    great spruce 186, 273
    large larch **56**, 274
    northern 192
    olive **56**
    pine 54, 192, 232, 273

silver fir 54, 273
six-toothed spruce **56**, 185, **189**, **192**, 232, 273
small spruce **56**
bats 13, 122f, 251
bee
carpenter 24, **76**, 323, **326**
leafcutter 77, **79**
mason **23**, **79**, **236**
beetle
ant bag 209
bee **26**, 72, **73**
black fire 57
blister **225f**, **289**
burying **89**, **93f**, **224**
capricorn **53**, 321
capuchin **63**
cardinal 84, **86**
checkered **181f**, **186**
click **72**, 84
darkling **72**, **82**
devil's coach-horse **127**, **141**
dor 98, **99**
dung **100**
false oil 31
flattened **324**
four-spotted carrion 141, **142**
fungus **95**
hermit **330**
lily **21**
malachite **98**
metallic wood boring 69, **70**
mountain pine 199, **247**, **288**, **289**
musk **66**
oak splendour **65**, 66, 291
pine shoot 54, **56**, 192
rasperry **42**
red-breasted carrion **105**, 106
rhinoceros 72, **74**
rove **153**
sawyer 72, 241, **292**
scarab 110, 112, **114**
six-spined engraver **198**, **210**
skin 106, 114, **115**, **116**
stag 69, **70**, **71**, 321, **324**
striped ambrosia 57, **229**
tanbark 64
tanner 69
timberman **51**, **59**
wasp 64, **65**
Bibio marci 109, **111**
biocontrol 11, 125f, 136, 139, 155, 174, 185f, 307
biting midge, see no-see-um

Blepharipa schineri **175**
Boloria euphrosyne 316
Bombus sp. 22, 24
Bombus terrestris **24**
Bombylius sp. **21**
Bombyx mori **293**, 297, **298**
borer
emerald ash 310
fan-bearing wood- **120**
oak pinhole **2**
ribbed pine **63**, 64
Bostrichus capucinus **63**
Brachyopa sp. 75
Brachyopa vittata **78**
Bracon sp. 170
brown
woodland 10, **314**, 315
bug
assassin **150**
birch catkin **33**
bronze shield- **149**
brown marmorated stink 310, **311**
common flower **151**
dock 33, **34**
green shield- 33, **34**
fire- **96**
forest **2**
oak lace **311**
spiny shield- 148
spruce cone **33**
sycamore lace 310
tree damsel **149**
western conifer seed 33, **311**
bumble bee 22, 24
buff-tailed **24**
Bupalus piniaria 116
Buprestis novemmaculata **320**
Buprestis octoguttata **59**
Bursaphelenchus xylophilus 279
Byturus tomentosus **30**
Caliroa cinxia **43**
Callidium violaceum **61**
Calliphora sp. 90
Calliphora vicina **90**
Calosoma sycophanta 138, **139**, **140**, **325**
Camberwell beauty **316**
Cameraria ohridella **311**
Camponotus herculeanus 55
Camponotus sp. 73, **75**, 118, **131**
cantharidin 289f
Carabus auronitens 138, **139**
Carabus coriaceus 137

Carabus depressus **138**
Carabus intricatus **137**, 138
Carabus irregularis 138
Carabus problematicus 138
Carabus sp. **138**
Carabus violaceus 138
carrion 8, 11, 14, 89f, 137, 141, 205, 224f, 290
caste 12, 142, 144, 202, 208, 214, 294
cavity, see tree cavity
cellulose 51, 53f, 72, 75, 108, 113, 226
centipede
    brown **114**
Cephalcia abietis 260
Cerambyx cerdo **53**, 321
Ceratophysella sigillata 11, **46**f
Ceruchus chrysomelinus 321
Cetonia aurata 30, 71, **74**
chafer
    flower **71**, 72, **74**
    garden **44**
    marbled rose **319**
    rose 30, 72, **74**,
Chalcophora mariana 318
Chalcosyrphus valgus **77**
chitin 115f
Chlorophorus herbstii **323**
Choerades fuliginosa **154**
Chrysis ignita **88**
Chrysis sp. **173**
Chrysobothris affinis **8**
Chrysobothris chrysostigma **8**
Chrysolina sp. 29
Chrysopa pallens **156**
Chrysopa perla **179**
Chrysopa sp. 154
Chrysoperla carnea 154, **156**
Cinara sp. 211
climate change 250, 273, 275, 286, 314
Clytra sp. 209
Clytus arietis **65**
Clytus lama **65**
Clytus sp. 64
Coccinella septempunctata **133**, **135**
cockchafer
    common **44**, 126, 262
    northern 262
Coeloides bostrichorum **191**f
Coloradia pandora 303
comma butterfly **11**
Compsilura concinnata 173
coneworm
    spruce 35, **36**

Coremacera marginata 152, **155**
Coreus marginatus 33, **34**
Corticeus sp. 186
Corythucha arcuata **311**
Corythucha ciliata 310
Cossus cossus 11, **54**, 55
Craesus septentrionalis **43**, **171**
cranefly **9**, 75, **76**, **113**
Cratyna sp. **78**
Creophilus sp. 94
cricket
    bush **95**, 157
    oak bush 157, **158**
Ctenophora festiva **76**
Ctenophora sp. 75
Curculio elephas **31**
Curculio glandium 31
Cychrus caraboides **139**
Cychrus sp. 138
Cydalima perspectalis **310**
Cydia pomonella 33
Cydia splendana 35
Cylindromyia brassicaria **175**
Cynips quercusfolii 13
Cynomya mortuorum **91**
damage 8, 13, 29f, 44, 101, 129, 176, 249, 255f, 309f
deadwood 27, 31, 52f, 55f, 147, 251f, 313, 317f, 321, 324
decomposer 43, 51f, 90f, 97, 108f, 277
deer ked 179, **180**
defoliation 38, 40f, 44f, 138, 231f, 237f, 257f, 310
Dendroctonus brevicomis 196
Dendroctonus frontalis 189
Dendroctonus micans 186, 274
Dendroctonus ponderosae **187**, **235**, 275, **276**
Dendroctonus rufipennis 196, 198
Dendrolaelaps sp. 189
Dendrolimus pini 259
Dendrosoter protuberans 192
dendrotelm 75
Dendroxena quadrimaculata **141**
Dermestes lardarius **103**
Dermestes sp. 94, 101
Dermestes undulatus **103**
detritus 10, 13f, 52
Diaea dorsata **173**
diapause 32, 239
Diaperis boleti 80, **82**
Dictyoptera aurora **85**
Dinothenarus fossor **141**
Dioryctria abietella 35, **36**

345

Index

Diplolepis rosae **117**
Dipogon sp. 170, **173**
dispersal 246f, 310
Dolichomitus mesocentrus **88**, **169**
Dolichomitus sp. 168
Dolichovespula media **147**
Dolichovespula sp. **144**
Dorcus parallelipipedus **69**, 71
Drepanepteryx phalaenoides 156, **157**
Drepanosiphum platanoidis 221
Dreyfusia nordmannianae 264, **266**, 307
Dreyfusia piceae 152
Dromius quadrimaculatus **185**
Dromius sp. 139
Drosophila
    spotted wing 310
Drosophila suzukii 310
Dryocosmus kuriphilus **306**f
Dryophilocoris flavoquadrimaculatus 149, **151**
Dutch elm disease 229, 234, 279
earthworm 105f, 137
earwig 157, **159**
ecosystem engineer 235f, 239, 251f
ecotone 7, 314
Ectemnius sp. 77
ectoparasite 163, 172f, 179, 190f
elaiosome 27f
Elatobium abietinum 264, **265**
emperor
    purple **315**, 316
    small **174**
    tau **7**
endoparasite 163, 172f, 175, 179
Enoplognatha ovata **162**, **166**
Entedon methion **195**
Epirrita autumnata 220
Episyrphus balteatus **19**
Erannis defoliaria 10, 40, 232, 259, **260**
Erebia aethiops 316
Erebia ligea 316
Ergates faber 321
Eridolius hofferi **171**
Eriogaster lanestris 287
Eristalis pertinax **20**
Eucallipterus tiliae 48, **49**, **153**
Euceraphis punctipennis 220
Eupeodes lapponicus **152**
Euproctis chrysorrhoea 116, **284**
Eupsilia transversa 157
excrement 8, 13, 21, 35, 64, 92, 94f, 168, 183, 296
Exocentrus punctipennis **66**
Exochomus quadripustulatus 136

Exorista grandis **174**
extraintestinal digestion 137, 148, 159
flagship species 315, 321
fly
    bee **21**, 174, **176**
    blow- **90**
    common horse **184**, 192, **301**
    flesh 111
    marsh **167**
    of the dead **103**
    robber **87**, **154**, **155**
    Spanish 289, **290**
    St. Mark's 109, **111**
    tachinid **174**, **175**, **176**
    toad- 180
    walnut husk 310
    yellow dung **99**
    yellow flat-footed **84**
Forcipomyia eques **179**
forest caterpillar hunter 138, **139f**, **325**
forest edge 6f, 10, 18, 22, 44, 118, 136f, 148f,
    157f, 211, 282f, 314f
Forficula auricularia 157, **159**
Formica aquilonia 111, 201, **203**, 220, 221, 240
Formica lugubris 201, **203**, **215**
Formica paralugubris 201
Formica polyctena **28**, 201f, **204**, **206**, 215f, 219,
    221
Formica pratensis 201
Formica rufa 201f, 216, 219, 221
Formica sp. 94, 107, 118, 120
fritillary
    pearl-bordered 316
    silver-washed **27**
fungi 51f, 64, 78f, 84f, 106f, 125f, 196f, 223f, 226f,
    251, 267f, 277f
gall mite
    cauliflower ash 29, **30**
gall wasp **25**
    bedeguar **117**
    chestnut **306**f
    knopper **34**, **301**
galls 11f, 29f, 35f, 82, 116f, 236, 299f, 306f
Gastrodes abietum **33**
Gastropacha populifolia **317**
Gilletteella cooleyi 307
golden net wing **85**
grasshopper
    Generoso mountain **45**
greenbottle
    common **91**, **291**
ground beetle **138f**, **185**

blue **137**, **138**
snail-killing **139**
violet 138
grub 44, 72f, 122f, 126, 262
habitat tree 53, 314, 317f
Haematopota pluvialis **289**
hairstreak 316
Halyomorpha halys 310, **311**
Harmonia axyridis **135**f, 311
hawk moth
death's-head 127, **128**
pine **7**, **176**, **256**
privet **25**
spurge **41**
Hemerobius humulinus **10**, 156, **157**
Hemipenthes maura 174, **176**
Heringia sp. 151
Himacerus apterus **149**
honeybee 22, **24**, **128**, 293, **294**f, 301, **306**f
honeydew 21, 48, 86, 128f, 134f, 145, 155, 191,
204f, 214f, 219f, 296
hornet **143f**
hoverfly **17**, **20**, 75, **77f**, **152f**
lesser hornet 102, 152, **154**
marmalade **19**
pellucid 102, **103**
snout- **20**, 21
Hylaeus sp. 22, 77
Hylecoetus dermestoides **58**, 274
Hyles euphorbiae **41**
Hylesinus sp. 190
Hylesinus taranio **56**
Hylobius abietis 277, **278**
hyperparasitism 167, 169, 174, 176, 192f
ichneumon **88**, **169**, **171**
giant 86, **167f**, **180**, 181
idiobiont 170
inquiline 217, 236
Iponemus sp. 189
Ips acuminatus 54, 192, 232, 273
Ips cembrae **56**, 274
Ips duplicatus 192
Ips sexdendatus **186**
Ips typographus **15**, 54, **181**, **223**f, **232**, 251, **252**,
255, 266, **267**
Ixodes ricinus 176, **177**, **281**f
jewel beetle **8**, **53**, **58**, **313**, 318, **320**
eight-spotted **59**
painted **320**
steelblue 54, **186**, 277, **278**
kairomone 182f
Kermes ilicis 299

Kermes vermilio 299, **300**
Kerria lacca 298
Kleidocerys resedae **33**, 35
kleptoparasitism 191
koinobiont 167
lacewing 155, **156**, **179**, **210**
brown **10**, **157**
common green **156**
Lachnus longirostris **119**
ladybird
eyed **137**
harlequin **135**f, **148**, 311
pine 136
seven-spot **133**, **135**
two-spot **136**
Lamprochernes nodosus 225
Laphria flava **87**
Laphria sp. 152
Lasius fuliginosus **75**
Lasius sp. 73, 94, 118, 120
leaf miner
horse chestnut **311**
leaf mines 263f, 311
leaf roller
European green oak 10, 30, 40, 116, 219, 259
Leptoglossus occidentalis 33, **311**
Leptura annularis **323**
Leptura quadrifasciata 64, **68**
Leskia aurea **174**
Lilioceris merdigera **9**
Limenitis sp. 316
Lipoptena cervi 179, **180**
Lithobius forficatus **114**
Lonchaea bruggeri **188**
Lonchaea sp. 188
longhorn
large poplar **52**, 54
wasp 64, **65**
longhorn beetle **72**, **73**, **74**, **76**, **77**, 81, 333, **334**,
335
Asian 118, **305**, 307, **308f**
black-striped 69
citrus 309
four-banded 64, **68**
red-brown **25**, **66**
speckled **67**
spruce **57**
two-banded **68f**
Lopinga achine 10, **314**, 315
Lucanus cervus 69, **70**, **321**, **324**
Lucilia bufonivora 180
Lucilia caesar **91**

347

Index

Lucilia sericata 290, **291**
Lucilia sp. 90
Lymantria dispar **39**f, 117, **126**, 138, **139**, **171**,
  232, **237**, **257f**
Lymantria monacha 40, **42**, 125, 138, **149**, 259
Lytta vesicatoria 289, **290**
Machimus sp. **155**
macrofauna 105f, 108, 113
Malachius bipustulatus **86**
Mantis religiosa 226
Marpissa muscosa **166**
maturation 189, 267f, 270, 279
Meconema meridionale **158**
Meconema thalassinum 157
Medetera signaticornis **187**
Medetera sp. **187**f
Megachile sp. 77
Megachile willughbiella **79**
Megastigmus sp. 31
Melanargia galathea **178**
Melandrya caraboides **72**
Melanophila acuminata 57
Meloe proscarabaeus **225**, 226
Melolontha hippocastani 262
Melolontha melolontha **44**, 126, 262
mesofauna 105f, 111f
Mesopolobus typographi 194
microfauna 105, 107f
microhabitat 236, 317
microorganisms 38f, 48, 108, 125, 182, 197, 226
millipede 4, 105, 108f
mineralisation 38, 45, 111f
Miramella formosanta **45**
Misumena vatia 160, **164**
mite 117
    Varroa 176, **178**
    velvet **166**, 176, **178**
Monochamus galloprovincialis **60**, 229, 279, **280**
Monochamus sartor **60**
Monochamus sp. 57
monoculture 255, 260, 314
monogynous 202, 216
Morimus asper 321, **322**
mosquito
    Asian tiger 282
moth
    autumnal 220f
    bee 102, 157, **159**
    box tree 309, **310**
    brown-tail 116, **284f**
    codling 33
    European goat 11, **54f**

garden tiger **123**
gypsy **39**f, 117, 122, 125, **126**, 138, **139f**, 169f,
  171, 174, **175**, 232, **237**, **257**f
hornet clearwing 55
larch bud- 40, 116, **238**f
leopard 55
nun 40, **42**, 125, 138, **149**, 259
pandora 303
pine 259
pine beauty 10, 259
small Eggar 287
winter 10, 30, 40, **116**, 221, 232, 259, **260**
yellowlegged clearwing 174
mottled umber 40, 232, 259, **260**
multiparasitism 167
Myathropa florea 75, **78**
mycangium 226
Mycetina cruciata **83**
Mycetophagus quadripustulatus **82**
myrmecochory 28
myrmecophily 211
Myrmica sp. **95**, 118, **130**, 157
Necrobia sp. 94
nectar 18f, 77, 94, 134, 145f, 151f, 173, 191, 226,
  237, 296
nematodes 111, 126, 189, 196f, 223f, 279
Nemozoma elongatum **185**
Neodiprion sertifer **37**, 260, **261**
Nephrotoma crocata **113**
Neriene radiata **164**
Nicrophorus sp. 92
Nicrophorus vespilloides **89**, **93**, **224**
Nineta sp. 155
nitrogen 40f, 48, 51, 97, 111f, 221, 243, 256, 264,
  272f
no-see-um **180**
Nothochrysa sp. 155
Nudobius lentus **185f**
Nymphalis antiopa **316**
Nymphalis polychloros 316
Ocypus olens **127**, **141**
Oedemera nobilis **31**
Oiceoptoma thoracicum **93**, 94
oligolectic 22
Ommatoiulus sabulosus **110**
Oniscus asellus **109**
Onthophagus sp. 98
Onthophagus taurus **101**
Operophtera brumata 10, 30, 40, **116**, 221, 232,
  259, **260**
Orchesella flavescens **113**
Orchestes fagi 263, **264**

Oreina sp. **29**
Orgyia pseudotsugata 42
Oryctes nasicornis 72, **74**
Osmia rufa **23**, **79**
Osmia sp. **236**
Osmoderma eremita **318**
Ostoma ferruginea **324**
Otiorhynchus apenninus **178**
Otiorhynchus sp. 126
Ovalisia rutilans 318
Oxymirus cursor **64**
Ozyptila atomaria **14**
Pachytodes cerambyciformis **67**
Palomena viridissima 33, **34**
Pammene fasciana 35
Panolis flammea 10, 259
Panorpa communis 94, **97**
Parasetigena silvestris 174
parasite 120, 134, 174, 179f, 217
parasitoid 86, 134, 147, 163f, 182f, 190f, 198f, 226, 240, 244, 251, 307
Pardosa amentata **165**
Pardosa lugubris **165**
parental care 92f, 98f, 157
parthenogenesis 35f, 265
pathogen 52, 125f, 196f, 223f, 229, 234, 266, 279, 281f, 289f, 310
Pentatoma rufipes **3**
Pericallia matronula **316**
Periphyllus testudinaceus 221
Peyerimhoffina gracilis **156**
Phaenops cyanea 54, **186**, 277, **278**
Phaeostigma notata **189**
Phalangium opilio **178**
Phengaris sp. 157
pheromones 182f, 186, 202, 208, 267, 269
Phobocampe unicincta 169
Pholidoptera griseoaptera **95**, 157
phoresy 223f
Phryganidia californica 40
Phryxe erythrostoma **176**
Phyllaphis fagi 264
Phyllobius sp. 30, **154**
Phyllopertha horticola **44**
Phymatodes testaceus 64
Physokermes piceae 264, **265**
Phytodietus griseanae **245**
Picromerus bidens 148
pine looper 116
pine wood nematode 229, 279
Pissodes piceae 232, **233**
Pissodes pini 249, **250**

Pissodes sp. 277
Pityogenes chalcographus **56**, 185, **189**, 232, 273, **275**
Pityokteines curvidens 54, 273
Placusa depressa 186
plant galls see galls
plantation 8, 262f, 277f, 301
Platypus cylindrus **2**
Platyrhinus resinosus **69**
Polistes dominula **145**
Polistes sp. **129**
pollination 12, 17f, 30, 237
Polydrusus sp. 30
Polygonia c-album **11**
Polygraphus poligraphus **56**
polygynous 202, 214f
polylectic 22
polypore 78, 80f
poplar lappet **317**
praying mantis
    European 226
predation 10, 14, 182f, 134f, 221, 224f
Prionus coriarius 69
Pristiphora abietina 262, **263**
Pristiphora geniculata **1**
processionary moth
    oak 220, **286**
    pine 286, **287f**
Prociphilus bumeliae **48**
Prociphilus xylostei **48**
Proctolaelaps sp. 189
propolis 290
Protaetia aeruginosa **74**
Protaetia lugubris **319**
Protaetia sp. 72
Protapanteles porthetriae **171**
Protapanteles sp. 169
Pterocomma salicis **206**
Pterostichus sp. 139
Ptilinus pectinicornis **120**
Pulvinaria regalis 311
Puncha ratzeburgi **189**
Purpuricenus kaehleri 321, **322**
Pyemotes sp. 189
Pyrochroa coccinea **86**
Pyrrhocoris apterus **96**
quality (food) 242f, 248, 269, 293, 303
recycling (nutrients) 38, 89, 108, 251
resin 35f, 37f, 52, 55, 80, 108, 211f, 232f, 266f, 271
Rhagium bifasciatum **68**f
Rhagium inquisitor **63**f
Rhagoletis completa 310

349

Rhingia campestris **20**
Rhingia sp. 21
Rhizophagus depressus 186
Rhizophagus grandis **185**, 186
Rhizophagus sp. 186
Rhogogaster punctulata **10**
Rhopalicus tutela **194**
Rhopalodontus perforatus **83**
Rhynchophorus ferrugineus **312**
Rhynchophorus sp. 302
Rhynocoris iracundus **150**
Rhynocoris sp. 149
Rhyssa persuasoria 86, **167**f
ringlet 316
Ropalopus clavipes **62**
Roptrocerus xylophagorum 192, **193**
Rosalia alpina **67**, **321**
Rosalia longicorn **67**, **321**
Rutpela maculata 64, **65**
Samia cynthia 298
Saperda carcharias **52**, 54
Saperda scalaris **62**
saproxylic 51f, 75, 80, 82f, 251, 314, 317f
Sarcophaga sp. **99**
satellite 157
Saturnia pavonia **174**
Satyrium sp. 316
sawfly **10**, **43**, 260
    birch **43**, **171**
    European pine **37**, 260, **261f**
    lesser spruce 262, **263**
    mountain ash **1**
    pine web-spinning 260
    spruce web-spinning 260
scale 298
    horse chestnut 311
    kermes 299, **300**
    spruce bud 264, **265**
scarab 98, **100**
    sacred 100
    taurus **101**
Scathophaga stercoraria **99**
scavenger 89f
Scoloposcelis pulchella 189
Scolytus multistriatus **14**
Scolytus ratzeburgi **56**
Scolytus scolytus **279**
Scolytus sp. 229, 234, 279
scorpionfly
    common 94, **97**
Scymnus sp. 137
Sesia apiformis 55

sheet weaver **164**
silk 158f, 166f, 284f, 293, 297f
silkmoth
    ailanthus 298
    domestic **293**, 297, **298f**, 303
Silpha sp. 94
Sinodendron cylindricum **71**
Sirex noctilio 8
Sisyphus schaefferi **100**
Sisyphus sp. 98
snail 105f, 138f, 152
snakefly **189**
snow flea **11**, **46f**
species number 2, 6f
Sphinx ligustri **25**
Sphinx pinastri **7**, **176**, **256**
spider
    crab **14**, 160, **164f**, 173
    cucumber green **163**
    European garden **143**, **160f**
    jumping **166**
    tangle-web **162**, **166**
    wolf **165**
spindle ermine **261**
springtail **11**, **46f**, **105**, **113**
Staphylinus sp. 141
Stenurella melanura 69
Stictoleptura rubra **25**, **66**
Stylops melittae 179
superparasitism 167, 170f
symbionts 51, 54, 168, 256
symbiosis 18, 28, 57, 128, 223f, 277
Symydobius oblongus 221
Synanthedon vespiformis 174
synchrony 243f, 250
Syrphus torvus **17**, **152**
Tachina fera 173
tannins 38, 43, 52, 298, 300f
Taphrorychus bicolor 185
Temnochila caerulea **186**, **198**
Temnostoma bombylans **77**
Tetropium castaneum **57**
Tettigonia viridissima 157
Thanasimus formicarius **181**, **183**
Thaumetopoea pityocampa 286, **287**
Thaumetopoea processionea 220, **286**
thermoregulation 214
tick **176f**, **281f**
timberworm
    large **58**, 274
Tipula maxima **9**
Tomicobia seitneri 193, **194**

Tomicus minor 54, **56**
Tomicus piniperda 54
Tomicus sp. 192, 273
tortoiseshell
    large 316
tortrix
    chestnut 35
Tortrix viridana 10, 30, 40, 116, 219, 259
Torymus sinensis 307
tree cavity 21, 71, 75f, 251, 317f
Trichius fasciatus **26**, 72, **73**
Trichogramma semblidis 190
Troilus luridus 148, **149**
Trombidium holosericeum 162, **166**, 176, **178**
trophallaxis 205f
trophic level 82, 84
trophobiosis 28, 128
Trypodendron lineatum **57**, **229**, 274
Trypodendron sp. 226
Trypoxylon figulus 77, **79**
ubiquist 135
Urocerus gigas **60**, 226, **227**
Valgus hemipterus **71**
Varroa destructor 176, **178**
vector 21, 189, 223f, 229, 277f, 281f
Vespa crabro **143**, 144
Vespula sp. **94**, 144, **146**
Vespula vulgaris **95**
virus 125, 167, 196f, 223, 240f, 277, 281f
vitality (tree) 231f, 260, 269
volatiles 18, 90, 168, 182f, 205, 266
Volucella inanis 102, 152, **154**
Volucella pellucens 102, **103**
Volucella sp. 102, 104, 152
wasp **94**
    crabronid 77, **79**
    cuckoo **173**
    digger **148**
    European paper **145**
    median **147**
    paper **148**
    rubytail **88**, **173**
wasteful feeding 40, 188, 240
web 38, 116, 158f, 237, 255, 261
webworm
    pine false **262**

weevil 30, 126, **154**, **178**
    acorn 32
    banded pine 249, **250**
    beech leaf-mining 263, **264**
    chestnut **32f**
    large pine 277, **278**
    red palm 302f, **312**
    silver fir 232, **233**
white
    black-veined 287
white rot 64f, 71, 80
windthrow 30, 199, 268f, 271
wood mould 71, 73, 108, 317f
wood pasture 248, 317
woodlice 13, 94, 105, 108f, 124
woodpecker 117f, 181, 189, 195f, 198f, 211, 217, 251
woodwasp
    giant **60**, **61**, 226, **227**, **228**
Xylocopa sp. 24
Xylocopa violacea 75, **76**, 323, **326**
Xylophagus ater **87**
Xylosandrus germanus **55**, 274, 307
Yponomeuta cagnagella **261**
Zeiraphera griseana 40, 116, **238f**
Zeuzera pyrina 55
zoophily 18

351

Index